Shroud of Secrecy

Shroud
of Secrecy

The Story of Corruption within the Vatican

The Millenari

Translated from the Italian by Ian Martin

KEY PORTER BOOKS

Canadian Cataloguing in Publication Data

Marinelli, Luigi
    Shroud of secrecy : the story of corruption within the Vatican

Translation of: Via col vento in Vaticano
ISBN: 1-55263-142-7

1. Catholic Church – Corrupt practices. 2. Vatican City – History. 3. Catholic Church – Government. I. Title.
BX1802.M37413 2000   262'.02   C99-933074-8

THE CANADA COUNCIL | LE CONSEIL DES ARTS
FOR THE ARTS | DU CANADA
SINCE 1957 | DEPUIS 1957

The publisher gratefully acknowledges the support of the Canada Council for the Arts and the Ontario Arts Council for its publishing program.
We acknowledge the financial support of the Government of Canada through the Book Publishing Industry Development Program (BPIDP) for our publishing activities.

Originally published in Italian in 1999 by Kaos edizioni Milano
First English-language edition published in 2000 by Key Porter Books Limited

Key Porter Books Limited
70 The Esplanade
Toronto, Ontario
Canada M5E 1R2

www.keyporter.com

Design: Peter Maher
Editorial: Amy Laird
Research: Laryssa Polika
Electronic formatting: Heidi Palfrey

Printed and bound in Canada

00 01 02 03 04 6 5 4 3 2 1

Editor's Note

The book that you now hold in your hands began its life in Italy in February 1999. Published by Kaos Editions, *Via col vento in Vaticano* made news as soon as it hit the bookstores. The marketing campaign—which heralded the book as a sizzling account of intrigue, homosexuality, and corruption within the Vatican bureaucracy—almost overshadowed the significance of the authors' message. For the first time since 1517, when Martin Luther posted his historic 95 theses in Wittenberg, Germany, the public could read a criticism of the Church written from within the Church itself.

Kaos Editions originally released 7,000 copies of *Via col vento in Vaticano*. When, in June 1999, Vatican officials issued an order to cease publication and distribution, sales soared to more than 100,000 copies. Sales continued to climb as both the Italian and international press picked up the story. As this book went to press, more than 200,000 copies of *Via col vento in Vaticano* were in print, and foreign editions were in high demand. *Shroud of Secrecy* is one such edition.

Translations present a number of challenges. First, *Via col vento in Vaticano* was written by a group of prelates whose native language is Italian, and whose training within the Church involves Latin. A literal and faithful translation would have been unreadable. Yet the editors of *Shroud of*

Secrecy were committed to giving the authors their authentic voice, and have edited the translation with that in mind. In addition, the authors of *Via col vento in Vaticano* assumed that their readers shared their knowledge of Church history, and had certain religious beliefs in common. Compared to many European countries, however, North America is decidedly secular—and in places where religion is important, it cannot be assumed that Roman Catholicism is the predominant system of belief.

To aid the North American reader, and readers who do not share Roman Catholic beliefs, we have provided marginal notes and a glossary. Both of these elements have been written to provide readers with information, not analysis. They are meant to help explain references, terminology, and allusions that may not be immediately obvious to some readers.

Finally, we are pleased to include, from the publishers of *Via col vento in Vaticano*, an afterword written specifically for this edition of the book to update readers on the events that have taken place in Italy since the original publication date. Clearly, this is a story that continues to unfold.

Table of Contents

Fighting the Silence

The measure of any critical work is the extent to which it is willing to question the status quo and suggest serious reform. Without subtlety and compromise, this work denounces the practices of the Vatican and attempts to cleanse what has become a festering wound.

These revelations of corruption may shock some and horrify others. Because this book was conceived and written by a team, it possesses both the merits and shortcomings of a work with many voices. To reflect the authors' different perspectives, some repetition of the most meaningful concepts occurs; however, repetition helps, especially for those unfamiliar with the world of the Vatican.

In these times, "where we die of certainties while those same certainties die" (Leonardo Sciasia), truth remains constant whether spoken by the most skilled or least experienced orator. Eloquence will not enrich it. Stuttering will not deplete it. Saint Peter warns the Church: *"For the time is come that judgment must begin at the house of God: and if it first begin at us, what shall the end be of them that obey not the gospel of Christ?"*

In the humblest of voices, this book exposes how those at the heart of the house of God have failed to follow the words and obey the gospel of Christ, and how the hierarchy and politics of the Catholic Church must undergo reform and renewal. Vatican II states: "The Church, unlike the

Saint Peter was the leader and spokesperson of the twelve apostles. His successors as bishops of Rome became leaders of the Church.

The **Second Vatican Ecumenical Council**, also known as **Vatican II**, convened in 1962 and continued until 1965. It sought to foster spiritual renewal and reconsider the church in the modern world.

innocent Christ, which includes sinners in its bosom, both holy and needing purification, never neglects its penance and its renewal. . . . The wandering Church is called by Christ to this continual reform of which, as a human and worldly institution, it is always in need."

The time has come for the Church to seek forgiveness, first from Christ, then from humanity, for the many infidelities and betrayals of its ministers, especially those at the top of its ecclesiastical hierarchy. The issue is not the divine institution, but rather the corrupt practices that risk emphasizing the structure rather than the substance of the Church. We must destroy the mechanism that imprisons Christ-centered truth. Reforming the Church in the new millennium will involve changing its bureaucratic structure, which is no longer effective. For Clemenceau, government meant bringing peace to good citizens, not to the dishonest ones. To govern otherwise would invert the natural order of things.

From its divine beginning, the Church was given the mandate and the capacity to exist in the world temporally, assimilating without corruption and growing without distortion. The Second Vatican Ecumenical Council allowed the Church to exist as such, and it began to run smoothly again. For many, however, the Council seemed only superficially effective. An irritated journalist charged: "Is it possible that in the same documents this Council was able to state everything and the opposite of everything, agreeing with everyone?"

The Church today exists as though it has suffered a nuclear catastrophe more devastating than the one at Chernobyl. While the Church remains structurally sound, it is physiologically subject to the harmful influence of a stifling dominant mentality. Let us sound the trumpet in anticipation of the new millennium and the two-thousandth anniversary of Christ's birth by setting out as Christians in search of our own salvation.

The difficulty lies in deciding how to proceed. Should we keep the secret knowledge to ourselves, or shout from the rooftops the evil that has infiltrated the Church? Although the old adage proclaims that silence is golden, a certain breed of silence is deadly. The silence that allows evil to continue to avoid a scandal can be confused with complicity. Silence that reinforces corruption only maintains the status quo, and does not challenge the rampant evil in the house of God.

Saint Giovanni Leonardi wrote to Paul V regarding how to appropriately effect Church reform: "He who wants to effect serious religious and moral reform must above all, like a good doctor, perform a careful diagnosis of the ills that afflict the Church so as to be able to prescribe each with the appropriate remedy." The renewal of the Church must occur equally among all people. It must begin with those who command, and then extend to their subjects. It demands that cardinals, patriarchs, archbishops, bishops, and parish priests have strong enough characters to be entrusted with governing God's flock.

Paul V served as pope between 1605 and 1621. He was a stern and uncompromising man who ruled the church using authoritarian decrees rather than diplomacy.

We did not decide lightheartedly to record these painful words expressing our collective, yet independent, anxieties about the Church, which has been devastated by an external postwar atheism and an internal theological desecration in the wake of Vatican II.

Because of the risks involved in revealing the unfettered truth, the team sent word of these concerns to an individual close to the pontiff to find out how he felt about this endeavor. He responded: "I wish you and the project that you intend to undertake well, because I can only begin to imagine how difficult it will be."

A Necessary Scandal

God's alliance with the poor and meek stands in stark contrast to the arrogance of the powerful church officials who condemn the innocent. This book expresses all that has gone wrong with the Catholic Church.

As a failed politician, Jeremiah was imprisoned whenever he tried to warn his people of what was to come. But as

The prophet **Jeremiah** preached in Jerusalem under King Josiah and condemned his contemporaries for committing social injustices and rejecting their religious beliefs.

a prophet, he sought to shed light on the path necessary to become true followers of God. A pacifist, he was chosen to confront a nation in crisis whose leaders opposed him because he questioned the security of the establishment.

Relentlessly persecuted, Jeremiah bravely resisted the lies and rejected the silence of shame, like Christ, who said: "Thou, therefore, gird up thy loins, and arise, and speak unto them all that I command thee: be not dismayed at their faces, lest I confound thee before them. For behold, I have made thee this day a defensed city, and an iron pillar, and brazen walls against the whole land, against the kings of Judah, against the princes thereof, against the priests thereof, and against the people of the land. And they shall fight against thee; but they shall not prevail against thee."

A recalcitrant prophet, chosen by God for a mission for which he felt ill suited, Jeremiah resisted and said: "Ah Lord God! Behold, I cannot speak: for I am a child." But the Lord said unto him: "Say not 'I am a child,' for thou shalt go to all that I shall send thee, and whatsoever I command thee thou shalt speak. Be not afraid of their faces: for I am with thee to deliver thee." Although Jeremiah suffered insecurity throughout his life, he proclaimed the urgent need for the radical renewal of Israel and ultimately heralded a new covenant.

Trapped between two forces, God and Israel, Jeremiah lived a difficult life. He lived as a simple man—neither king nor politician, pontiff nor mercenary. Both weak and strong, he was an enviable example of a man of God who remained pure under the most powerful forces. Jeremiah remains the most Christian of the saints of the Old Testament—the most vulnerable, the most fraternal, and the closest to sinning and divided hearts.

Inspired books clearly show that prophets are more than men of the temple and servants of the Lord; they are God's voice urging humanity to be continually reborn. Often, these saintly men become victims of Church officials when they condemn the obvious sins committed by

Judah was a southern Jewish kingdom that was constantly at war with the northern kingdom of Israel.

these officials. Savonarola, Rosmini, and Padre Pio serve as examples of pious men who have suffered this fate. If God grants someone the character to denounce the privilege, corruption, and indolence of the clergy, the accuser must expect an equally ferocious attack from these men who, enveloped in mystical zeal, guard the sanctity of the Church. Clergymen always consider their consecration to be a human investment, and they form a contract with God, bargaining out of self-interest.

On the contrary, the eccentric nonconformists who are willing to reveal oppression, opportunism, and obsequiousness often become isolated and marginalized. The establishment mistrusts and condemns them, since their refusal to adhere to rigid, one-sided principles is contrary to the Chinese proverb that states: "When the wind blows, the reeds must all bend in its direction." Nonconformity sentences one to derision and insinuation and condemns one to silence against the conformists. It is one thing to read about such an existence, but quite another to live it daily, as the authors have.

Many judgmental people will point an accusatory finger, offended, disgusted, and stunned because we have chosen this book as a form of redress. We should have exercised greater discretion! When subtle criticism becomes a serious and valid protest, the authorities rally the support of the majority and present a strong defense. By enlisting the most faithful supporters, the authorities exhort loyal followers to obey the Church by combating its enemies. Due to servile conformism, these severe judges rush to condemn such a book. For authoring such a work, we have been considered inept, rebellious, insubordinate, dissatisfied, spiteful, contemptible, and more. Just as Priam's daughter Cassandra accurately predicted the destruction of Troy, various narrow-minded individuals discounted and discredited her catastrophic predictions.

A new idea that opposes the prevailing one is generally rejected outright by the majority, and is not considered seriously. Because we usually value familiar concepts, the opposite applies to the unfamiliar. Good and evil only exist in opposition, and it is confusing to determine which is which. We are taught from an early age to hide what is ugly and unnatural and to suppress what the majority considers undesirable. Nobody denies the existence of evil and corruption, but why expose it? Uncovering the evils and shortcomings of the Church will undoubtedly generate hate, vendettas, and persecution, and many believe that it is best not to interfere.

Conventional thinkers maintain that publicizing such potentially dangerous information, aside from scandalizing and discrediting the Curia, could also have serious consequences elsewhere. Some believe that it is best to conceal everything, just as the events at Fatima were kept secret. Opposing the idea that silence is the best tactic, René Laurantin declares: "The insistence and virulence of Christ's prophets and the apostles often scandalized the conformism of their contemporaries. In order to impose certain intuitions it is, at times, necessary to shock." Teixeira agrees that change is effected through profound measures: "The true friend is not the one who wipes away your tears, but the one that stops them from falling."

Scattered and sterile souls condemn those who express enthusiasm. Challenging the status quo—a common virtue of people of character—is mistakenly confused with insubordination, a serious offence that must be censored by the papal court. Eventually, those who refuse to cater to unjust statements and practices must pay for their behavior. People who value the truth believe in the saying: "Pay no heed to who does the talking, but to what is said! If it corresponds to an incontestable reality, then exalt the truth and not its concealment."

Those who throw a stone into the river must anticipate its effect. Each stone, regardless of its size, is carried by the current and eventually comes to rest on the riverbed. But all of the stones eventually form a bank that dictates the

The **Curia** is the body of tribunals and offices through which the Pope governs the Roman Catholic Church.

After six reported apparitions of the Virgin Mary to three shepherd children in 1917, the community of **Fatima** in central Portugal became a Roman Catholic pilgrimage site.

course of the river. Even small accusations can help change the secular course of the Church.

Our spirituality must be restored to a purer state, and wrenched from the idleness into which all religious families have sunk. This task is profoundly revolutionary, but cannot be delayed. Too many idlers dwelling in God's house proclaim at his expense: "Here we shall live well."

The clergy often become content with less—a disposition that encourages sloth, a lack of energy, and an unwillingness to work. When examining these religious families, we must ensure that there isn't a facade concealing the reality behind their vows. Reform is inevitably postponed. As convents grow in wealth, the true spirit of sanctity is extinguished and replaced by ease and indolence (Pietro Friedhofien).

Everyone, wealthy or poor, layman or clergyman, enters the kingdom of Christ only on the recommendation of the needy: the travelers we have sheltered, the thirsty we have quenched, the sick we have healed, the prisoners we have visited, the quarrelsome we have calmed, the dead we have buried. Without commendations from the people we have helped, we will not enter the kingdom and we will be rejected at its gate with the words: "In truth I tell you, I do not know you."

Primo Mazzolari said that neither speech nor silence is witness to what resides in the heart. Because both good and evil originate in us, one who criticizes is no less devout than one who only and always praises. Spoken words do not reveal true devotion.

Saint Augustine teaches us that: "We follow this apostolic rule passed on to us by the Fathers: if we find something true even in evil men, we correct the evil without violating that which is good in them. In that way, in the same person, we correct the errors, starting from the truths that they admit, and avoid destroying the true with the false."

The authors do not intend for these writings to be hurtful to the reader, and we apologize for any pain we may

Saint Augustine (354-430) was one of the founders of western theology. His extreme and controversial beliefs dictated that people must ultimately align themselves with God or Satan.

inadvertently cause. The truth must be proclaimed not only when it is convenient, but also when it is right. This message does not belong to us. In fact, it is so much greater than us that we are overwhelmed by our own insignificance. These revelations seem to flow from mysterious evangelical sources.

Those reveling in the present will say: "Yes, they are professing the truth and the right path, but it's not yet time to declare it. It's not worth it: it would do more harm than good on the eve of the Holy Year. We would bring persecution upon ourselves. Why incite scandal?"

Christ said: *"It is necessary that scandals occur when it is for the good of all."* Jesus challenged the privileges of the ruling class and shocked his disciples when he explained they would soon be shamed for his dishonorable death on the cross.

According to Chesterton, divine ideas are corrupted when those who oppose the kingdom of heaven use them for different ends.

A Stew of Corruption

This book is not intended for the majority of those in the Vatican Curia who have performed their duties and been rewarded for their devotion by being left to serve the Church in silence and indifference. We praise them wholeheartedly for their past and continued service to the Church of God.

Like Christ their model, the silent and modest prelates are like cornerstones of the Church that were discarded for the use and consumption of the Church's builders. But, because of their silence, the Vatican has marshaled many Curial conformists. The well-deserving priests have endured a difficult passage between Scylla and Charybdis, stuck in the middle to avoid choosing one side, just as the eagle of Ippona warned: "If you go one way you will wreck your ship against the rocks, on the other side you will be devoured by the waves: stay in the center in order to avoid the traps of Scylla and Charybdis."

Some people have considered erecting a shrine to the Mother of the excluded members of the Curia beneath Michelangelo's dome. At her feet, the marginalized clergymen would repeat the cry, "I have no man," which in "vaticanese" means lacking an appropriate dignitary to support and pull strings for you.

However, establishing such a shrine would involve the most enterprising group in the Church, since those closest to the people in power are most successful at getting what they want. This principle applies to every society in the world, including the Church. No human hierarchy is foreign to this concept, including the most prominent and supposedly most pious.

The Church is in crisis because it exists in the world, and because the world exists in it. Its troubles resemble those of the Middle Ages, when individuals mixed the quaintness of the religion with a destructive secularism. Because of this tendency, the same person could exhibit both sin and compassion; for example, proud ostentation and humility, or lust for power and generosity. Ecclesiastical history is replete with these passive wrongdoings.

Values never change, but the culture that maintains those values does, like the constant sun covered by clouds. Presently, there is a crisis surrounding moral values in that the most important appointments in the Curia are being auctioned off to the highest bidder inside or outside the Church.

The world needs the Church to resolve its recurrent crises. Ernest Bloch stated: "Without the inner roads of the spirit, one can't walk upright and with dignity on the roads of the world." The Church has been given the mandate to call everyone to attention and to encourage a return to the spiritual from the material. *"For all flesh is as grass, and glory of man as the flower of grass. The grass withereth, and the flower thereof falleth away: But the word of the Lord endureth forever."* The Church is the guardian of the Word of the Lord, but when the Church lowers its guard, it easily slips into crisis.

The Pope's Mule

S atire and humor are important reflexive tools for any healthy society. Dictatorships, however, do not understand how to appreciate these tools. A government that does not tolerate conflicting opinions eventually becomes a dictatorship, and implies that its citizens must approve without dissent. A government intent on growth and improvement encourages participation and values constructive criticism; conversely, a government intent on stagnating and stifling its people discourages the circulation of ideas and critical humor.

A tyranny exists where suspicious and jealous people attempt to silence the values and voices of the able and qualified. Democracy accepts a certain amount of satire. The despot, obsessed with maintaining power, silences the satirist who can reveal the deficiencies of the despot's reign.

To those who challenge a prelate in a position of authority, their Rasputin, let us quote Alphonse Daudet regarding the kick that the Pope's mule gave his young groom in Avignon: "When one speaks of a rancorous and vindictive man, one says: 'Beware of that man! He is like the mule of the Pope, who waited seven years to kick him.' . . . There is no better example of ecclesiastical revenge."

Uncontrollable backbiting and sarcastic comments are rampant in Church offices. Such criticism is a rough hand that ruffles the delicate feathers of senior Curia members.

Located in southeast France on the Rhone River, **Avignon** was the papal city from 1309 to 1378.

Apparently, to appease and entertain his subjects, Ferdinand II of Naples once circulated gossip about himself.

The Roman Curia doesn't customarily appreciate freedom of expression, and often it accepts the grotesque in place of the sublime. But even the limited power of dissidents should not be overlooked.

Dissatisfied Curia members instinctively hide behind exaggerated, often unwise, criticism. This criticism is a great whispered rumbling, like the rhythmic drone of a swarm of bees. However, the critics are rebellious more in form than in substance, and do not affect the power structure or the person in the seat of power. Suggesting that it is important to effect change from the center and not from the periphery, Renato Rascel observed: "One should tickle the brain, not the armpit."

The Pillars of the Church

We often ridicule Pope John Paul II's love of the Slavs and his "Polandification" of the Church. Many Polish priests arrived at the Vatican in an attempt to secure powerful positions. They were endorsed and praised wholeheartedly by the prelates of the court who were eager to endear themselves to the Pope, who is Polish. Certainly, those same people who supported the promotion of the Polish priests will remove them after the next Pope is inducted.

Elected in 1978, **John Paul II** is the first non-Italian Pope since the sixteenth century.

The armored-car hoax in Via della Conciliazione is a particularly memorable incident regarding the promotion of Polish priests in the Vatican. On a cold January morning in 1991, the police reported a rudimentary camouflaged armored vehicle parked next to Pius IX school in Via della Conciliazione. Given the circumstances, the road was cordoned off, traffic was re-routed, and students were sent home. As a precaution, the bomb-disposal unit was called in. After alerting everyone in the vicinity and expecting the worst, the authorities waited, but nothing happened. When an explosives expert eventually inspected the vehicle, however, it turned out to be nothing more than a wreck covered hastily in soldered sheet metal.

The car was supposed to have been a gift to the Polish monsignor who, at a holy luncheon, had succeeded in convincing the Pope to institute a military bishopric in Poland, offering himself as the first bishop to the forces. With this armored-car prank, his friends ridiculed him and clearly displayed their disapproval of his useless mission.

The diplomacy of the Vatican immediately influences any states with which it has diplomatic ties. In fact, when troubling relations arise, the paperwork is filed and buried where it can be easily or not so easily accessed, depending on the situation. The most experienced Vaticanologists attempt to understand the workings of this monarchic, religious state but are not always successful.

According to journalist John Cornwell, Monsignor Paul Marcinkus described the state as "a village of washerwomen: they wash the clothes, they beat them with their fists, they dance on top of them, and they manage to get all of the dirt out. In everyday life, people have other concerns; in these places, you know that if someone tells you a story it is because he wants you to tell him one too. It is a place filled with not entirely honest people."

Antonio Bacci

was Archbishop of Colonia de Cappadocia in 1962. He attended Vatican II and participated in the 1963 conclave.

The brilliant Latinist, Cardinal Antonio Bacci, said: "Vatican diplomacy was born one sad evening in Jerusalem, in the atrium of the highest priest, when Peter the apostle, warming himself by the fire, came across a young maid who, with finger pointed, asked, 'Are you not also a follower of the Galilean?' and Peter gave a start and responded, 'No, I don't know what you are talking about.' This was a diplomatic answer with which neither faith nor spirit was compromised."

The Vatican state influences the behavior of other states to the degree that hypocrisy becomes both the cause and effect of each state's success. The epitome of institutional hypocrisy, this small state contains in its governmental practices one of the most serious global environmental hazards.

The Vatican is an island where law, power, good and evil, and the violent abuse of the defenseless coexist in equal measures. In the Vatican, it is easier to see the evil in the good rather than the good in the evil. In short, the Vatican state contains a strange amalgam of age-old intrigues, as the following passages demonstrate.

A diocesan bishop once ended his pastoral visit with the celebration of the Eucharist, where he declared to God: "I am not worthy." The parish priest took note, and from that day on, in every Eucharistic prayer, he exhorted his parishioners to pray for "our unworthy bishop." When word of this reached the bishop, he demanded that the priest stop this practice immediately. But the young priest claimed that he had learned it from his very lips, and if the bishop had said it out of convenience, then he, instead, said it with conviction in the hope that God would convert him.

> The consumption of consecrated bread and wine during Catholic mass is known as the **Eucharist**. Catholics believe transubstantiation occurs during the blessing—that the bread and wine become the literal body and blood of Christ.

One is obliged to bow in the presence of a Secretary of State employee, as with the aristocratic elite; but, in the presence of one who has surpassed the tenth Curial level, a genuflection is in order. This gesture almost mocks the pomp, superiority, and legend of the caste that does all it can to maintain its status by traveling the world in expensive cars and jets.

Once, to quote a passage from the gospel, the Cardinal Secretary of State asked for a bible. His personal secretary returned having failed to find one. "Not even from the monsignor's assistant?" asked the cardinal. His secretary answered: "It was in fact he, who somewhat taken aback, replied: 'What does the Gospel have to do with anything here?'"

> **The Cardinal Secretary of State** serves as head of the Secretariat of State.

A well-known prelate, highly concerned with the
morality of others, but vulgar and licentious himself,
confided in his closest friends that he had taken
an "oath of homosexuality" so he would avoid
chasing women.

On Good Friday in 1985, during the procession of
prelates that follow the Pope, a Polish master of
ceremonies happily saluted the cardinals and bishops
by shouting, "You, you are the pillars of the Church,
the pillars, the pillars, thank you!" One old prelate,
who was hard of hearing, asked his neighbor, "Whom
is he calling pullets?"

A **pullet** is a
young chicken.

The most reverend cardinals have their own protocol
of remaining sedentary or raising their precious
posterior weight according to the importance of their
visitor. If, for example, the Secretary of State should
present himself, the cardinals can't move quickly
enough; with their equals, their movement is slow and
deliberate; with dignitaries of a lower status, they lift
themselves no more than a few inches off the
cardinal's chair; with an up-and-coming monsignor, a
smile and handshake will do; and with a nobody, a
disinterested wave is enough to make him understand
the burden of his presence.

Marianna Roncalli, whose son had recently become a
monsignor, explained to one of her friends about the
prelate's clothing he wore: "If my son is dressed like a
bishop without being one, don't trouble yourself about
it, it is stuff that priests work out among themselves."
She is exactly right; there is no point in trying to
understand what priests decide within their circles.
Honor is to the clergy as sight is to the blind.

For about a decade, a doctor's report was circulated throughout the Curia. The doctor's cardinal-patient was the head of an important Curial ministry. When the cardinal arrived at functions, stunned and unaware of what was happening, he was likened to a horse sleeping standing up. With Moses' veil over his face, the juridical ideas and issues sailed over his head; yet, occasionally he would comprehend that he didn't understand what was happening. He started traveling without any real destination, until, one day, the police found him and called the Vatican to come and collect him.

Dazed and confused, the cardinal would often visit his doctor, confiding in him: "Doctor, for some time now, I feel I have something in my head. I can't explain, but I sense something up there." His kindly doctor responded: "Your Eminence, stay calm, I have already told you many times, relax and don't worry yourself: you, Eminence, have absolutely nothing in your head!"

And so, the cardinal convinced himself that his head contained nothing of importance.

Ironically, the pensioner leaving his position in the Church, soliloquizes: "My day is Done, it is evening. The dying sun is at my back. Lord, it is already late! I am no longer useful to your vine. There is only darkness around me. Goodbye, Lord, see you on the other shore!"

A nun, who kept house for a powerful cardinal, repeated the following prayer to Mary: "Madonna, how many times must I tell you: do not choose ignorant, insignificant people when you appear to deliver your messages. If you continue to do so, you will always be challenged as you were at Fatima and Medjugorie.

Meaning "between the hills," **Medjugorie** is an area in Bosnia-Herzegovina that became famous in 1981—when six youths witnessed apparitions of the Madonna.

Instead, try to appear to an eminent prelate of the church, like my cardinal! He would let the whole world know what it is that you want; what Jesus whispers in his ear, he would blurt out to the world. Nobody would dare deny the supernatural stature of such an apparition. Amen, and let it be so!"

After the Pope's skiing trip to the Adamello, a number of prelates prayed: "Lord, grant us, Adam's poor sons, a safe descent down the mountain toward our desired goals. Amen, and let it *ski* so!"

In the absence of a democratic system and an open forum for opposition, less controllable criticism occurs. Such criticism should not be disregarded, but rather be examined despite the risks it may cause both the meek and the strong. Every absolute monarchy must pay a price when it tramples the liberty and rights of its subjects.

"Your Death Is My Life"

In the Vatican, as elsewhere, some persecute their fellow monsignors to both humiliate them and raise their own images according to the saying, *"mors tua vita mea"* (your death is my life).

The newcomer who attempts to succeed and gain seniority is prevented from doing so as soon as he faces a rival who enjoys greater support. Stalled by a lack of support, the newcomer idles, waiting to exact revenge.

In response to a careerist who wanted to know what was involved in getting ahead, Cardinal Domenico Svampa is rumored to have answered: "Intelligence and a little devil to see you along." Apparently, the careerist replied: "Your Eminence, I have the intelligence, and you are the devil that can see me along."

Eighty percent of those in the Vatican accept that they will never attain the positions of the privileged class and will remain forever in the anthill with the workers. They are outclassed by the cunning and vainly wait as a grumbling, discontented lot.

The other twenty percent enter the bottleneck of a winding staircase, considering themselves the chosen ones in a regal priesthood. Nevertheless, these fortunate individuals must, in order to eliminate their adversaries, play their cards carefully throughout their career.

A title and office conferred upon a male cleric by a Pope, **monsignor** is used as a form of address for the position, and is prefixed to the clergyman's name.

As he nears his coveted goal, the hopeful cleric refines his strategy, blending craftiness, humility, hypocrisy, and false charity. The world of promotion is based on rivalries and hierarchies rife with real and vicious battles.

Those marked for successful careers—the go-getters, the pretenders, the favorites of their charismatic protectors—are few. They appropriate the merits of others and remain remarkably self-assured. The words of the Holy Spirit, *"We do not seek vainglory provoking and envying one another,"* do not apply to them.

V. Bukovsky said: "In that place there will never be a war, but there is always a similar battle for peace." If by peace we mean an ideal, imagined state, then apathy is the enemy of the Curia's aspiring members, who are spoiled by a false sense of security.

Indifference does not encourage solidarity between those who are taken advantage of or discriminated against. Many puritans and courtesans ensure that suspected dissenters are distanced. Such isolation further marginalizes them, and the silence around them becomes oppressive.

When church officials want to isolate someone in their office, they make life impossible for them, so that any contact with that individual becomes increasingly difficult. The dignity of the person in question is undermined, and he is alienated by his colleagues' indifference. The process is similar to a merciless stoning as he experiences a barrage of unfounded accusations of guilt. The dissenter will invariably bend under the pressure and, frustrated, will question his own capacities and mental stability. He will begin to accuse himself of the worst type of presumption and insubordination, and will eventually persuade himself that he has become ill.

The Vatican Curia needs men not who loudly champion justice, but who are true, good men. Christ called blessed not those who possess justice, but those who hunger and thirst for it.

The **Holy Spirit** is the third aspect of the Trinity in Christian doctrine, and is defined as the side of God present in the world and in human beings.

"Moreover, those who want to live piously in Jesus Christ will be persecuted. But the wicked and the impostors will always go from bad to worse, deceivers and deceived at the same time." The notion of bad to worse, in this sense, means in terms of their wickedness and falseness, not in terms of their careers, where they manage just fine.

IF A SUBORDINATE MONSIGNOR IS OVERLOOKED, he often believes that his worth and ability to be promoted have been neglected. He is nothing more than an island. Some joke that the root word of monsignor is derived from the Latin *mons ignoratus*, an ignored mountain. Hence, the strategy of conquering the subordinate monsignors is to divide them and dissuade them from forming any type of union. The mildest penalty for forming such a nefarious group would be lifelong segregation from that organization.

A geophysical theory explains that originally the continents were located closer together and therefore travel was simpler. The Vatican continent, however, prefers that individuals remain islands so that they can be closely monitored from the papal observatory.

If one is not forbidden to seek promotion, recognition, and dedicated service—a desire inherent in man—then the criterion for hiring and advancement is left at the discretion of the superior. This superior is often pleased with the mediocre and malleable, rather than the strong and principled. Although mediocrity was never a goal or standard for society, the Vatican Curia relishes it, since all of its dependants are men without aspirations.

The superior's standard for promotion follows the law of mediums; on average, ninety-nine percent of the clergy are mediocre and submissive. The other one percent is considered an aberration and is suppressed. For a long period, one ministry undersecretary used a divining rod to regulate his affairs and to determine the trustworthiness of his staff. He also used it in the kitchen and in restaurants—under the table, of course. Thanks to the rod, he claimed to have never made a poor decision. A fainthearted and wishy-washy character, he refused to watch television, but never missed the daily Vatican radio bulletin with news of recent dismissals and promotions. For the rest of the day, he would sit by a window and record all of the prelates who passed by that corner of the Vatican.

Heraclitus said: "One man, if he is the best, is worth more than ten thousand." This principle bothers the insignificant superior who feels deficient when confronted with an intelligent and qualified subordinate. A handful of men, who govern with absolute and limitless authority, reduce the body of Curial employees to an assembly of automatons whose sole function lies in ratifying decisions. The subordinates learn to assent without challenging, as in *The Dialogues of Plato*, where Adimanto always agrees in a soliloquy that is disguised as a dialogue: "Very well . . . that is true . . . of course . . . well said . . . clearly. . . ." A morally subjugated servant will never hold office in a state governed by the Rule of Law. In the Vatican, however, the law is flexible and constantly changing.

The rights that God granted to his people are less important than those invented by the superiors regarding appointments, promotions, and dismissals. In the United States, in Arlington National Cemetery, the monument of the Unknown Soldier reads: "Unknown to all, except to God." A similar statement in the Vatican would never be credited.

Such an environment allows people to coexist without ever fully knowing or valuing one another. Though they work side by side, the Curialists love each other superficially, for rational rather than emotional reasons, in a bureaucratic interdependency that makes them indifferent to their neighbor's condition. They are hollow men, content to praise the system and undermine the personal dignity of their rivals.

Christ's teaching is very different. His love for humanity, both earthly and divine, celebrates the whole man,

Plato's teachings are among the most influential in the history western civilization. Taking the form of conversations (hence the **Dialogues of Plato**), they cover most philosophical issues.

enriches him from within, and places him in communion with others. The Holy Spirit does not promote the monotony of similarity; it imbues in each person a different vocation according to his personality, fully acknowledging that such differences may lead to permanent struggle, pitting one person against the other. The unity that the Spirit demands is not uniformity, but the notion that each person, though different, retains an individuality for the common good. In the dynamic of this exchange, the Church builds from within and grows for the common good.

Every clergyman, animated by the same Spirit, must remain united in faith with others who live in the freedom of the Son of God: *"To each is given a particular manifestation of the Spirit for the common good: to one the language of knowledge, to another that of science, to one the language of faith, to another the gift of healing, to one the power to perform miracles, to another the gift of prophesy, to another the ability to contact spirits, to the other the gift of tongues, and to another still the gift to interpret them. But it is the Spirit that chooses and appoints them."*

The Roman Curia is a strange compendium of uncodified and uncodifiable practices centered on traditions mixed with diplomacy. The Curia considers its staff as representatives but shapes its workers in an undesirable way, creating an environment where truth accompanies falsehood, and where prejudice and suspicion accompany common sense. Rather than considering an individual's merits, the Curia values an individual's public behavior.

When one's professional experience occurs in a nondemocratic context, relations become strained. Blaise Pascal remarked: "Plurality that rejects the concept of unity is lost, and unity that doesn't depend on plurality is tyranny."

For outsiders, the Roman Curia is considered the most perfect government in the world, where social justice is applied evenly and fairly. To state the contrary might seem defamatory, but it isn't. The insiders who are privy to the secrets, and who have given their best, see themselves over-looked and surpassed by others who advance without modesty and humility.

To build a career in this environment involves double-crossing your colleagues, and this savage competition undermines evangelical charity and fraternity. These practices lead to the loss of ethical and social standards, and mask human will as divine will. He who is unable to succeed in the Curia in such a narrow-minded and treacherous environment becomes a pariah who is unable to advance.

THE EMPLOYEE WHO HAS BEEN UNJUSTLY OVER-looked experiences feelings of inferiority and a weakened spirit. Unable to fulfill a profound vocation, he slowly withers and retreats into himself, resigned to the fact that all hope is lost and that he will not be justly treated.

Eighty percent of the clergy, the silenced subordinates, are disadvantaged because they convince their superiors that their power is unlimited and inviolable. Selection, promotion, and dismissal are at the superiors' discretion, even if it is sinful and abusively arbitrary.

We must learn to give voice to those who do not know how to proclaim the inalienable rights of man, especially when the environment breeds silence and submission. The dependents who have fallen behind, the ones excluded from the protective shield of the clan, too often retreat into the silence of Curial glaciation.

Quo vadis Domine is a Latin term meaning "Where are you going, Lord?" Here, it refers to the biblical passage John 13:36, where Simon Peter queries Jesus before his death.

When flames threaten the house of God, the Church, all of the faithful must fight the fire. Whoever watches as Rome burns from the hilltop, as Nero did, contributes to its destruction. *Quo vadis Domine?* in this new millennium? *"I am going to destroy Satan who is setting my Church ablaze."*

While the evil treat the good with utter indifference, the good compromise themselves with disinterest and inaction, believing that they are serving God. And so, everyone, believing himself justified, proceeds with good conscience.

God, who can judge the sinner, becomes impotent in the face of those who justify themselves on their own terms.

Several prelates in the Curia manipulate events in the Church according to their moods, whims, and shifting ambitions, and, as a result, sow seeds of discord and resentment. Absorbed by their own preoccupations, they presume to interpret the thoughts of others, and consequently perpetuate the conflict.

The history of the Curia is replete with colorful examples of clergymen who have tried, and who continue to try, to use the Gospel to justify their acquired privilege, and to manipulate divine will to correspond with their own interests. These men of the Church who give orders, gladly invoke the will of God, identifying it in some way with their own ambitions, which all of their subordinates must embrace without question.

Matters worsen as the hierarchy, including authorities, friends, jurists, psychologists, aesthetes, and many others, becomes involved in this political web. It reaches the point where one no longer knows how to obey one person without disobeying another.

The Gospel is the message of Christ, the kingdom of God, and salvation—particularly as expressed in the four books of the New Testament.

I V

The Hierarchy

This reference to the **Eastern Fathers** and the **Western Fathers** alludes to the schism between the church of Constantinople (east) and the Church of Rome (west) that took place in 1054. The separation resulted in six centuries of disagreement over issues such as married clergy.

The Eastern Fathers of the Church do not appear to have had as unified a concept of the Church as the Western Fathers. Western theology was largely conditioned by the genial image of Saint Augustine, who expressed his thoughts on the great truths of humanity and influenced future generations' conceptualization of society and the individual.

But the truths masterfully proclaimed by the eagle of Ippona had to be adapted to meet the intellectual standards of subsequent generations. Any serious scholar recognizes that the Church is for humanity, not humanity for the Church.

The Eastern Fathers compare the Church to a great indestructible ship, much like the original image of the *Titanic*. Whoever embarks on it in a tempestuous sea will enjoy a calm passage, unlike the other ships caught in the storm. In Western thought, all of those who are not on board the indestructible ship of the Church attempt other means of reaching salvation, such as the rafts, lifeboats, and life jackets of other religions that promise salvation. While they strive for salvation with more difficulty, what is important is their hope that they will reach it.

The Second Vatican Council stated: "This, God's universal plan for the salvation of humankind, is not realized in only one way, secretly in the minds of men who variously search for God with groping efforts and who ignore the fact that he is so far from us." It further noted that "this statement could constitute a valid pedagogical program toward the true God or in the preparation of the Gospel."

Instead, the Western Fathers became conditioned somewhat by the clear-cut Augustian definition that maintains: *"Beyond the Church there is no salvation."* This is a theologically sound assertion, but not the only valid one. This axiom has become incontrovertible dogma, according to which Latin theologians, to save the four billion unbaptized souls, endorse the notion of baptism by desire, which designates unknowing people as Christian. In the West, we safeguard the theological concept that there is no salvation without the Church.

For example, when Jesus established the Church, he promised to make Peter its leader: *"You are a rock, and upon this rock I will build my church; and the gates of hell shall not prevail against it. And I will give unto thee the keys to the kingdom of heaven; and whatsoever thou shalt bind in and along the polygonal walls of this social edifice, shall be bound by in heaven."* Jesus intended that the Church be built on one rock alone, alluding to a specific polygonal geometric figure on which he placed Peter, his vicar.

Jesus returned to childhood memories of the marvelous Egyptian pyramids that continue to challenge us, and whose geometric figure, according to the theory of Nobel-prize winner Louis Alvarez, is a powerful repository of unifying cosmic energy, as the ancient Egyptians and Persians recognized long ago. Before returning to Nazareth, Jesus spent his early years in Egypt and certainly would have accompanied his parents, Mary and Joseph, to the renowned pyramids of the pharaohs, a tourist destination even then. Like all children, Jesus must have been indelibly marked by the pyramids. Required to provide humanity with a model of the Church he intended to establish, he identified the geometrical form of the pyramid as the best point of reference for his divine project—a structure that

Baptism by desire is the act of officially declaring people baptized to save their souls. In Catholicism, only baptized souls enter the kingdom of heaven.

A site of tourism and pilgrimage, **Nazareth**, in northern Israel, was the home of Jesus.

physically communicated a sense of unity and cohesion for the entire family. The pyramidal shape better corresponded to the characteristics that Christ, through the Holy Spirit, conferred upon the church.

The Church more or less concurs with this hypothesis. The sociological composition of the Church is pyramid-like, since the Pope is unquestionably united with the bishops, priests, and faithful followers. Dividing the Church's constituents would contravene its original nature and intention, and pervert its basis.

The Church is a living structure, essentially an indivisible one. This unity was the wonderful achievement of the originating Church Fathers and of medieval Christianity, of which the marvelous cathedrals are a prime example. To erect tall and proud spires, engineers, technicians, painters, sculptors, mural artists, geologists, physicists, doctors of theology, priests, poets, musicians, saints, and the faithful had to cooperate in a harmonious and joyous union. Since then, praise and glory for the unity and trinity of God has been constant. Moreover, the mystery of the Holy Trinity recalls the geometrical figure of an equilateral triangle, which is also pyramidal.

The **Holy Trinity** is a key Christian doctrine that purports that God exists in three equal and eternal elements: God the Father, God the Son, and God the Holy Spirit.

Very often, though, this guiding structure is divided into different ranks—the masses and the hierarchical authorities. So, when referring to the Church, it is easy to focus on the upper part of it, as if it were the only expression of God's will.

Our present-day theologians, like their Renaissance counterparts, like to consider the Church's base as composed of an amorphous, unrefined flock of sheep at the shepherd's command. So, when one speaks of the Church, it is more or less a reference to those at the top of the hierarchy, specifically comprising the Pope, cardinals, bishops, Roman Curia, and high-ranking prelates who are invested with power and authority. Many of these church officials frequently compare their mission to Christ's offering himself on the cross for all humanity.

This theological indiscretion corresponds to the erroneous expression: "The Church wants, the Church doesn't want; the Church permits, the Church doesn't permit; the Church orders, the Church obliges; the Church approves, the Church disapproves; the Church prohibits, the Church admits; the Church confirms that phenomenon, the Church finds nothing supernatural in that apparition or in that individual." This statement refers only to certain clergy who exercise control and manipulate the balance of power. In many instances, these clergymen have incorrectly appraised the historical truths of certain people and phenomena.

The real dichotomy in thought lies here. On one hand, the Church affirms that the authorities and the faithful represent one body and, consequently, an injury to any part directly affects the entire mystic organism. On the other hand, when some members of this body, particularly prophets interested in Christ's compassion, denounce corrupt practices, they are rebuked as insubordinate, rebels, and heretics who must be silenced. After time passes, and after useless contrition and belated pardons, it will become apparent that it was wrong to have judged these dissenters.

But who benefits from the silence? Why doesn't someone intervene? Is it just a case of wanting to leave things as they are, so that we continue to err? The Church is either united in base, sides, and summit, or it is not the Church ordained by Jesus. Jesus didn't establish his Church based on a domineering, all-controlling government.

The Church of Christ governs in one way only: it must serve. Dignitaries and cardinals should have no other ambition or aspiration than to serve: *"But so shall it not be among you: but whosoever will be great among you, shall be your minister: And whosoever of you will be the chiefest, shall be servant of all."*

WHEN JESUS' CHURCH ACTS AS A SERVANT TO its people, it achieves its most divine and complete expression as the protector of humanity. Theologically speaking, God is infinite. However, though a divine creation, the

Church is finite. Consequently, the Church cannot recognize the infinite nature of God. If it knew the infinite omnipotence of the Absolute, it would have to contain him and incorporate his infiniteness. *"See, the heavens and the heavens of the heavens can't contain thee, or imagine this house that I have built!"*

Even God cannot create an institution capable of grasping and encompassing his infinity. To do so, he would have to create another god. Our minds, infinitely weaker than the Church, cannot possibly comprehend the infinite omnipotence of the Creator.

When he founded the Church, Jesus endowed it with enough grace to ensure that men throughout time could draw from it the salvation necessary to save themselves and others. He couldn't, however, grant the finite creation of the Church the capacity to contain the infinite good that God dispenses widely, liberally, and protectively throughout the world.

The Church cannot act as God's guardian, locking him behind the door of a tabernacle and distributing him at its leisure and when it sees fit. The Church's mission is to be more like a theater that displays Christ to man, without appropriating him or his voice. The Absolute has the power to manifest himself in infinite ways to all of his creatures, both inside and outside the Church.

In the Roman Catholic Church, a **tabernacle** is a small, ornamental, locked box that holds the consecrated elements of the Eucharist.

The Holy Spirit periodically reveals the omnipresence of God in the universe through divine apparitions and special graces such as miracles. Such signs formulate the divine language through which the Lord expresses his messages to individuals and all of humanity. Part of a natural divinity, these miracles could not have been created even by a divine institution such as the Church. The perfection of the Church cannot circumscribe God's infinite might.

What, then, is the role of the Church when it is faced with a miracle or a divine message? The Church must interpret it according to the rule of fallibility dictated by Jesus: *"A good tree cannot yield bad fruit, nor can a bad tree yield good fruit."* The Church should adhere to general principles and denounce what are not divine symbols, but it must remain careful not to impose the oversights and prejudices of certain churchmen on God's true works.

Historical facts and divine symbols will only be absolutely clear at the final judgment. Throughout history, God has manifested himself without undermining his divinity or uprooting the temporal world, so that Revelation is possible at the same time as the Incarnation, as prophesied by the Apocalypse (Ottorino Pasquato). How many times have ecclesiastical humans tried to instruct God on how to intervene in the world, and how many times has God's divine intervention been overlooked or cursed by those who originally requested the intervention?

We have often arrived at the absurd notion that the person at the head of the Church is always right, contrary to the messages God has sent through men, saints, and supernatural apparitions that church officials proclaimed to be false. Jesus says to such officials: *"Ye hypocrites, ye can discern the face of the sky and of the earth; but how is it that ye not discern this time? Yea, and why even of yourselves judge you not what is right?"*

Later, the successors of these officials were obliged to accept those previously dismissed supernatural phenomena, with great confusion and embarrassment. This was the case with Galileo Galilei, Saint Joan of Arc, Saint Teresa of Avila, Saint John of the Cross, Saint Joseph of Copertina, Girolamo Savonarola, Antonio Rosimini, Padre Pio of Pietrelcina, and the miracle at Medjugorie, where millions flock to purify themselves while thirty churchmen continue to condemn its authenticity.

The Church has committed many blunders throughout history, and these are some of the more recent ones.

The reference to **Revelation** alludes to the last book of the New Testament, which describes visions of heaven and the Last Judgment.

Incarnation is the union of divinity with humanity in Jesus Christ.

A Judeo-Christian writing dating from 200 BC to AD 150, the **Apocalypse** predicted an imminent cosmic cataclysm in which God destroys evil and raises the righteous to life in a messianic kingdom.

Church Blunders

At the beginning of the century, the Virgin Mary appeared to three small, illiterate children in Fatima, Portugal. She revealed that the Church was rotten at its core and that, to the Pope's great despair, bishops were pitted against bishops and cardinals against cardinals. She revealed that the Church had been ravaged and dishonored by ambitious prelates who had participated in a court conspiracy. Although the statute of limitations for prosecuting the offenses declared in the prophecy had expired, the Church sought to conceal the charges.

During the apparitions at Fatima, Cardinal Antonio Belo Mendes, the patriarch of Lisbon, publicly disavowed what was allegedly happening in that village. He even forbade his priests from making pilgrimages to the site. Now, Popes visit Fatima on pilgrimage. What part of the Church originally viewed the events at Fatima correctly—the summit or the base?

PADRE PIO OF PIETRELCINA WAS, FOR FIFTY years, alternately considered a saint by the growing number of people who followed him and a "dangerous mystifier and corruptor of morals" by the Holy Office. The Church ministry repeatedly warned everyone, especially the clergy, to avoid Padre Pio, who was eventually excommunicated for his visionary and miraculous saintliness.

In response to Padre Pio's visionary claims, the office in charge of confirming miracles took the abnormal (never before or since repeated) initiative to forbid Padre Pio from contacting his spiritual father (June 2, 1922). Still dissatisfied, the same supreme congregation issued a declaration against the monk on March 31, 1923, stating: "Do not verify the supernatural occurrences" surrounding the mystical phenomenon of Padre Pio's stigmata. This decree was published in the *Osservatore Romano* on July 5 of that year, for the whole Church to see. Again, which part of the Church was justified—the top that condemned, or the base that venerated him and continued to flock to him in opposition to the authorities' directives? The declaration

The **Holy Office** is a tribunal of the Curia that deals with the protection of faith and morals.

Stigmata are bodily marks or pains resembling the wounds of the crucified Christ.

The **Osservatore Romano**, or *Roman Observer*, is the newspaper of the Vatican.

claiming the absence of a supernatural occurrence was later published in the pamphlet *Analecta Cappucinorum.* When Padre Pio read it, it brought tears to his eyes.

To end the scandal, the not-yet-satisfied ministry prohibited the monk from celebrating mass in public and secretly planned to send him to Northern Italy or Spain. These charges were resumed with greater vehemence in 1960, when that saintly man, at age seventy-three, was accused of immorality for allegedly having sexual relations with some of his penitents. This accusation was later confirmed by several doctored reels of tape, apparently placed in Padre Pio's confessional by an apostolic visitor who had clearly overstepped his boundaries.

"For so is the will of God, that with well doing ye may put to silence the ignorance of foolish men: as free, and not using your liberty for a cloak of maliciousness, but as servants of God."

Thirty years after Padre Pio's death the ministry that opposed him for fifty years still tries to conceal its scandalous conduct and justify its actions. Those men who supported the infallibility of the Church were unable to reconcile the saintliness of this miraculous man with the charges laid against him, which still haven't been retracted.

Now Padre Pio is a saint. The same man that the Church described as a mystifier and corruptor of morals still draws millions of believers and nonbelievers from all over the world to his tomb, in the hope of witnessing his extraordinary miracles. Which part of the Church behaved properly in this situation—the base or the top? Can the Vatican institution that declared for fifty years "Do not verify the supernatural occurrences," and that was detached from the base of the Church's faithful followers, claim that it can recognize divine works and people? To believe that the Church alone has this ability would be to claim that the individuals and faithful followers who comprise the base of the Church lack the ability to perceive God, which is untrue.

ONE MORNING, DURING PADRE PIO'S CELEBRATION
of mass, the congregation filled the church to capacity so that
parishioners were crowded up against each other in the
small, limited space. Among the crowd was a young deacon
who had attended mass there for years, ignoring his superiors' admonitions. The cleric claimed that there was nothing
wrong with observing the marvels of God at work in one of
his servants. But the Church judged his conduct severely and
insisted that he obey the prohibitions imposed by church
officials who possessed greater knowledge than he did.

Kissing Padre Pio's hands, whose stigmatized wounds
were covered with eschar, was not an easy task. He always
covered his hands with half-gloves, which he would remove
in the sacristy before celebrating mass and put on again
after he put the chalice away. Apparently, the Lord had
given him these instructions, and he obeyed them rever-
ently. As a result, only the person who approached him as
he replaced the chalice in the sacristy would experience the
miracle of his stigmatized palms. The young deacon, distracted by the intense seriousness of the occasion, first
planned to take communion from Padre Pio, and then
planned to thank him in the sacristy as he was putting away
the chalice with his gloves removed, so that he could kiss
his scarred hand.

When the mass was finished, a flood of people poured
into the sacristy, shoving their way through the crowd.
Resisting the onslaught of people, the deacon found himself a meter and a half away from the minister who was
overwhelmed by parishioners eager to kiss his hand.
Disappointed by the failure of his plan, the deacon planned
for the next day. Then Padre Pio, shouting at the others,
raised his right hand, lowered it on the deacon, and offered
it for a kiss, saying: "Hurry, be quick about it." He then
turned to the others and said: "Enough now, enough."

The Lord gave Padre Pio the ability to see into the hearts
of others. He could read the hearts and minds of those in

Eschar is a dry scab
that forms on the skin
after it is burned, or
after a corrosive
substance has been
placed on it.

Also known as a
vestry, the **sacristy** is
a room in a church
where sacred vessels
and vestments are
kept. It is here that
the priest dons his
vestments before mass.

his presence, and could unveil the thoughts and sins of those before him. That morning, he had wanted to satisfy the spiritual conviction of that deacon, now a priest, who still recounts this experience with tears in his eyes.

THROUGHOUT THE 1920S, THE CANONIZED Don Luigi Orione, founder of the Little Work of Divine Providence, without ever meeting Padre Pio, took up his defense to the ministry of the Holy Office in Rome. Many clergymen valued the judgment of this holy man due to his holy life, charitable works, and extraordinary deeds. For Orione, Padre Pio was a true saint regardless of what others claimed, including the Curia. Toward the end of his life, Don Orione was also persecuted for expressing immoral weaknesses toward the opposite sex, just as Padre Pio had been.

The **Little Work of Divine Providence** is one of many foundations formed by, or based on the ideals of, **Don Luigi Orione**—a religious man known for helping the poor in the nineteenth and twentieth centuries.

Wherever Don Orione traveled, the crowds were so large that the police could barely maintain public order. For this reason, he was required to notify the police of his plans to venture outside. Nevertheless, detailed written documents surfaced that accused him of carnal relations with several women. Since nobody would substantiate the accusations, the advocates decided to concoct physical evidence.

Don Orione began to experience a general malaise throughout his body. His doctor confirmed that he was suffering from syphilis. As a result, he was to have contact with no one. He was committed, under strict surveillance, to a convent in San Remo, where he spent the last years of his life. He died there without ever explaining how he had contracted syphilis, insisting that he had never had sexual relations. Although everyone continued to revere him as a saint even after his death, strict orders were imposed against his canonization because of the disease.

Years later, after the affair had been put to rest, a barber-surgeon in Messina asked a priest and two witnesses to help him right a wrong that had been kept secret. The barber had taken refuge in the boarding school of the Orionini of Messina, after the earthquake of 1908, and he was often asked to cut and shave the head of its founder, Don Orione. Incited by a member of the confraternity, the barber agreed to accidentally nick Orione's head and disinfect it with the contents of a small bottle, which he later discovered had been tainted with syphilitic pus.

TWO SAINTLY MEN, DON ORIONE AND PADRE PIO, once accused of immorality by the Church, are now being venerated. At twilight, the sun's rays are at their longest and most beautiful. The course of sainthood is imperfect, but it is designed with precision and care.

For Giambattista Vico, the epitome of cunning was the willingness to use all available resources to achieve one's own end, deliberately lying and defaming others, and twisting the gifts of Providence for diabolical purposes. On this matter, Dostoyevsky reflects: "There are many men that have never murdered, yet they are much worse than those who have murdered six times."

While alive, Padre Pio and Don Orione, profoundly blessed by the Lord, were regarded by church officials with suspicion and diffidence, if not open disapproval and persecution. After their deaths, their lives have been recorded, their saintliness verified, and their prophetic messages diffused. The difference between mortals and saints is that mortals are preoccupied with problems, while saints live in the realm of solutions.

As soon as the announcement from Rome was issued that Padre Pio had committed a miracle, the media informed the world that he was to be beatified on May 2, 1999. God accepted him, despite all those who had been hostile to him. "Woe unto you also, ye lawyers! For ye build the sepulchres of the prophets, and your fathers killed them. 'Master thus saying thou reproachest us also' . . . Woe unto you also."

V

Weeds in the Wheat

The Ten Commandments are the largest guide that God has provided humanity to help individuals reach salvation. However, God provides an infinite number of other guides to individuals who still need deliverance.

We know that the Commandments are valuable and important, because they are products of God's infinite goodness. Yet, God is not limited by the finite good of the Ten Commandments, which are but a small part of him. The infinite love of God is incarnated in the love of good described in the Decalogue. Many people who adhere to and live out the Commandments still remain far from God, just as many people who believe in goodness fail to follow the Ten Commandments.

Each person has different weaknesses and vices due to his or her temperament, personal experience, and genetic makeup. Even a stopped clock tells the correct time twice a day, meaning that each of us possesses both a shadow of humanity and a glimmer of conscience. As a result, everyone has different obstacles to overcome, and the measures of guilt are not quantifiable in the Ten Commandments alone. Morality is judged according to respective scales: one scale measures conscious knowledge; the other, divine paternity.

The **Decalogue**, or the Ten Commandments, is the summary of the divine law given to Moses by God on Mount Sinai.

The **First Council**
of **Jerusalem** was
the meeting in
AD 50 where Peter,
Barnabas, and Paul
made speeches
defending Gentile
Christians and claimed
that faith in Jesus as
the Messiah was not
exclusively Jewish.

Morality is not static; it is a process in which values are constantly being sounded and tested in different contexts. At times, these ethical values are rediscovered in the light of contemporary experience. At others, they no longer apply and need refashioning according to the message of Christ.

At the First Council of Jerusalem, the apostles Syria and Selenica wrote in the first letter to their brothers at Antioch: *"For it seemed good to the Holy Ghost, and to us, to lay upon you no greater burden than these necessary things; that ye abstain from meats offered to idols, and from blood, and from things strangled, and from fornication: from which if you keep yourselves, ye shall do well. Fare ye well."* Today, no moralist would impose such strict definitions of sin. In those days, however, such regulations were considered necessary, and were accepted as dictated by the Holy Spirit in apostolic revelation.

The concept of decency is also dynamic rather than static, in which multiple elements of theory and practice, science and humanity, and instinct and behavior compete in differing measures. Don Primo Mazzolari said: "The Lord also makes use of misfortune. We do not know precisely what effect our sins have on God, and where he places the foundations for a bridge on the return road." Saint Isaac Siro reassuringly echoes this statement: "God is not fair, but he is endless Love."

In 1789, Stefano Avtandilian, the Armenian bishop of Tiflis, taught: "A silent tolerance of corrupt morals, however reprehensible, can be useful, particularly when dealing with a sterile and prohibitive pastoral teaching. In fact, the Gospel teaches that a deeply rooted weed that hasn't corrupted the wheat planted beside it, if eradicated inopportunely, would result in the uprooting of the wheat and a barrenness of the whole field. In this case, it is better to leave the lone weed as opposed to upset the whole field of wheat."

Saint Bernard's Teachings

Every Pope should learn to repeat, by heart, the advice that Saint Bernard wrote to his Cistercian disciple, who eventually became Pope Eugene III. If the reigning Pope is unaware of the materialistic movements within the ranks of the Roman Curia, then that ignorant Pontiff should recite what Saint Bernard wrote in his *Consideration IV* as often as he recites the breviary.

Eugene III never thought of becoming Pope; he preferred the rigorous monastic solitude of the Cistercians who refused to become involved in the earthly matters that had already compromised the Church. Eugene III was one of Saint Bernard's best disciples and was himself called Bernard. After his death, he was beatified and canonized in 1872. Saint Bernard sacrificed his solitary monastic life and provided his insights to the Church to help reform it.

Although already Pope, Saint Bernard continued to teach Eugene III as though he had never left his school, and continued to impart harsh lessons on life. We cite here Saint Bernard's most salient lessons—not to console those who degrade the Curia and present-day Church, but to exhort the reformers and address the revelations of the Madonna at Fatima.

Saint Bernard told Eugene III: "You must now reflect on those things that surround you, particularly your Curia. Here is the wound; it is up to you to cure it. Perhaps you smile because you think it is incurable, but do not be discouraged; you are expected to treat it, not heal it.

"Where should you begin to treat this illness, you may well ask. Do not pay attention to riches, since they influence some of the most serious abuses. Can you show me one man who has received you as Pope who hasn't been given generous sums of money or the promise of some in the future? Do they not expect the world to be given to them? They claim to be Christians only to do more damage

Pope Eugene III was exiled from Rome in 1146. While away, he reformed the clerics of western Europe. He led the second crusade and was beatified in 1872.

The **breviary** is a book of prayers, hymns, psalms, and readings for the canonical hours.

to those who trust them. You will have no secrets or plans that they are not privy to. They are incapable of doing good, and are masters of evil. They are impious toward God, impudent toward sacred things, cruel to one another, and envious and unforgiving of their neighbors. No one can love these people, because they love no one; and, while they pride themselves on being feared by all, it is absolutely necessary that they themselves be fearful. They will not be ruled, yet they have not yet learned how to govern.

"I have digressed, but it was only to open your eyes. Let's get back to the point. What is this business of buying favors with the spoils of plundered churches? And, what about the rich who squander the lives of the poor? Is it true that this practice started with you, and that heaven wants it to end with you? Look at you, the shepherd, bedecked in gold and ermine. What advantage does your flock have? I would dare say that it is more a flock of demons than of sheep. Was Peter like this? Did Paul amuse himself this way? Do you see that ecclesiastical zeal is all about prestige and careerism? Everything is done for one's career, and very little for holiness.

"You must find yourself a devoted man who will take charge for you, not with you. If he proves unfaithful, he will become a thief; if he is not prudent, he will be robbed. You must therefore look for an honorable and prudent man to head your family.

"You cannot be the last person to know about disorder in your house. Raise your hand to the guilty, since a lack of punishment breeds recklessness that opens the door to all kinds of excess. Your brothers, the cardinals, must learn by your example not to keep young, long-haired boys and seductive men in their midst.

"I am not counseling you not to be severe, but to be serious. Severity is for those who are weak-minded, but seriousness and sobriety keeps the reckless in check. The former is hateful, but the absence of the latter makes one a laughingstock. In any event, moderation is the most important. I don't want you to be either too severe or too weak. In the Palace, behave like a Pope; among your closest friends, behave like a father.

"Let me summarize. The Roman Church, which governs by the will of God, is the mother of the other churches, not their mistress, and you are not the master of bishops, but one of them. You must be an example of justice, a reflection of holiness, a witness to truth, a defender of the faith, a teacher of people, a guide to Christians, the one regulator of the clergy, a refuge for the persecuted, a defender of the poor, an eye for the blind, a voice for the mute, the priest of the Almighty, the vicar of Christ, the Lord's Anointed one, and, finally, the god of Pharaoh."

Saint Bernard wrote this and more, accurately representing the Roman Curia and its protagonists: Popes, cardinals, bishops, archbishops, dignitaries, prelates, careerists, crooks, and even the train of pretty young boys.

The Case of the Missing Dossier

In early 1974, Paul VI, who observed the corruption at the core of the Church, found himself forced to form a special commission to reorganize the administration of the Roman Curia. Instead, he entrusted Curia members with the secret mandate of ascertaining exactly what corruption existed.

Archbishop Edoard Gagnon, an upright and sincere Canadian prelate, was chosen as president of this special committee. He chose for his secretary (or rather was saddled with) Istvan Mester, a German monsignor and head of the Congregation of the Clergy. They went through almost all of the departments of the Curia, inviting employees to freely express their views on their superiors and the management of their offices.

Put at ease, many Curia members willingly disclosed deeds and misdeeds that had occurred in the workplace.

Elected in 1963, **Paul VI** continued John XXIII's vernacular reform of the liturgy. He also attempted to reassert papal primacy, despite growing dissent from within the Church.

The information gathered was both interesting and revolutionary. Monsignor Gagnon spent three months drafting a voluminous report, which the Vatican Freemasonry immediately found insulting, damning, and dangerous, because the names and hidden activities of certain Curia members appeared in it. The Curia decided it was necessary to do something so that the report would not reach Montini, the Pope, who was already in bad health. The interception of the report was to be executed with the utmost discretion, and a plan was hatched and carried out.

Once he had assembled the findings of the inquiry and concluded various parts of his report, Gagnon asked the Secretary of State to make an appointment with Paul VI, so he could share his findings on the corruption in the Vatican. Days passed, and Gagnon received no response. He finally decided that, given the confidential nature of the material, he should give the entire dossier and final report to the Congregation of the Clergy, where Mester would safeguard it in a solidly built, double-locking cabinet in his office. Although the archbishop didn't fully understand why, he obeyed the order.

On the morning of Monday, June 2, 1974, Mester entered his office and immediately realized that something was amiss—papers were on the floor, books were out of place, pamphlets were scattered everywhere. He then noticed that the cabinet adjacent to his desk was unhinged, and the dossier and all of the documents pertaining to Gagnon's investigation were missing. The weekend had been more than enough time for the thieves to calmly purloin the dossier.

Everyone was sworn to pontifical secrecy on the matter of the missing dossier. The Secretary of State and Gagnon were notified of the incident, and Gagnon, surprised, promised that he would immediately draft a second copy of the report. However, he was relieved of the task, and the head of security, Camillo Cibin, was asked to investigate the theft and

Freemasonry refers to the teachings and practices of the secret fraternal order of the Free and Accepted Masons. The Roman Catholic Church discourages membership in this liberal and democratic society that supports anticlerical attitudes.

report his findings to the Secretary of State. The Pope was informed of the break-in and the loss of the dossier, and absolute silence was ordered regarding the case.

Yet, by early afternoon on June 3, news of the break-in had already started to circulate, stating that thieves had forced open a cabinet and stolen some important documents. Journalists skeptically accepted the version of events presented to them by the Vatican press-office spokesman, Federico Alessandrini. Those who are well informed understand that when somebody at the Vatican claims to be unaware of what is being asserted, something is going on.

News of the missing dossier spread quite rapidly. In fact, the *Osservatore Romano*, the quasi-official newspaper of the Holy See, issued the following reassurance: "It was a real and proper burglary, perpetrated out of malice. Unknown thieves entered the office of a prelate and removed some dossiers kept in a sturdy cabinet with a double lock. The theft is sensational." In truth, the Masonic lodge knew both the perpetrators of the crime and those who had issued the order to steal the documents.

The mood in the Roman Curia at the time was very tense and Gagnon's report didn't alleviate the situation. A foreign head of the department wanted the five commission members interrogated and thrown out, but a cardinal opposed any investigation of his personnel. The dossier contained opinions and judgments on the personnel, superiors, and the administration of the entire Curia; hence, the robbery had been carefully planned and executed.

Even though he was never asked to resubmit his report, Gagnon drafted another one and requested a private audience with the Pope, which he was refused. He then asked the Secretary of State to forward the report, in secrecy, to Paul VI. Once again, the package was not delivered because the Pope had been told that the stolen papers had disappeared. The conspirators in the Curia had decided that the Pope was never to see or hear of the contents of that report.

Literally translated as "holy chair," the **Holy See** refers to the actual seat or residence of the Pope, with the various ecclesiastical authorities who constitute its central government.

Realizing that he had been deceived, Gagnon terminated his involvement in the affair. He consulted a few wise and morally upright individuals, and made the radical decision to return to Canada and retire with all of the privileges of his office. But, once Pope John Paul II was informed of the rectitude of this man, he was recalled to Rome and made a cardinal so that the Pope could consult with him on cleaning up the Vatican, which was steeped to the core in evil.

"For many walk, of whom I have told you often, and now tell you even weeping, that they are the enemies of the cross of Christ."

V I

The Cradle of Vatican Power

At the last consistory of the twentieth century, John Paul II, handing the biretta and the ring to his newly chosen twenty-nine cardinals, asked them in front of the world to assist him in guiding Peter's boat, knowing that he had little strength for the task. Because the Holy Father must trust his collaborators, they, for that reason, can take advantage of their position.

Strangely enough, the investiture of those cardinals coincided with the Carnival of Viareggio on February 22, 1998, when enormous papier-mâché masks and caricatures of infamous people are paraded through the streets. Ironically, the media indifferently televised the ungainly faces mounted on the parade floats in juxtaposition with the smiling faces of the satisfied and attractive cardinals.

In that speech, the Pontiff invited all the cardinals and dignitaries of the Curia to be converted, since the Church contains many allegorical characters who every day parade triumphantly behind large, expensive masks that are dignified on the outside but empty and dark on the inside. "Theater and life are not the same thing," say the clowns. Dante echoes this sentiment: "And he said to me: foolish creatures, how much ignorance will offend you."

The greatest future Pope will be the one who has the courage to remove the useless and corrupt from the atelier of the Church, who today fill the halls of the College of Cardinals.

A **consistory** is a solemn meeting of Roman Catholic cardinals convoked and presided over by the Pope.

A stiff, square cap with three or four ridges across the crown, a **biretta** is traditionally worn by the Roman Catholic Church's clergy. Priests wear black, bishops wear purple, and cardinals wear red.

The **College of Cardinals** is the body that elects the Pope. Its members are appointed by the Pope to help govern the Church.

According to the English saying, middle children cry more than their brothers and sisters to get more attention. The Pope knows this ordered system of patronage all too well, but he lacks the courage to remove anyone from the Curia. He understands that control is slipping from his trembling hand and that he has become too weak to remove the schemers with whom he invested so much power.

"But what can I do?" confided John Paul II to a Polish family member. "The offenders are many and high-ranking; I can't remove them all from office, especially in such a short amount of time. The press would never stop talking about it." As usual, history and propriety can wait; what remains important is that the story doesn't break.

In his pontifical yearbook, John Paul II records the names of political clique members, and the cardinals and dignitaries present in the Curia: Achille Silvestrini, Pio Laghi, Vincenzo Fagiolo, Luigi Poggi, Carlo Furno, Gilberto Augustoni, Dino Monduzzi, and so on—men who have inherited and continue to exercise the power that once belonged to Baggio and Casaroli. The present Vatican elite includes characters of both questionable associations and shaky spiritual integrity.

These dubious characters occupy positions of authority, having been made cardinals and bishops by the present Pope during his lengthy papacy. It would have been easier not to elevate them in the first place than it would be to demote or discredit them now. Every Pope is faced with the warning that Saint Catherine of Siena addressed to her beloved Christ: "I understand that here you have made some cardinals. I think that it honors God that you have applied yourself to making virtuous men. You know that better than I. The contrary would be an affront to God and compromise the Holy Church. I pray that you do what you must, energetically, with fear of God in your heart."

When cardinals, the department heads of the Curia, are well qualified and strong, the Pope can afford the luxury of being weak. However, when the heads of departments are weak and mean, the Pope must determinedly see to their removal.

Saint Catherine of Siena (1347-80) was an Italian mystic and diplomat who influenced Pope Gregory XI's termination of the "Babylonian Captivity" of the papacy, and persuaded him to return to Rome.

Insidious Plots

Every time a new Pope is elected, especially if he is not from the Curia, the cunning Curia members immediately recognize his weaknesses and determine how to win his favor. They then instruct the Pope to distrust everyone, except for them, his helpers and confidants.

The cardinals in the Curia know how to get what they want. To create a power vacuum at the top, they encourage the Pope to immerse himself in apostolic visits. They also arrange for him to be accompanied on these visits by two principal companions, the Secretary of State and the deputy, so that they don't stay behind and meddle in Curial matters. They pester the Pope obsessively with the Curia's foreign affairs in order to reserve the administration of internal affairs for themselves.

With this arrangement, the Pope's public appearances have become staged performances featuring thousands of dancing youths, VIPs from around the world, and unbearable music. When Providence wants to accurately represent itself, it will do so without pomp and circumstance.

The ecstasy of the huge crowds, the parades in city squares, and the monuments celebrating the Pope are too much. All papal regimes have profited from this lavish attention, and some have even used it to justify repression and violence. The following examples carry stinging but memorable lessons.

Once back in Rome, bewildered and dazed by the rush of the crowd, ears still ringing with delirious hosannas, it is virtually impossible for the Pope to discover the intrigues of the court. Even if he had some inkling of Curial matters, they would pale in comparison to dealing with exhilarated masses. The Pope lets the Roman Curia continue its abuse of power as he addresses the laity.

The true face of Christ's Church isn't the systematic production of parades and festive celebrations; its true face reflects and encompasses the child, the young, the sick, the worker, the family, and others. The celebrations and parades

Shouts or cries of fervent praise, **hosannas** are used to express adoration to God.

Pius XI's (Pope: 1922-39) pontificate was marked by great diplomatic activity. He spoke out against nationalism, racism, totalitarianism, and their threat to human dignity.

Pius XII (Pope: 1939-58) attacked totalitarianism, and excommunicated Catholics who joined the Communist Party.

Aiming to continue the work of Vatican II, Pope Paul VI (Pope: 1963-78) instituted the international **Synod of Bishops**, which assembled bishops to discuss relevant church concerns.

Cardinal Jan Pieter Schotte has been Secretary General of the Synod of Bishops since 1985.

mask the Church's decline, just as the thick facade of Saint Peter's Basilica attempts to hide its massive proportions.

In the meantime, though, pastors are poorly chosen. A Rwandan proverb teaches: "Even if God watches over your flock, try to entrust it to a vigilant shepherd." Taking advantage of the power vacuum at the Church's core, its officials generate piles of paperwork on incredible projects and proposals to submit to the Pope. When the Pope returns, steeped in glory, he is too tired and distracted to notice the insidious conspiracies hidden in the documents he signs. Everyone drafting the documents knows that the aging Pope won't absorb the notes on the report.

These politics suit the Prince of Darkness, who encourages these practices while leading Christ into temptation: *"Again, the devil taketh him up into an exceedingly high mountain, and showeth him all the kingdoms of the world, and the glory of them; and saith unto him, all these things will I give thee, if thou wilt fall down and worship me."*

DRAWING ON THE TEACHINGS OF PIUS XI AND Pius XII, the Second Vatican Council glorified a communal Church government directed by the bishops and the Pope, who would support each other reciprocally. Paul VI, pressured from various sides, established the Synod of Bishops in 1965. This assembly of bishops chosen from all over the world was supposed to meet periodically to help the Pontiff recognize and resolve the problems and questions of the growth and well-being of the faith.

This Synod cannot settle and enact laws without the Pope's consent, but the bishops consider the Synod a binding force that keeps Cardinal Jan Pieter Schotte (the iron fist of the ecumenical vision) and the episcopate of the whole world under observation and control. The Pope doesn't enforce restraint, but the Curia does, particularly the Secretariat of State.

Since the principle of reciprocal support has been inadequately applied, Cardinal Jan Pieter Schotte does all he can to gain clout for the College of Bishops. He attempts to attain the same privilege and responsibility enjoyed by the apostles of Christ who were encouraged to contribute their thoughts on the construction of the Church, even though Christ had infinite wisdom, did not need counsel, and occasionally reproached them: *"You do not know what you say!"*

Many bishops were eager to express their thoughts in this kind of forum. One such bishop was the Archbishop of San Francisco, Monsignor John Raphael Quinn, who, at age sixty-eight, resigned without animosity, professing his fidelity to the Pope. Courageously, Quinn invited the Pope and the Curia to review the matter of supremacy, which he no longer considered viable for the next millennium.

According to Vatican II, the real concept of church government, which is practiced today *sub Petro*, must be understood and practiced *cum Petro*. Failing to trust in the Holy Spirit, the episcopate has become a model for control. Structural reform is necessary, particularly regarding the relations between the Pope, the bishops, and the present administration of the Roman Curia. Nobody denies that the Pontiff, as head of the Church, has the right to teach in an appropriate manner. Rather, the question is when and under what circumstances should he prudently exercise that right.

While some emphasize the doctrinal aspects and prudence of supremacy, Quinn maintains that bishops don't feel free to present to the Synod of Bishops their perspectives on the subjects and issues on which they want to comment, such as divorce, remarriage, sacraments to the divorced, and general absolution.

The Church does not offer bishops the opportunity to discuss the most serious questions posed to the judges and doctors of the faith. This perpetuation of a medieval Vatican mentality prevents constructive dialogue on ecumenism. Many Orthodox, and numerous other Christians, are skeptical of a full communion with the Holy See, not because of its prejudice toward doctrinal or historical questions, but because the Roman Curia conducts itself as a controlling force rather than as a partner in faith.

Headed by the Cardinal Secretary of State, the **Secretariat of State** works closely with the Pope and is the most important body of the Curia.

A Latin term meaning "under Peter," **sub Petro** suggests government of the church under an authoritarian leader.

A Latin term meaning "with Peter," **cum Petro** suggests government of the church in conjunction with a democratic leader.

A **sacrament** is a rite—such as baptism, confession, marriage, or last rites—that is believed to have been ordained by Christ and that is a sign or symbol of a spiritual reality.

Absolution refers to the formal remission of sin imparted by a priest.

The supreme mission of the Church is not to gain political control. The real question of supremacy and community lies in the answer to the question: "What was it that God wanted for Peter?" To find the correct theological answer, perhaps another council must search for a response that better corresponds with the beliefs of Christ's followers and fraternal ecumenical dialogue.

POWER, BY ITSELF, IS NEUTRAL; IT IS ONLY defiled when it is coupled with self-interest. Humanity corrupts power with its love, passions, tastes, opinions, courage, artifice, and spontaneity. The group that holds power determines the conditions and behaviors of those who live within the power structure.

Ideology and bureaucracy rob the individual of conscience, humanity, and freedom of thought and expression, and replace them with the dictates of the power structure. Power structures are grounded in ideological fiction and legitimize everything without ever using the truth. Nobody ever truly possesses power, because power possesses and conditions everyone.

In such a closed environment, dissent is rejected outright. He who has the courage to dissent knows that he does so at great personal risk. To others, he is an insubordinate, someone who creates confusion and, because of this, he is marginalized, distanced, and suppressed.

The power in the Vatican Church originates in and emanates from the Secretariat of State. The Curia preserves itself by training its members, who have been chosen because they are supported and favored by influential superiors. These members will become the Pope's representatives to countries that maintain diplomatic relations with the Holy See. Such training and promotion guarantees that nothing changes. The Cardinal Secretary of State, assisted by his deputy and entire internal and external service, wields the power to determine who is accepted into the Curia.

Everyone knows that the Pope is the head of the Church; however, he doesn't personally govern it. He relies on the honesty of others to fairly govern the Church, particularly his Secretary of State, who governs the rest of the Roman Curia and, at times, the Pontiff.

The dangers and risks of authoritarianism include the pandering to personal and particular interests, the seeking of material profit, and the atrophying of personal responsibility and social insight.

Curial members-in-training are groomed in the pontifical academy, a school where hopefuls learn the protocol and haughtiness of diplomats and are instructed in polite conversation and self-assurance. The true diplomat is formed when he ignores what he knows and knows what he ignores. He must also learn to take advantage of his position by spying on the powerful dignitaries to whom he was recommended.

Nothing happens in the Vatican unless the Secretariat wills it. Virtually all of the department heads are at the command of the Secretary of State and his deputy, as well as the aspiring underlings of the Secretary. The Roman Curia should not be under the control of the Secretariat of State, but should be directly under the control of the Pope. In diplomatic life, both inside and outside of the Vatican, reputation is everything. Many concessions are made to people who hold power and enjoy status. By inflating the value of power, one often ends up inflating an individual who doesn't deserve attention.

Christ didn't want to study the structure of diplomacy; in fact, he modeled the opposite in the temple. Christ needs to return to whip the vendors of the temple, who have transformed the Church into a den of thieves.

His Majesty, Chance

Angelo Giuseppe Roncalli was a Catholic priest devoid of all careerist ambition. This son of a simple farmer was neither in charge of a respected group, nor did he know how to

As Pope John XXIII (1958-63), **Angelo Giuseppe Roncalli** made many reforms including stressing the pastoral duties of the clergy, actively promoting social reforms, and advancing cooperation with other religions.

appeal to a group of dignitaries to gain promotion. By pure chance, he had been appointed the apostolic delegate to the forty thousand Catholics of Bulgaria.

The Secretariat of State viewed Roncalli's conduct as a failure. He was looked down on because he often adapted the directives to accord with his good nature and personal ethics that reflected the maxim: "Exist without challenging one another, meet without fearing one another, entertain without compromising oneself." As a result, Rome often found itself in diplomatic situations that didn't correspond with the proper protocol for relations with Bulgarian and Turkish authorities.

The Secretariat often had to remind Roncalli that as an apostolic delegate in Bulgaria and Turkey, he wasn't a diplomat with full accreditation, but rather a papal delegate to local Catholic priests and bishops. Nevertheless, rather than conforming to the rules of the diplomatic code outlined by his superiors, he continued to involve the Holy See in situations that the Secretariat of State wanted no part of.

For example, in those years, it was unthinkable that a papal representative should cultivate friendships with the heads of the Orthodox churches beyond the strict rules of protocol. Without a second thought, Roncalli took his secretary, Monsignor Francesco Galloni, who later replaced him in Bulgaria until his expulsion in the fifties, to visit several patriarchs and dignitaries, inviting them to lunch, making friends, and ending any misunderstandings.

Despite his rank, Roncalli would visit government ministers to plead on behalf of the poor of every religion. To succeed in this project, since he never carried any money, he implored his secretary, saying: "Don Francesco, give a good tip to the bailiffs of this office so they will treat us better and recommend us to others!" And things always went just the way he wanted.

A deferential dignitary, Roncalli knew that he was not well regarded in Rome; but he was so averse to ambitions, aspirations, and honors that he was indifferent to outward appearances and formalities. When visiting his superiors in Rome, he would arm himself with patience, as he often noted in his diary. In the Eastern Congregation, they would send him to visit Monsignor Antonio Spina, the official responsible for Bulgaria and Turkey, who would say to his administrator: "Monsignor, that chatterbox Roncalli has arrived, go and see what he has to say. If he wants to see me, tell him I am busy!" Despite this, Roncalli's wonderful mildness, self-mastery, and spiritual profundity were recognized.

The Secretariat of State waited for the appropriate moment to relieve Roncalli of his diplomatic appointment and offer him an early retirement. While those in Rome sought to consummate their plan, Roncalli carried on: "What do I care?" he confided to Galloni.

In Paris during those years, Charles de Gaulle was at odds with the apostolic delegate, Monsignor Valerio Valeri, over the thirty French bishops who de Gaulle claimed had collaborated with the government of Pétain, and for which he was demanding Valeri's resignation. The Vatican would never agree to such a proposal, and it instructed Valeri to firmly oppose it. Relations between the two sides reached a breaking point, and de Gaulle demanded and succeeded in obtaining the removal of Valeri, who, when he was recalled to Rome, was immediately made a cardinal.

The Vatican was displeased with de Gaulle's behavior and, out of spite, delayed appointing a new delegate. The fastidiousness of the French president made the new appointment very difficult. In the Secretariat, they considered which pontifical representative would suit him, but nobody available at the time would suffice. For de Gaulle, the long delay was a bitter diplomatic pill that he swallowed unwillingly.

One day, the French president was meeting the Ambassador of Turkey and, after the official protocol, the conversation shifted to the diplomatic difficulties that confront heads of state when they deal with competing interests from a foreign body such as the Holy See. Needless to say, this conversation fueled the fire. The Turkish government, to spite diplomatic orders contrary to the Koran, makes itself an enemy to half the world, including the Vatican.

Interested, de Gaulle inquired: "How do you manage?" The Turkish diplomat answered: "My government orients itself according to the individuals that represent the Holy See, which ranks as one of the most important international powers. For example, the apostolic delegate that we have now is among the best we have ever had—Monsignor Giuseppe Roncalli, a kind, humane, and cunning old devil, like all priests." De Gaulle noted this and asked the Turkish official to recount some other anecdotes, such as the one about the three hundred children whom Roncalli declared baptized so that they would be saved. Two hours after their conversation, a message was sent from Paris to the Vatican expressing the French government's pleasure in accepting the apostolic delegate of Turkey as the new representative in Paris.

Monsignor Domenico Tardini, a member of the foreign relations directorate, who viewed Roncalli as a bungling and chatty delegate, was astounded by the request from Paris. Given the tense relations with France, Tardini could not see Roncalli managing such a delicate and complex situation, where the most able diplomats had already failed. The Vatican decided to consider the matter and delayed its response.

In December 1952, not long before Christmas, de Gaulle was supposed to receive Christmas greetings from the Dean of the diplomatic corps who had not yet been designated. In the Dean's absence, he was to be replaced by the vice-Dean who was, as luck would have it, the Russian Ambassador and an outspoken Communist.

Given de Gaulle's ultra-right-wing politics, an appointment of this nature was unacceptable, and the Vatican recognized this. De Gaulle contacted the Vatican and demanded that it remedy the matter. Tardini, pressed into action, wired Roncalli in Istanbul and requested that he

The **Koran** is the sacred book of Islam revealed by God to the prophet Mohammed. It is the Muslim equivalent of the Bible.

return immediately to Rome to prepare for his new appointment as the delegate to Paris. Roncalli, who had repeatedly heard rumors of his return to the diplomatic corps, thought it was all a bad joke at his expense and responded that he was amused and that he wished everyone a Merry Christmas and Happy New Year. Tardini's next message was much more explicit; he insisted that the matter was serious and that Roncalli return to Rome before Christmas. Roncalli left immediately.

Pope Pacelli cautioned Roncalli against saying too much in his speech at the beginning of the year; in fact, he suggested that Roncalli send a draft to the Secretariat of State for approval before delivering it. Roncalli promised to do his best, but said he wouldn't have enough time to organize his ideas and put them into draft form before leaving for Paris.

Once there, one of Roncalli's first orders of business was to visit the vice-dean, the Russian, who had invited him to dinner. Over several courses and glasses of wine in the dimly lit room, the two struck up a friendship. Roncalli seized the opportunity, and asked his Russian friend: "Mister Ambassador, what would you have said in the speech, if I hadn't arrived in time?" The vice-Dean immediately placed a duplicate copy of his speech in the hands of the new Dean who read it, memorized it, and delivered it to de Gaulle and the ambassadors of the French diplomatic corps, who were amazed by its subtle sensibility. Only the Russian smugly knew what had transpired.

Everyone was pleased with the outcome of the appointment, and the fate of the thirty bishops was secure. Relations between De Gaulle and Rome became conciliatory, and Roncalli became a mediator for any delicate situation that arose between the Holy See, France, and the countries behind the Iron Curtain, whose problems seemed to disappear with his good-humored intervention.

In 1956, when it was time to replace the now-elderly delegate, Pope Pacelli made him cardinal and Patriarch of

Venice, where he was to have spent the rest of his days. The Curia felt that he had sown and reaped a wonderful life, without even wanting it and carried by luck and fortunate circumstances.

A **patriarch** is a high-ranking bishop with authority over other bishops. The title is conferred on four prelates, including the Archbishop of Venice.

When Pius XII died, the Patriarch of Venice, now aged seventy-six, was at the bottom of the list of candidates for promotion. The Armenian Patriarch, Cardinal Gregorio Agagianian, appeared to be the front-runner for the papacy. This large and kindly fellow, both shepherdlike and ascetic, had spent much of his life in the West in the Roman Curia, whose ways and customs he knew well. But everybody knew that whoever enters the conclave as the prediction for the next Pope usually leaves as a cardinal.

A **conclave** is the meeting in the Sistine Chapel where cardinals are secluded continuously while choosing the next Pope.

Instead, the Holy College thought it wise to elect an older cardinal, who wouldn't disrupt matters and who would leave the necessary Church reform to his replacement. On the third ballot, Roncalli was elected. He took a name that nobody expected, John XXIII. Tardini, who had held Roncalli in such disregard, now found himself faced with him as Pope. He fully expected to be dismissed; instead, Roncalli made him a cardinal and appointed him Secretary of State.

From the very first days, John XXIII revealed himself to the world as the true prophet that he was. Stimulated, enlightened, and nourished by a sense of history, he organized the Second Vatican Council for whose success he was wholly responsible. In a letter to Voltaire, Frederick the Great wrote: "His Majesty, Chance accounts for three-quarters of the work in this wretched world." In this instance, the Lord accounted for the fourth quarter of Roncalli's success.

The Laundered Past

Two monsignors who were very good friends—an American and an Italian—worked together in the same office of the Secretariat of State. At the beginning of the seventies, they bought an apartment and moved in together, with a house-keeper to care for them both.

The American had started to dabble in drugs, lightly at first and then heavily. His Italian monsignor friend tried to discourage him, but the American was either unable or unwilling to quit. More and more frequently, the American would be found lying ill in bus shelters around the city. When he could manage, he would ask someone to escort him home. Other times, he would be brought unconscious to the emergency ward, where his Italian friend would immediately collect him and whisk him off to a private clinic, where his name would never appear on the register.

At the office, the Italian would tell his colleagues that his American friend had returned to America for a family crisis and, to those in the apartment, he would say that he had gone on a mission for work. These stories worked temporarily, but many people had other suspicions.

When the Italian celebrated mass in the mornings, the American would stay home. When he had celebrated morning services, often the drugs from the night before had not worn off, and he had distressed those in the congregation, since, in a stupor, he would distractedly skip the most important parts of the mass, even the consecration.

> The blessing and transubstantiation of the Eucharistic bread and wine during mass is called the **consecration**.

Notwithstanding some love letters written by the American prelate to a woman that appeared in the newspaper, the powerful Italian monsignor managed to plead his case and that of his American friend so well that they were both made nuncios, and important ones at that. The Italian has since died, but the American continues to enjoy an ambassador's pension.

> A **nuncio** is a high-ranking papal official who is permanently assigned to working with a civil government.

So, in the Secretariat of State, a person's past is of no consequence—it emerges from the wash as clean and white as a baptismal stole. Moreover, the dirt remaining is not to be mentioned, since all members of the Secretariat are pure.

V I I

The Bureaucracy

The term **post-conciliar** refers to the period following Vatican II.

The post-conciliar Roman Curia has developed an international character, as if it were something new. The Curia has always been international; that is, Catholic. The difference is that, before, both Italians and foreigners alike began their ascent of the Church's hierarchy from the lowest level. Today's foreigners don't like to rise through the ranks, and they set their sights on prestigious and powerful appointments, trampling that eighty percent of saintly officials whom John Paul I defined as "the indispensable mechanism of the clock that knows how to indicate the correct time in the history of the Church." The remedy to these inappropriate ascensions is proving to be more damaging than the illness.

Born Albino Luciani, **John Paul I** was elected in 1978 and ruled for only 34 days before his death.

Experts of nothing, the new foreign superiors, especially the Polish ones, allow themselves to be manipulated by their secretary-monsignors. These superiors, almost always unqualified and feeble, are kept on a tight leash by their lackeys. Every prelate manipulates and abuses his superior regarding important matters, often to gain promotions and even to dismiss others.

Everyone knows that the Church belongs to Christ, but that God loans it to the brave. The careerists are ready to take total control of it, in an attempt to make it their own.

The Excellent, the Excellers, and the Excellent Thieves

After the Secretariat of State, the key ministry in the Curia is the Congregation that nominates bishops for the Pope, led by Cardinal Sebastiano Baggio. In reality, the Pontiff signs only the first name he is presented with in a triad, and the rest is arranged by the one who has managed to climb his way to the top. This ministry is important because it is a strategic position in the Church that, along with the Synod of Bishops, attempts to divest the Pope of as much power as possible. To reach the episcopate today, successful candidates fall into the following categories:

1. The Excellent: ecclesiastical figures whose saintly devotion and dedication to study are beyond reproach; priests suited to the episcopate, armed with diocesan or Curial degrees, who are considered worthless by their superiors; men considered saintly by most, even if cast aside or if they refused advancement because they felt themselves unworthy;

2. The Excellers: the few dignitaries who become bishops even though they do little or possess nothing to deserve the nomination; many of these men have modestly claimed not to be up to the task entrusted to them;

3. The Excellent Thieves: those who have secured ecclesiastical rank through furtive ways such as friendly attention to those in favor, questionable donations to prelates, allegiances and service of all sorts, expensive gifts for influential people; these individuals are conceited and proud to have reached the top by any means possible.

These candidates to the episcopate are a plague on Christ's true Church. When church officials claim they have done nothing to secure their position, they insult their listener since they have always done something to secure it. The episcopal nomination only arrives to those actively seeking promotion, who then claim to accept it only to submit to God's will.

At the same time, the dignitary responsible for this appointment strives to convince others that the promotion was deserved and that he was justified in making the appointment. These practices only confirm the prejudices of the evil-minded.

Few in this post-conciliar period are rewarded for actual personal merit; most are promoted for glaringly obvious intrigues and extraordinary services.

Miters without Heads

Miters are headdresses worn by Christian bishops.

The Congregation of Bishops recommends candidates for bishoprics and establishes dioceses.

Before the Second Vatican Council, bishops were named by the Congregation of Bishops, assisted by other countries in the ministry for the propagation of the Catholic faith. Those from the Eastern Church observe another code that is also plagued by intrigues and corruption.

Since Vatican II, the process for selecting candidates for the episcopate occurs in two phases and on two consecutive levels. The process begins in both national and regional episcopates where nominations are blessed by the apostolic nuncio of the country, passed to the appropriate ministry in Rome to ensure there are no serious impediments to the candidatures, and finally submitted to the Pope for approval.

The new post-conciliar process falsifies or silences facts about candidates. The meddling in this promotion process must be better defined and controlled.

With this new standard, the responsibilities among the episcopal conference, nuncio, and ministry in Rome are often skillfully manipulated. The nuncios distance themselves from the national episcopates so as not to ruin their careers, especially when candidates supported by certain bishops turn out contrary to how they had been presented.

For thirty years, the Church has selected bishops that it deserves, and now many miters are running around without any heads to support them.

The appointment of bishops must be revisited and perfected, so that it becomes an inclusive and participatory event for the whole Church. Divine right demands that one bishop be placed in every local church. Choosing the bishops is a human ecclesiastical right that, over the centuries, has taken various forms. Until 1829, the policy of the Holy See was to leave the appointment of bishops for vacant dioceses to the regional bishops. After the death of Leo XII, only twenty-four of the 646 diocesan bishops were directly nominated outside of the papal state. For the most part, these direct appointments were due to the difficulties in countries such as Albania, Greece, and Russia.

Not every candidate is referred to the Pope; only the favorite who appears highest on the list. On paper, that candidate is described marvelously, even if in reality he leaves much to be desired. As mentioned earlier, the reports presented to the Pope are so dense that he can't possibly wade through them in the time allotted, which is deliberately kept short. How can he fairly judge the 5,000 people nominated as bishops? Trusting blindly, he affixes only the date and his signature to the document, which becomes pontifical approval of the appointment of the newly elected bishop. Certainly, this procedure is not stringent enough to ensure that the elected monsignor is worthy of the position, whether in a diocese or the Roman Curia. It is even less able to ascertain whether the appointee belongs to one of the Masonic lodges or some other underworld organization.

For the appointment of bishops, Pius XI, the scourge of Mussolini, gathered information from other channels before consenting to their approval. That resolute Pope replied to one of his cardinals who highly praised one of his

An unpopular Pope (1823-29) who condemned Freemasons and other secret societies, **Leo XII** lacked insight into the politics of his age and consequently implemented measures that would hinder his successors in resolving issues during their papacies.

own protégés whom he desperately wanted to become a bishop: "Cardinal, my only objection to your candidature is that your Eminence seems so interested in its outcome!"

Before Vatican II, the ministry selected qualified individuals for the various offices in the core of the Church. Because of this, appropriate individuals were appointed to govern dioceses or the Curia. The success of the original procedure is evident in the noble and saintly figures of the Italian and European episcopate in the last decades of the previous century and the first ones of this century, many of whom were or are being venerated.

In the last decade, there has been a tendency to reverse this selection process. For example, in 1984 the French episcopate introduced *recentrage*, which called for a return both to the centrality of Rome and to the bishop within his diocese. At present, the selection of bishops has been limited to territorial parameters, where each, often regional, episcopal conference—as in Italy, Spain, France, and Latin America—advances its own preferences, all chosen from their local favorites.

Most of these selections are opportunistic and competitive. Obviously, the secretary-chauffeur of the diocesan bishop is likely to secure a promotion to the episcopate. The young ambitious priest who offers himself to the bishop as secretary-chauffeur always anticipates future rewards from the well-served bishop.

At episcopal conferences, bishops rarely oppose a candidate for fear of being in the minority. The actual vote is just a formality. The vote on the nominee, who is unknown to most, is granted in faith to the bishop who nominates him, who then acknowledges his debt to his brothers at subsequent conferences.

So, the eventual choice of candidates is based on blind faith, not on who deserves the appointment. Saintly men averse to exhibitionism never gain the position, but always those eager for success and power. Rarely does a man of culture and saintly example pander to his bishop, although he knows that by not doing so, his possibility of promotion is minimized.

When a bishop takes undue advantage of a priest, it is obvious and natural that the servant will petition his superior for future favors. After ten or fifteen years of such symbiotic, opportunistic service, the bishop cannot easily release his aide without a suitable reward. If the bishop feigns ignorance, his servant reminds him, first indirectly and then directly, that he expects something in return for his dedicated service.

A forgetful cardinal, whose personal secretary came from outside the priesthood, was reminded by his aide of the many years that he had served him with only a bishop's nomination to show for it. The cardinal would have tried to secure a bishop's position for him, but because of the servant's past, he couldn't. When the cardinal advised him that he should not aspire to some goals, the prelate responded aggressively. He reminded his master that when the cardinal appointments had been delayed and he had almost had a heart attack because of the wait, it was he, his servant, who had reassured him and told him to have patience and faith in the Pope. The cardinal was in no mood for such a lecture from someone in that position.

Occasionally, a dignitary will indifferently cast aside a servant for which he has no further use. Eschewing every possible debt of gratitude, he rejects his faithful and useful follower, an action as despicable as falsely promoting him.

A TELEPHONE CONVERSATION BETWEEN TWO bishops on the eve of a conference contained the following exchange: "Excellency, you remember that last time you asked me to endorse your candidate at the ballot? This time I would like to ask you to do the same for my good secretary, who is an excellent candidate for the episcopate. For about fifteen years, he has also been my chauffeur and I can vouch for his unconditional commitment in the service of the Church. You, Excellency, can understand that such priests must be rewarded for their dedication to the bishop. Imagine if I had hired a layman for the same amount of years: I have saved the diocese a considerable amount of money!"

Votes are counted and recounted before the bishops meet at the episcopal conference to usher in their favorites, so that they can withdraw a candidate and wait for a better occasion to represent him. The outcome of these conferences is predetermined, and the actual event is often rushed. Too many religious men are willing to sell their souls in support of the Curia, whether legitimate or illegitimate, ethical or unethical.

What is the value of the votes that appoint bishops or other elected church officials? Are the votes credible? Are the participants conscious of and dedicated to their voting responsibilities? These questions are serious and deserve an authoritative answer.

Cardinal Joseph Ratzinger has held the position of Prefect of the Congregation for Doctrine of the Faith, and was President of both the Pontifical Biblical Commission and the International Theological Commission.

According to Cardinal Ratzinger, the truth cannot be elicited through a vote. To believe so would be like substituting the truth of power for the power of truth. A unanimous vote does not constitute the truth, but acts as evidence against it. It follows that an episcopal conference cannot vote on the truth of something, because their decision is always in perfect agreement.

In many episcopal conferences, the majority, dictated perhaps by the desire to live quietly or to conform outright, accepts the positions of an enterprising minority that determinedly drives toward preestablished goals. The majority adopts a false uniformity, and says: "We want what you want, and vote for what you vote for." This amorphous majority would never end this uncomfortable allegiance, since making enemies with powerful members, however much in the minority, is the last thing it wants.

Ratzinger, on the question of this silent complicity, said: "I know bishops that confess in private that they would have decided differently if they had been alone. By accepting the law of the group, they avoid appearing outmoded or close-minded. Voting in unison seems innocent enough, but often this *togetherness* borders on scandal and folly. Today, more than ever, bishops need to ensure that the individuals appointed to serve the Church are fair and capable."

We have witnessed situations where different bishops have sought the same goals for their ambitious priests. These priests are often sent to Rome to attend one of the pontifical universities, to gain an advantage over their rivals. Mark Twain accurately represented the absurdity of this action when he stated: "The cauliflower is nothing but the cabbage that studied at Harvard." In Rome, we often see miters on empty heads as a result of decisions made at conferences and secretly prearranged over dinners or through telephone calls.

At the Market of Monsignors

In a fully funded Roman college in India, three priests, who were all close friends, shared everything they studied and desired, including erotic fantasies. The priests would wake up around three a.m. to watch risqué homosexual and heterosexual pornography, making note of the various positions and participating in reciprocal exchanges of their friendship. Spied upon and followed by one of their brothers, this priest reserved the right to discuss their encounters, but never betrayed them to the authorities.

Once back in Italy, two of these priests were immediately made auxiliary, then diocesan bishops. The third one had to wait a little longer before enjoying such privileges. So far, no one has complained about their pastoral conduct, but there are rumors about their indulgence toward young obliging clerics.

AMAZINGLY, ALL OF CARDINAL ACHILLE SILVESTRINI'S personal secretaries and public relations attachés have had successful careers; they are now all bishops, nuncios, and dignitaries of the Curia. His current personal secretary also hopes to receive his reward before his master passes away.

IN THE FOLLOWING PAGES DEDICATED TO fraudulent degrees and theses, we will refer to the promotion of one of Silvestrini's personal secretaries who cunningly achieved the position of archbishop. This protégé of Silvestrini had been falsely awarded a degree based on a thesis that he hadn't even read. This isn't an invention, but God's truth.

When the prefect of a ministry considers his office a personal kingdom, his arbitrary choices and abuses of power become blatant and beyond reproach. In this case, too, Saint Bernard is worth quoting: "A lack of punishment breeds recklessness that opens the door to all kinds of excess."

A MONSIGNOR IN THE CURIA KNEW THAT THE bishops of his country had systematically left his name off the list of candidates for the episcopate as a result of his amorous adventures. With admirable resourcefulness, he vied for a promotion despite his reputation. He invited cardinals, ambassadors, and politicians to attend dinners and lunches at his house, where they mingled with some of the highest-ranking church officials from the Vatican and elsewhere. At the end of these events, he would ask them to sign a guest register so that they could see the names of previous guests.

The monsignor arranged a meeting between his ambassador to the Holy See and the head of his ministry, who had a weakness for swindling the Curia and the Pope. The diplomat endorsed the monsignor, who he suggested should not have to wait much longer for his episcopate. The cardinal promised the ambassador that he would soon be nominated. The diplomat immediately sent word of this to the monsignor.

When the list of candidates for the episcopate reached Rome, the name of the monsignor was missing. Within three days, the head of ministry compiled a falsified dossier of information on the candidate and asked three of his bishop friends to submit reference letters on his behalf. As an argument for his promotion, one of the bishops said it had been rumored that the monsignor had already been made the bishop of a diocese, and that his village had already celebrated; therefore, they might as well make him a bishop. The only problem with the story was that it couldn't have referred to that particular monsignor because, at the time of the claim, the candidate wasn't even a priest.

An entirely new office was created and, disregarding the normal procedure, the cardinal slipped the name of this monsignor to the Pope along with the others who had been properly elected. The monsignor was granted his episcopate with papal approval.

A disaster ensued because the new bishop became troublesome to his endorser. The cardinal was rebuked for the serious intrigues that were being attributed to *his* bishop. Finally, unhappy with not being promoted to another important archdiocese, the new bishop convinced a number of priests to sign a petition rejecting the candidate who had been elected by the Synod, proposing that he replace him. The nomination took three months to be decided, but he didn't succeed.

A MANIC-DEPRESSIVE UNDERSECRETARY, WHO was prone to dramatic mood swings, was known in the Vatican for his attempts to make money through corrupt schemes. At one point, he was illegally buying fake Russian icons with ministry money and selling them as authentic relics.

AN OLD AMERICAN PARISH PRIEST HAD REALIZED the weakness for gifts and rewards of many Curia members. He had spent his life serving corrupt monsignors, Curialists, and prelates of his country, treating them lavishly with impressive results. Because he was aging, he had someone in the registry office change his birth date, subtracting years as he gained them.

When he arrived in Rome, it was as though Santa Claus had arrived. He visited the most influential people and dined them in Rome's most expensive restaurants until one of these officials advanced his name for an episcopate. When people questioned his age of seventy-two years, his supporter replied that a little bit of the Holy Spirit couldn't hurt anyone. In no time, he was invested with the episcopal miter.

This appointment was a scandal to the priests and faithful of that and the surrounding dioceses. He squandered millions of dollars and sold many diocesan possessions, including the bishop's residence and the cathedral. When he died, it was discovered that he had given them to his birth-daughter, who had been blackmailing him with her paternity.

This corrupt and corrupting bishop had paid the undersecretary to intervene on his behalf and ask the Pope not to accept his compulsory resignation. Because he was already riddled with cancer, his request to maintain his position was denied.

Unbeknownst to the cardinal, the undersecretary ordered the deputy of the nunciature to write to everyone telling them that the bishop was returning to his diocese with full powers of jurisdiction. He lied, knowing that the Pope had ordered the opposite.

Having discovered the truth through the grapevine, the Cardinal Prefect summoned the undersecretary and placed photocopies of the documents he had written under his nose, asking him to justify his actions, which he was unable to do. The cardinal reproached him: "Monsignor, if you betray the decisions of the Pope like this, I tell you that there isn't room here for the two of us: it's either you or me in this office!"

The **Cardinal Prefect** is the head of a group of cardinals.

The undersecretary protested all the way to the third level of the Vatican loggia, asking what he was supposed to have done. For a clerk of insignificant rank, the answer should have been simple—dismissal or transfer to a lower office. Instead, he was promoted and one of the ranking officials suggested that he find a nuncio or secretary to write to the Pope on his behalf, presenting him as a candidate for a nuncio. If the letter reached the Pope's hands, the official would ensure the desired result.

Despite the reprimand for insubordination, the undersecretary became nuncio in an eastern country, where he remained for a short time before being dismissed for the many rumors surrounding his ascent. The higher you climb, the harder you fall; but you can still climb.

AN UTTERLY INCOMPETENT MONSIGNOR, EMPLOYED in the ministry where bishops are trained, was the nephew of an enterprising bishop. Despite this timid nature, he knew how to captivate the benevolence of his superiors.

Because of his sheepish temperament, he enjoyed the protective company of a community of nuns, and he received the solicitous attention of the Mother Superior. Their relationship began to attract attention, and his superior asked him to find another chaplaincy. Once established in a new community of nuns, and having been confronted with the same injunction from the same official, the crafty monsignor realized that he was risking his career.

In the early eighties, he decided to ask for a one-year leave to do missionary work in Kenya. Instead of being humiliated, this estrangement from the nuns gave him an opportunity to earn back some credit.

He lasted there less than three months. He was secretly joined by a nun and was convinced to return to Rome. Meanwhile, an undersecretary position in the ministry became available, which, by seniority, would go to a colleague of his age. Not attaining that position would be tantamount to ending his career, so he and his uncle moved in skillful synchrony to secure him the promotion.

Half an hour before the papal decision was announced, the monsignor rightfully in line for the nomination was informed by the prefect that he would be granted a diocesan episcopate while the other monsignor, in recompense for his missionary work in Africa, would be appointed undersecretary.

This news met with little approval since the new undersecretary was devoid of intelligence and ability. The poor fellow lasted only a few years in that position before he was offered the bishopric of a small diocese in the outskirts of Rome, just to remove him from the ministry.

AROUND THE TIME THAT PADRE PIO DIED, ANOTHER monsignor, also the nephew of a deceased bishop, sought to win the nomination for papal administrator of the Hospice for the Relief of Suffering, in San Giovanni Rotondo. Years passed, but nobody considered making him a bishop. He would appear regularly in Vatican circles, but he was ignored. He understood that more was required of him to attain the position, and he began to ply the officials with gifts.

The monsignor filled vans, which were at his disposal from the hospital, with everything imaginable. He would personally deliver items to cardinals and influential dignitaries of the Curia, in hopes that they would help him become a bishop despite his age. By now, the arrival of these relief vans was well known in Vatican circles, and people would cruelly say that the Magi had arrived bearing gold, frankincense, myrrh, and a little something extra.

One of his protectors from the Roman Curia, a cardinal well provided for by the relief vans, disagreed with a Curial member who had stated that the generous monsignor's age precluded him from becoming a bishop. The cardinal retorted that it wasn't too late for him and that something would soon happen regarding his nomination to bishop. Mammon was becoming a prophet.

Knowing that he was receptive to gifts, the aspiring bishop continued to lavish gifts on the cardinal. Aware of the excess, he wittily quoted Jeremiah: *"You seduced me God, and I allowed myself to be seduced!"* All men have a threshold that, once crossed, makes them corruptible.

A few months later, news of the monsignor's nomination was revealed. The generous corruptor, in his sixty-eighth year, became an auxiliary bishop to an archbishop fifteen years his junior. Despite the age difference, the old fellow was to assist the young archbishop who was in excellent health and had never dreamed of asking Rome for an assistant.

Shortly after the archbishop's ordination, he had to run to the bedside of his assistant who, ironically, was recovering from a heart attack that had placed him in the very hospital where he had begun his aspirations. None of this was made public.

Mammon is an Aramaic term meaning worldly riches.

UPON LEARNING OF SOME DUBIOUS NOMINATIONS, the eminent professor of history at one of Rome's most prestigious seminaries, Monsignor Pio Paschini, ironically observed the following to his students: "The Holy Spirit has made this man a bishop! Can you imagine how badly we make the Holy Spirit look before the eyes of the world?"

It is difficult to communicate the strange ways of the Holy Spirit to a rational world.

Corruption Included

Aspiring bishops will do just about anything to secure support for their candidatures, regardless of price. Their sponsors herald them as valuable, but instead of enriching their own diocese, they generously present them to others.

When the bishops finally arrive at their destination, they are like time bombs placed in greener pastures.

An archbishop who had ensured the promotion of four of his favorite priests, claimed that he had forwarded the candidature for the fifth bishop, now in his forties, ten years earlier, but that the officials in the appropriate department had advised him to let the young priest mature in the ministry. They agreed to reconsider the matter ten years later, which is precisely what occurred. The protector must have lost track of time and a sense of proportion, since he had believed that his charge was worthy of promotion to the episcopate at age thirty-one, after only eight years in the priesthood.

THERE ARE ALSO THOSE BISHOPS WHO DO THE opposite and block every nomination to the episcopate for the duration of their tenure because of too many scruples, because of jealousy, or because nobody meets their standards. In these cases, the best and brightest priests lose out.

It has been said: "In less pleasant and fiercer times, thieves were hung on crosses; in these less fierce and more pleasant times, crosses are hung on thieves."

The Church must abandon its sordid ways, its privileges, and its securities so that it may become pure and calm.

A Christian cannot believe if he is not believable, especially if he chooses to live out his apostolic vocation in the priesthood or the episcopate.

VIII

Episcopal Candidates and Cardinal Baronies

For 2,000 years, the Church has gathered information on the lives of episcopal candidates from their most influential patrons. Once it is established that he has no children, no hereditary illnesses, that he isn't insane, that he is an able administrator, and that he is obsequious, then he is fit to be bishop of any diocese on earth.

This practice cannot continue as we enter the third millennium. Ridiculously, while society is preoccupied with computers, information technology, and interplanetary exploration, the Church still selects its bishops based on the recommendation of those directly interested in their promotion. Newly appointed bishops are entrusted with clergy and believers whom they subject to improvisational and inventive leadership. The incompetent neophyte wonders what a bishop does and, to worsen matters, finds himself coveted and pursued by others who want to ascend the ranks.

Since the fifth and sixth centuries, the Church authorities understood that they would be unable to confront the pastoral and spiritual problems of the faithful without well-trained priests. So, it created environments where diocesan and religious clerics could be trained before being ordained. Over time, they perfected these institutions, which were later called seminaries and novitiates. The Council of Trent was instrumental in this endeavor and implemented severe reform in these institutions.

The nineteenth ecumenical council of the Roman Catholic Church, better known as the **Council of Trent**, was convened in 1544 to deal with the crisis of the Protestant Reformation.

How has the Church instructed and shaped the candidates for the episcopate over these 2,000 years, other than accept them on the merit of their prelate friends? Is it still acceptable to use this outdated method of appointing bishops who typically lack proper training and thorough schooling? Without similar institutions, how can these individuals succeed in reforming the Church and become true fathers and pastors?

This arbitrary and corrupt standard of selecting priests and suggesting that they are intelligent and capable enough to perform a bishop's duties is no longer enough. This practice is especially questionable since it accepts recommendations from those most likely to benefit from the success of those promoted. The Church should have recognized the need for change long ago and, surprisingly, the Church hasn't already found a more suitable form of selection before now. Strangely, until now, not a single Pope, nor any of his collaborators, has thought to undertake a project of this nature and importance, which is still urgently needed. We also need to establish a training center for those nominated to the episcopate, with a specialist program intended for the ecclesiastical sector.

Many will oppose such a comprehensive proposal and, without reflecting, will view it as unfeasible and unmanageable. These opponents would be the ones thwarted and deprived of the power that they presently hold in their corrupt hands.

Justly, all people should be able to consider the young clerics preparing for the priesthood, so, if they have something to contribute, they can do so at the appropriate time. Rightly and fairly, the faithful should be equal partners and participants in the selection of priests that the Church proposes as possible candidates for bishops.

Since the Church recently began to ask the clergy and the people for their advice on elevating a simple cleric to the priesthood, why does the Church maintain rigorous papal silence regarding promoting a priest to the head of a diocese?

We must end this practice that favors manipulators. By establishing a school to train all aspiring clerics, these young men would be visible to the faithful and could be carefully judged and approved by all. By the same token, candidates could also be denounced, perhaps because of an association with a Masonic mafia sect or party, as commonly occurs.

Enrollment in the school would not guarantee the student a career, a prelacy, or even a bright future. Students would be advised that most will remain in the service of their parishes and to dispense with any visions of grandeur.

Such instruction could be divided into two consecutive sets of courses. The first set would teach candidates to be bishops and would include lessons on required qualities, spiritual and cultural pastoral preparation, fiscal management of the diocese, social and interpersonal skills, and so on. The second set would be reserved for candidates who have already been appointed to an episcopate, to complete their formal episcopal instruction. It would include specific theoretical and practical lessons related to applying their instruction to their particular diocese, or the office where the bishop would be responsible for exercising power over subjects or peers.

In this second set of courses, the successful candidate would learn what was expected of him as bishop of that diocese, the priests with whom he would interact, the faithful entrusted to him, the works and programs he would continue, the properties to maintain, the obstacles to overcome, the qualities and virtues to demonstrate, and whatever else is deemed relevant.

WHEN A NEW BISHOP TAKES OFFICE, CONSCIOUSLY or unconsciously, he orders that everything be done opposite to his predecessor's methods to make his presence felt, even if he doesn't say publicly: "Behold, I make everything new."

A particular bishop, still practicing today, had a habit of destroying everything in order to build it up again. Since he worked almost exclusively in the area around the Rubicon, where he pressed his clergy and parishioners for their money, they placed the words: "I came, I saw, I destroyed!" on his bishop's seal.

"I came, I saw, I destroyed" is a play on Caesar's Latin words *"Veni, vidi, vici"* ("I came, I saw, I conquered"), which he pronounced on his easy defeat of Pharnaces II in Syria in 47 BC.

Legitimate businesses don't change their methods whenever a new director arrives, to the detriment of their profits. If well-functioning companies don't adopt this practice, neither should the dioceses, whose sole purpose is the salvation of the faithful.

The Church still selects its bishops with the same senseless procedure contingent on recommendations that it adopted 2,000 years ago. Today's bishop steers a middle course between two banks—he is either convinced that he is capable of the task, or else he knows that he cannot manage and places his trust in the first enterprising secretary who comes along.

These risks and excesses, which have plagued the Church for centuries, must be eliminated before the Church enters the third millennium. There is no more time to simply close our eyes and claim that the problems don't exist. The problems are too numerous and too serious to ignore. What good does burying the truth do when the same problems will eventually resurface with greater force and urgency?

Christ's Church must become strong and reject the mediocrity and falsity that it continually perpetuates. The Popes of the next millennium cannot avoid answering the pressing questions at the heart of the Church. We must restrain those presumptuous individuals who, though different in character and approach, cultivate an apparent and morbid ambition for power.

That infinite God who spilled his blood at Calvary for the salvation of all humanity cannot allow his most significant work, the universal Church, to be ruled by gangs and crooks, today from Brindisi, yesterday from Piacenza, tomorrow from other scarlet-clad conspirators. The Church's infinite richness rots and is sullied by those in power.

The time has come to free God's Church from the fetters of a system that imprisons it.

Baronies, Cartels, and Clans

The barbarity of some cardinals' baronies are worth emphasizing, especially some that are currently at their worst. Each cardinal tries to convince the others that God has granted him the task of liberating the Church from the materialistic movements in the Vatican. For many of those cardinals, God is an infinite well of riches that the Church mines and exploits.

At the top, the Curia is divided in two—those in power and those who anxiously wait for the power to shift hands. According to members of both groups, the split originated with the Apostles, who frequently argued among themselves for primacy in the Church. Apparently, they also sought to reach the pinnacle.

Monsignors of the Curia rarely remain isolated; however, the prelate keeps to himself and avoids political issues. The complicity and servility demanded by those in power marginalize the nonconformists, leaving them open to persecution.

Curialists who want to establish themselves must choose their adoptive family early on, and pledge to it their unconditional allegiance and devotion. They must prove their undying commitment to the clan in words and deeds that exclude the possibility of changing sides. Dissent is unthinkable; repentance is impossible. In the Curia, it is all for one, and one for all, just as in the Mafia.

In the political workings of the Vatican, a clever game of point and counterpoint keeps the members of the two opposing clans in check. The rivals have realized that they cannot eliminate each other, so they divide the spoils—this promotion to your man, this position to my gang, and so on.

A fountainhead of Christian doctrine, **Saint Paul's** views of Church doctrine as the mystical body of Christ and of justification by faith alone were imperative to the formation of the Christian faith.

Saint **Timothy** was an early Christian and a friend and companion of Saint Paul.

Many Curial dignitaries belong to these clans, which are composed of many greedy and power-hungry cliques that engage in petty corruption and protect their own interests. These groups that are determined to reach the top are all dominated by a gang lord, usually a cardinal.

The nature of the Curia fosters resentment and divisions. Saint Paul's admonition to Timothy isn't enough for them: *"I charge thee before God, and the Lord Jesus Christ, and the elect angels, that thou observe these things without preferring one before the other, doing nothing by partiality."* For members of these clans, the rule states that when a gift, a promotion, or an award is received, it should at least be repaid with servile availability. Nothing is free in the Curial world. Wonders are achieved with an insignificant man, and the clan's lofty ideals.

Struggles within the Vatican

Humanity is tired of empty words without meaning and substance. In this tormented age, a religion of words, documents, and papal edicts is useless. The concrete truths of the Church, conceptualized and expressed through a human medium, are all that remain to challenge the chaos.

It has been said that words are the embodiment of life. Saint Gregory the Great said: "Knowledge of this world depends on shielding one's own feelings with shrewdness, concealing thoughts with words, showing the false to be true and the true to be false." Bacon wrote: "Men believe that their minds govern their tongues; but it is the tongue that governs the mind." Words have a power that can make us victims of oppression and control.

George Orwell drew attention to the danger of doublespeak; that is, manipulating the human mind by charging words with other meanings. Such a system leads people to believe that all valid motivations and experiences reside in the governing body and its leader. The ideal subject, then, is one whose reasoning conforms to the leader's, who obeys in silence, and who eschews any mental or social development. By so doing, he frees himself from any responsibility for error and blame.

The Curia retains and passes on a language with private lexicons and its own code; it has a closed-circuit jargon with

Known for his spiritual and political leadership, **Saint Gregory the Great** served as Pope from 590 to 640. He enforced papal supremacy and supported monasticism, celibacy for clerics, and the exemption of the clergy from civil trial.

idioms, passwords, slang, idiosyncratic phrases, and a communication system reserved for those who know the code.

The Curia promotes a technical way of thinking and a specific vocabulary. The different forms for fetish-words, prejudice-words, judgment-words, rhetorical-words, and mystic-words are familiar and reassuring to the Curia members who share this secret language.

The Latins used to say: "Words bind men as the rope binds the bull by the horns." Anyone who fails to use the Curial language finds himself marginalized by the others who consider him someone who thinks differently. Although we live in an age that celebrates open dialogue at every social level, and that is surrounded by an abundance of communication media and devices, Curial members find themselves victimized by a dictatorship that dominates and enslaves the minds of those who succumb.

The Latin language with which the Church has expressed itself for 2,000 years, until a few decades ago, has all but disappeared from the Roman Curia. Very few true Latinists remain, and the number of those who understand Latin is decreasing steadily. Schopenhauer claimed that Latin refined general linguistic competence, and Bergson said that the Latin language taught students to delve into the meaning of things. Nobody speaks of Latin as the language of the Church anymore.

For those employed in the Curia, the doublespeak is so transparent and self-evident that there is no need to belabor it. For outsiders, though, some examples are in order.

Attempts to Divide Power

To reach the top of the Roman Curia, you must remain in a compact and cohesive group with a lead climber, to whom team members must remain loyal and subservient. It takes years, even decades, to assemble a team of ecclesiastics of the same nature, from the same region; however, it is a flexible practice that admits numerous prelates according to their interests and sympathies.

So, we witness the cycle of prelates, who, to reach the summit first, must obstruct access and interfere with the other lead climbers. Anything goes when it comes to undermining the opposing team. When these clergy arrive proudly at their designated ministry, it is not because they are considered competent, but because they arrived there first. Instead of illuminating the office with their presence, these leaders disorient and hinder it. In the name of God, the prophet Hosea rebuked them with these words: *"And as the troops of robbers wait for a man, so the company of priests murder in the way by consent: for they commit lewdness."*

In these struggles for power, Curial members try to eliminate aspiring adversaries by quietly and skillfully pulling the rug out from under them. *"We have been with child, we have been in pain, we have as it were brought forth wind; we have not wrought any deliverance in the earth; neither have the inhabitants of the world fallen."*

The excluded underhandedly attempt to guess the members of the ascending team, their tactics, their allegiant supporters, and the success of their results. Disgruntled and critical, they grumble their opposition to the ascent, but there is nothing more to do. In the Curia, it costs nothing to ruin someone's reputation. Dignified and decent people are trampled, denigrated, or cajoled depending on their position in the political world. The decent people symbolically contradict those who act despicably and whose claim "I am not worthy" is as severed from sincerity as John the Baptist's decapitated head is from his body.

The groups still aspiring to reach the top watch the other groups' ascent and gather information on how to groom their own candidates. These actions don't display the Church's strength; instead, they show weakness and a sign of our times.

THE PREFECTURE OF THE PAPAL RESIDENCE IS an office that no self-respecting ascender could ever refuse.

Hosea was a prophet who preached against sins in northern Israel during the eighth century BC.

A Jewish prophet and the forerunner of Jesus, **Saint John the Baptist** (d. AD 28) received the divine call to preach, baptized Jesus, and was beheaded at the request of Herod's wife.

In rank and importance, the prefecture is second only to the Secretary of State. The prefect of the papal residence, if capable, guides the Pope in almost every action.

The prefect determines with whom and when the Pope has appointments—both with laypeople and cardinals. Many cardinals are excluded from audiences with the Pope for months because the prefect has orders not to include them, as opposed to the cardinals and prelates of his preference, who easily attain appointments. When a clan possesses the prefect of the papal residence as a member, it knows that it has the right man in the right place and that it can settle many of the group's interests without passing through the State.

In light of the benefits of this influential position, we can understand the assignation of this prefecture to a cleric from Piacenza during the reign of the Nasalli Rocca family, and to Dino Monduzzi from Brisighella of the Emilia Romagna clan, who is now a cardinal in the Curia responsible for the election of bishops and conclavists. These strategic games go unnoticed by the ignorant foreign prelates, who are more likely to be used as pawns in the game than to play the game themselves.

Emilia Romagna refers to a region in northern Italy whose capital is Bologna.

The transition of Monduzzi from prefect of the papal residence to cardinal left the Prefect's office without a suitable replacement. Not surprisingly, the emergency replacement was another devotee of the Emilian clan—the youngest of the three De Nicolò brothers, Paolo.

With Monduzzi as cardinal, the Pope selected three pawns—an American, a Pole, and a colleague from Piacenza—to whom he granted the positions of pre-, pro-, and sub-bishop, to fill the one position of residential prefect. The Pope seemingly still enjoys the ability to reward his own aspiring favorites.

When the next Pope is elected, he will have to contend with the reigning clan. The clan will convince him to send home the three "prefixed" prelates and place control in the hands of the able Paolo, who will guide the Pope in the determined Vatican plot.

Knowing that power will soon transfer to a new Pope, the newly elected man for Piacenza, Piero Marini, who is devoted to scandal, schemes, and pragmatic genuflection, has already made it clear that he's no longer satisfied playing altar boy to the sickly Pope. He claims to be due for a prominent position in some ministry.

Church politics are a Masonic game that no one would attribute to the Holy Spirit. However, Satan is familiar with and enjoys playing such games.

A COMPARISON OF VARIOUS PAPAL YEARBOOKS over the last twenty years would reveal the overwhelming influence the Church has endured at the hands of harmful, conniving people.

With this kind of ruling influence, the ways of the Lord are few, and the followers of those with power adorn all of the Curial ministries with their presence. They are almost all either members of the gang from Piacenza or from Emilia Romagna, whose names, even as simple priests, appeared twenty years ago on the Masonic list.

One need only peruse the index of the Papal Yearbook for 1998 to find the names of Cardinals Achille Silvestrini, Carlo Furno, Dino Monduzzi, Edoardo Martinez Somalo, Vicenzo Fagiolo, and the number of appointments that each one has made to Curial ministries. One made twelve appointments, another fifteen, and Pio Laghi even appointed eighteen people! Thanks to this cooperative system, you can guess the relational extent of the dignitaries and how the power of numbers politically directs the Church in a style everyone calls "Vaticanism."

Let us revisit Saint Bernard's admonition to every Pope: "All of these people, who urge with more force, attack with more fury, and threaten to reduce us to nothing, visit you with greater regularity, knock at your door more frequently, and solicit you with more petulance. These are the people who have no compunction about waking the beloved before she wants to. Can you show me one of them who, once he has declared his allegiance to you, doesn't pretend more power? From that moment, you will have no project for which they do not feel themselves suited; you will have no secret that they will not want to share. I would dare say that this is more a flock of demons than of sheep. I have allowed myself to get carried away, because I wanted to open your eyes to those who surround you."

The protector who wants to enlarge his circle of influence and the protégé who expects consideration and promotion encourage intrigues and favoritism for their benefit. The puppet-master who pulls the strings isn't necessarily the superior; in fact, it is often his meddling secretary.

Cardinal Richelieu (1585-1642) was the chief minister of Louis XIII. He gained control of the government and asserted a domestic policy that aimed to consolidate and centralize royal authority, while disempowering the nobles and Huguenots.

According to Cardinal Richelieu, a believer in absolutism of the State or Gallicanism, he who is in power must surround himself with men whom he can trust. This idea suits Vaticanism perfectly, since the Curia selects its members and God confirms them. The swirling currents of the corrupt Vatican sea are flooding the Church of Jesus.

Because Curial associations with clans are evident, there is no need to list them all, just the ones that involve ranking prelates. Although the collaboration between the different clans seems well organized, the rival clans plot to unseat each other.

Many Vatican promotions occur in August when the distracted prelates are on holiday. The most curious prelates remain tied to their cellular phones, and even if they are vacationing in the snowy mountains, on sunny beaches, or on ocean cruises, they listen to every Vatican radio broadcast for the results of the nominations.

All ecclesiastical promotions have a specific protocol, and the most anticipated ones occur at a specific time. The August promotions, and those of other Curial equinoxes, are not as much for the experienced vaticanists who are promoted as the need arises. The August promotions are the most absurd ones, because there is no way of punishing the perpetrators who operate according to the axiom that superiors are never wrong, even when they compromise the Pope.

At the time of Pius XI and Pius XII, the Roman Curia was led by prestigious cardinals by right of birth and formation: Pietro Fumasoni Biondi, Pietro Ciriaci, Paolo Giobbe, Luigi Traglia, Alfredo Ottaviani, and others. They were well-respected Roman dignitaries known for their faith and service to the Pope and Church, and for their intelligence. As that Roman group's numbers dwindled, the importance of the two clans from Piacenza and Emilia Romagna increased, and under Tardini, the Secretary of State, they continued to square off at every turn, alternately divvying up the positions of the Curia.

The Gangs from Piacenza and Emilia Romagna

The gang from Piacenza is likened to the Ursa Minor of the Curia's northern hemisphere, except that it is always visible.

In the sixties and seventies, the archdiocese of Piacenza boasted five living cardinals, one of which was the Secretary of State, Agostino Casaroli. He was accompanied by Rocca Nasalli, Silvio Oddo, Opilio Rossi, and Antonio Samoré, who were later joined by Luigi Poggi. Some of these cardinals were quite frightening-looking, but even ugly characters can become pleasant cardinals. A varied and diverse group affects the nature of the Curia and the Church, as well as important positions such as the Secretary of State.

Many different members of the Curia, and the world, live in a symbiotic relationship based on mutual respect. If support weren't reciprocated between various members, they would find it difficult to govern. However, seven cardinals in the Curia, and as many bishops and prelates, chosen from one diocese is a bit much. Observers began to notice such nepotism in the papal court. Such favoritism typically lasts twenty years before it is replaced, which is long enough to steer Peter's boat toward the next conclave and to recommend the successor to Peter's Chair.

Presently, the gang from Emilia Romagna is considered the Ursa Major of the Vatican. This clan is the most visible in the celestial hemisphere of the Church and has the most influence and ability to secure the candidature of the next Pope when its conclavists have been alerted.

The Emilians include monsignors of all shapes and sizes from around the world. They are especially well represented by bishops such as the Gaetano brothers, Amleto Cicognani, and Marcello Mimmi, as well as Gaspare Cantagalli (elected Archbishop of Pompei before he died of a stroke), Aurelio Sabattini, Achille Silvestrini, Pio Laghi, Dino Monduzzi, and Luigi Bettazzi. Then there are the three De Nicolò brothers—Piergiacomo, Mariano, and Paolo—who have been placed at the disposal of the Secretary of State in Rome. Greedy for money and ambition, each brother possesses an episcopate and holds a high office in the Curia. And let us not forget Claudio Celli, the last of this group who, needless to say, enjoys similar privileges. What blessings the Lord has bestowed.

The Emilian gang gained other members during the August promotions, such as Renato Martino, an observer at the United Nations; Riccardo Fontana and Edoardo Menichelli, both secretaries of Silvestrini; and Mario Rizzi, whose name already appeared on the 1978 list of Masonic prelates, and who is untrustworthy and given to petty gossip and harmful slander. Other members include Pietro Giacomo Nonis from Vicenza, Arrigo Miglio, Lorenzo Chiarinelli, Attilio Nicora from Verona, Benito Cocchi in Modena, Cesare Bonicelli in Parma, Italo Castellani in Faenza, the man from Brisighella, Silvano Montevecchi, and others. All of these men were promoted by the ring leader, Silvestrini, to balance the number of Curia members from the Piacenza gang.

The overtaking of all the Church's prestigious appointments is similar to a dormant volcano that erupts at precisely chosen intervals. Unbridled hidden powers typically extend their roots until they invade the whole body of the Church.

Recently, one of the members of the team, Monsignor Andrea Cordero Lanza from Montezemolo, a close friend of Silvestrini, was made nuncio of Italy. This appointment meant that he could facilitate his friends' nominations for bishop and reject those of his adversaries.

In February 1998, Cardinal Giuseppe Siri thought it probable that a Pope singled out by the Masonic sect could be manipulated. But even if the next conclave were to elect a Pope of different character, the new Pope would have to compromise regarding the Church and its government, since all of the important positions in the Curia are held by the influential group from Emilia Romagna.

In his writing "Service, Not a Career," Silvestrini himself confirms his associations: "At the juridical seminary of Sant'Apollinare there were three of us from Faenza enrolled in the faculty of 'Utrisque Iuris' of the Lateran, Don Dino Monduzzi, Laghi, and I. A few steps away from the seminary, in the Capranica College, Don Franco Gualdrini was finishing his theological studies at the Gregorian University. The four of us were bound in a friendship that continued to unite us throughout life. This was the *career* that Don Pio Laghi, and others like him and me, entered." So, the family from Faenza was united even then, as we learn from its spokesman and lead climber. Social-climbing dignitaries are often at the command of a leader, who has a compass in hand and magic wand at the ready. These men are all in place and, as long as they remain united and harmonious, they will await the orders for the next conclave.

These associations are also signs of the time. As the Vatican leader, Silvestrini extracts previously selected candidates for promotion and craftily submits them to the Pope for approval so they can be set free to scavenge the decaying body of the Church. These predetermined candidates are

Sant'Apollinare is a sixth-century church in Ravenna, Italy, ornamented with mosaics.

The Lateran is the name applied to a group of buildings in southeast Rome that were presented to the Church by Constantine and built on land once belonging to the Laterani.

all chosen for earthly and materialistic reasons in stark contrast with divine will. The superiority complex of this particular head clansman undermines his rapport with the other cardinals; yet, his inferiority complex ruins his rapport with the other prelates.

In the divine drama of Calvary, we saw the confusion of the Roman soldiers as they divided the few spoils of the crucified Christ. Two thousand years later, they are performing the same tricks—dividing the garments of the Church by voting and drawing lots.

Since the Cicognani brothers (Cantagalli, Silvestrini, and Monduzzi) all hailed from Brisighella, the satirical priests of other clans would jokingly say: "Christus brisighellatus est," which loosely translates as "Christ is from Brisighella."

The ambitious Renato Bruni, also from Brisighella, served and was served by the Emilia Romagna gang for twenty years. He enforced the law and set official procedures to the point that he took over an important ministry in the Curia during the reign of three physically unstable cardinals. Although everyone was disgusted by this man, none of the top leaders dared denounce his indecency because he was too valuable a figure in the clan.

Periodically, when there is an important position to claim, the members of the two gangs square off in public. In these instances, the battles are fought without the weapons used behind closed doors. Then, everyone returns to his respective camp.

Fierce Competitors

First Amleto Cicognani from Emilia Romagna, then Agostino Piacentini from Piacenza held the position of Secretary of State at the head of the Church. Sadly, Achille Silvestrini, who coveted the position, narrowly missed his chance at succeeding the latter.

When the two Cicognani brothers disappeared from the Vatican scene, Silvestrini, even though he was well placed as the Secretary of the Papal Council for Public Affairs of the Church under Casaroli, felt that his appointment to a cardinal's position was overdue. To remind his superior of his expectation, he planned to hold a solemn annual ceremony in Brisighella for the blessed souls of the cardinals, pretending to pass as their nephew. But the townspeople knew that the three men were unrelated, regardless of how much he insisted.

Once the date for the ceremony was established, the brave Achille began his plan. Renato Bruni, not yet in disgrace, and Mario Rizzi, an Emilian of the worst type, filled a caravan of vintage cars with as many big shots from the town as they could muster, to participate in the intercession planned by the confident "great-nephew," on behalf of those two souls. The Pope learned of the event and the names of those who participated in the mourning from the *Osservatore Romano*. Regarding Silvestrini, members of the Secretariat of State said to themselves: "That fellow cries for the dead and steals from the living!"

The anxious nephew of the Cicognanis was cautioned, perhaps in a dream by his false uncles, that there were to be no more intercessions for the two deceased cardinals. Strangely, this warning coincided with the date when John Paul II made him cardinal in the June 28, 1988 consistory. This investiture occurred no thanks to his two unrelated uncles, or Bettino Craxi, the socialist Mason with whom Achille had collaborated to organize the famous 1984 Disconcordat between the Vatican and Italy, signed just prior to the flight of that deserter to Tunis.

ORIGINALLY, THE PRESS DOCUMENTED THE STRONG opposition of all the cardinals and bishops in the Italian Evangelical Commission (IEC) to the Disconcordat, which was drawn up by the socialist Bettino Craxi and Silvestrini. The public knew of the extremely violent clash between said prelate of the Curia and the placid Patriarch of Venice, Cardinal Albino Luciani, who was the spokesman for the ecclesiastics, and the Catholic laity who openly opposed such a discordant text.

Its opponents defined the Disconcordat as a classic example of a document drawn up to satisfy the two contracting parties, completely oblivious to the sociohistoric context and without considering the clergy in the diocese.

When Albino Luciani was unexpectedly elected Pope, taking the name John Paul I, Silvestrini couldn't find it within himself to appear before the new Pope, knowing that he had probably lost his chance to become a cardinal. Given the new Pope's reputation for moral uprightness, it was clear that he would be unable to corrupt him.

The sigh of relief was long and deep when the Pope was found dead in his bed after only thirty-three days. That excellent prelate from Emilia Romagna could again peacefully hope for promotion. O blessed death, you have never been as welcome as this! Since the opponents of the Disconcordat would not be silenced even after the signing of the document, Silvestrini drew up a plan. He entrusted Vincenzo Fagiolo with the task of singing the praises and merits of the pact to the press and the world, while he recruited ecclesiastics from the clan to convince the clergy and bishops from the most resentful dioceses through conferences and seminars.

When scrutinized, the Disconcordat revealed its incongruencies and superficiality that today, without all the frills and laurels, appears even more serious and troubling. The protagonists of that intrigue, even though cardinals, stand in judgment before the court of history.

RETURNING TO THE MATTER OF THE SUCCESSION of Casaroli, the two contenders, Silvestrini and Martinez Somalo, engaged in open conflict. They exchanged insulting letters to their mutual discredit, and were encouraged by their supporters who were directly interested in the victory of their preferred leader. The government of the Church continues amid silent battles between competing factions.

An example of one of Silvestrini's insulting letters to Somalo, which reached many dignitaries of the Curia, included the following: "Overcome by the race to get to the top . . . one has to be dismayed by the shrewdness and skill with which you have discredited your possible rival, Achille Silvestrini, fabricating all manner of things against him . . . sharp tongue, your greatest virtue is disloyalty. . . ." The biting Somalo provided a copy of the same letter to the dignitaries with the following comment at the foot of the page: "Mafia announcement, signed, With Much Malice, Achille and his dear friend Giovanni Coppa."

In the breviary of those days, the priests read: "*Destroy thou them, O God; let them fall by their own counsels; cast them out in the multitude of their transgressions; for they have rebelled against thee. But let all those that put their trust in thee rejoice: let them ever shout for joy, because thou defendest them: let them also that love thy name be joyful in thee.*" Prelates of every rank sink to terrible lows when their place in the promotional pecking order is threatened. Low blows, even if underhanded and cruel, are so common now in the Curia and elsewhere that they have almost lost their appeal.

Those groups call upon each other only to initiate conflict. When the competition to eliminate the other becomes ferocious, the noble and capable one succumbs and the cunning one triumphs, regardless of whether it is right. In the final throes of battle, the strong overcome.

THE READER WOULD BE JUSTIFIED IN WONDERING how that "dear friend Giovanni Coppa" from Alba wound up in the gang from Emilia Romagna. He was one of the closest associates of the omnipotent deputy Giovanni Benelli, who was called "Your Excess." The Benelli gang was truly something else.

Monsignor Benelli called Coppa to the Secretariat of State and made him a councilor, appointing him to a position that observes and tracks everyone in the Vatican. He trusted Coppa blindly, even though Benelli was only partially blind due to several retinal operations. Giambattista Re also claimed stake to the office of councilor, given that he too was now a fixture in that house. But neither Benelli nor Coppa would yield. Setting aside the succession in Florence for himself, Coppa tried to remain at the helm of the Church during those delicate final months of Paul VI's life.

Dogs don't willingly give up their bones, which is precisely why Benelli's successor refused to go to Genoa as cardinal—because he preferred to keep his position as councilor in the Secretariat. Fifty years ago, the Secretariat of State of Pius XII, Pope Pacelli, was more streamlined because it was less top-heavy with cardinals; today, Sodano and Re aren't as efficient because they are always off with the Pope.

One day, while waiting in the refectory for food, Coppa's housekeeper confided in her friend that her prelate was still sleeping because he had waited in the office until two o'clock a.m. for Benelli to arrive and replace him. This watch had been ongoing for several nights because the aging Paul VI was suffering from a very high fever and could expire at any minute. It was imperative that they keep vigil in the event that they had to remove documents if the Pope died unexpectedly. A gossipy monsignor, who was standing behind the women, pricked up his ears and spread the news, which is what typically happens with papal secrets.

Once the Pope had regained his strength, Benelli realized there was no time to lose and he pressed the elderly Pope to convene an emergency consistory to immediately nominate him as cardinal and Archbishop of Florence. Benelli also included three other names for nomination to make the procedure appear valid. One year later, Paul VI passed away.

With the passage of Benelli from the Secretariat to Florence, Coppa and all his other protégés were orphaned. Each one sought out a new benevolent patron to take him in, and Coppa found Silvestrini who was more than willing to have him as his lackey. Silvestrini managed to give him the very office that he had held, the most secret and most important in the Secretariat, the so-called "Personnel Office," which houses the dossiers on the highest-ranking Church officials in line for promotions. Of course, the dossiers are conditioned and guided according to the instructions of the leaders, and the Pope approves them without suspicion.

In this office, the trustworthy in line for successful careers are entered into the *white book* with their dossiers white and clean. On the other hand, the rejects, which are those destined for the catacombs, are entered into the *black book* with opaque, shadowy, and dubious commentary. Needless to say, those whose names appear in the *white book* are selected in advance to reach the snowy summits of the ecclesiastical offices.

Because of his meddling in the business of the Curia, including arbitrarily nominating prelates from Alba to pontifical universities and ministries, Coppa was relegated to nuncio of the small Czech Republic in 1990, where he continued to fend for himself in close contact with his protector Silvestrini. It should suffice to note that in less than eighteen months, without political or religious reason, he managed to arrange three Papal visits to that country. He is patiently waiting for the winds to shift in his favor.

In all of these cases, the same meddling cardinal from Emilia Romagna always profits. He has positioned himself to lead the shadow government of the Church, believing himself more than capable of doing it on his own, whether or not the leader of the Secretariat of State is present.

Subterranean vaults and galleries used by the early Christians primarily as burial crypts, the **catacombs** are also used as hiding places, shrines to saints and martyrs, and for funeral feasts.

X

Vatican Spin

Cardinal **Giuseppe Siri** (1906-89) was almost elected Pope twice in 1978.

Upon the death of Paul VI, the media announced as the next Pope the Archbishop of Genoa, Cardinal Giuseppe Siri, well known for his pastoral abilities, intellect, consistency between his faith and his life, and loyalty to the tradition of the Church, even before he entered the conclave. In Rome, in the days prior to the conclave, Siri was scheduled to meet with cardinals, ambassadors, politicians, and prelates from around the world. The modest archbishop, whose quiet and precise words are as cutting as a double-edged sword, listened without many illusions since he knew he was disliked by one Masonic group in the Vatican. He couldn't guess, however, what curve they were planning to throw at him to remove him from the favor of the press's predictions and the public's consensus.

On the morning of the conclave, Siri learned from the headlines that he had given an interview, which in reality he hadn't given, regarding the actions of the next Pope and what his concerns should be. During the interview, some delicate and risky passages were attributed to him, which were enough to jeopardize his chance of becoming Pope. The Archbishop of Genoa wasn't even able to deny the remarks before the doors of the conclave closed behind him. That gang's message echoed throughout the conclave and was promptly gathered up by the Court of Assizes who, for the sake of prudence, voted against Siri.

SIRI DIDN'T JUST MISS OUT ON BECOMING POPE. Not everyone knows, but he also failed to become the Secretary of State at the beginning of the papacy of John Paul II.

The Cardinal of Genoa's secret archive contains a letter from a Roman prelate addressed to him after the election of John Paul II. The letter reveals that several cardinals had expressed a desire for Siri to fill the office of Secretary of State, and that the archbishop should sacrifice his position in Genoa to courageously accept the position of excising suspect prelates from the innermost recesses of the Roman Curia. The cardinal answered the letter on Christmas Eve 1978. Begging forgiveness for his tardiness, he stated: "As for me, I have always obeyed even when obeying cost me dearly; I don't intend to change my tune in the last years of my life. I am at your service. But I have the impression that the orders will not arrive." His subtle humor apparently wasn't appreciated by the Curia.

In the first and second conclaves, Benelli and Baggio were the main contenders, but their respective groups were so acerbically pitted against one another that their choice for Pope almost eluded them. The two groups, devotedly loyal to their own candidate, wouldn't allow their respective votes to fall on the other. The makeshift solution was to eliminate Siri from Genoa. The bureaucratic hesitation allowed providence to select John Paul I, Pope Luciani, who died on the thirty-third day of his papacy. One is left to wonder whether it was a death of natural causes.

At a newly convened conclave, the factions squared off again, only in a manner worse than before. Taken by surprise, the pious cliques made a quick head count and realized that Cardinal Siri would have easily won that day, even though Baggio had garnered more supporters. So, the order was given to throw all the votes, those for Benelli and those for Baggio, behind the foreigner who had received seventeen votes in the previous conclave.

While the Curia looked kindly on the Polish invasion, it was shocked by the unexpected death of the vice-Pope Jean Villot. After his death, even magicians and clairvoyants wondered whether a real disease had felled him so quickly.

IN THE VATICAN, EVERY CHANGING OF THE GUARD is accompanied by the composition and decomposition of families who are well aware that things are only temporarily stable, and that only the deceitful are trustworthy.

When, for unknown reasons, one group is displaced by another, then the prelates of that party disappear and patiently wait for their turn for success. This hibernation could last an entire papacy or until one of their cardinals enters a high office.

The closing years of every papacy are always difficult for the elite of the Church, like the long agony of Christ between the thieves. The death of the Polish Pope, who is already quite ill, is anticipated with great hope for radical change in the future. According to Aristotle, hope is a waking dream. These prelates plan their attack so that, when the time arrives, they are more prepared and aggressive than ever.

In the Vatican, God plays at creating contrasting paradises, where powerful dignitaries are ambushed by ascending parties.

"Christ between the thieves" is a reference to Jesus' crucifixion where he was crucified between two thieves named Dismas and Gesmas.

Intrigues, Clients, and Recommendations

Immoral behavior leads to corruption and extortion. The magistrates of "Clean Hands," in Milan, had the courage to denounce, to Italy and the world, the extent of the corruption in the country. Political, aristocratic, and industrial VIPs were all arrested and the authorities moved in on political parties, Masonic lodges, and the Church. It was a timely housecleaning, even if the *Osservatore Romano* didn't approve.

Unfortunately, an anticorruption squad of that kind will never be let loose in the heart of the Church, since the cancer that infects the entire mystic body of Christ would be revealed. Regardless, the Church would deny any corruption and would continue to suffocate in silence.

In the Vatican, morality is infested with intrigues and corruption. We have already alluded to the corrupt practice of appointing bishops, but the process of career promotions in the Roman Curia, instead of being governed by competitions and the merits of experience, is conducted according to the indecent whims of patronage and recommendations.

As is well known, every successfully promoted employee in the Curia is more charmed than charming. But what does it matter? This corrupt promotion also happens elsewhere. How many bishops, interested in certain ecclesiastical promotions, incorrectly advise the nuncio in a given country? Somebody said that only two categories of people need protection in their careers: prostitutes and monsignors anxious to make their way in the Vatican.

Like every other employee, those in the Curia have ambitions. Conscious of being unable to realize them alone, they set out at whatever cost to find a protector. Promotions become marketable goods and are bargained with as if they were thoroughbred horses.

Curialists attribute the divine origin of the recommendation, trust in a prestigious prelate to advance a career, to the fact that some Greeks asked Philip and Thomas for a recommendation to see Jesus. Assessments of the candidates' suitability, or the competition's, don't exist. Promotions are based solely on exchanges of favors between the powerful, according to preference. Every official of the Roman Curia, being grounded and temporal, remains at the mercy of his superior. The superior may advance, defer, and discriminate

Philip and **Thomas** were two of the twelve apostles.

against whomever he chooses within his office. He need not explain himself to anyone; his will is law. The enterprising employee of the Curia convinces himself that he is carrying out divine will when he makes decisions for his personal benefit, and he believes these decisions have received confirmation from above.

A superior is not always impartial and fair-minded. He doesn't believe he must reward his collaborators according to their merits, seniority, or ability. His decisions do not conform to a code, but follow the whims of sympathy and antipathy, affiliations with clans and families, or other unhonored debts.

THE LUNCHES AND DINNERS OF CERTAIN PRELATES throughout the ages have entered the annals of history; however, the meals hosted by prelates of our age are nothing to scoff at. For example, the banquet for John Paul II's fiftieth anniversary in the priesthood was quite an event, organized by the Secretary of the Ministry of the Clergy, Monsignor Crescenzio Sepe. The party was exquisitely planned down to the succulent menu and the Pope was plied with several courses, wines, and even toothpicks, along with 2,000 happy priests.

Power meetings and power lunches are held regularly in the Vatican. Often, proposals are successful over a bowl of soup and a good glass of wine, even if they've failed in the past. The Church is increasingly becoming a ministry of meals!

Plans are hatched over meals with good food, with excellent wine, and in the company of people who casually linger until the victorious candidate or winning thesis emerges. Over dinner, everything is discussed, including the reforms and appointments to be instituted immediately following the meal. Often, details are confirmed as the food is being digested. In agreement on how to make their plans successful, the diners celebrate their success with generous servings of wine.

Most monsignors are connoisseurs of good food and drink, especially if someone else pays for their meal. The guests and the hosts understand that an invitation to a meal has its price; but, until they must produce the desired results, they leisurely satisfy their hunger and satiate themselves.

The lunches held in honor of senior Curial members often replace internal competitions. At a meal, securing the presence of a VIP often means a position, advancement, or degree for the aspiring prelate. The aspiring examinee must be present at the head table, seated surreptitiously next to the examiner, who will decide the aspirant's future. The examinee must know how to make his move while eating, modestly showing his worth. The examiner also behaves cautiously, pretending to be an objective delegate evaluating the prelate on his merits. But, if the food is good, it is considered a done deal.

Many prelates meet gladly for working lunches, especially to take in the food and wine. In these settings, promotions and recommendations advance more quickly. The most trusted professional waiters furtively notice that even the most demure prelates become more lively with each glass of wine.

At exclusive dinners in private rooms, waited upon by only the most trusted staff, the spiritual and the material worlds become better acquainted. Missions are accomplished and goals are achieved between jokes, entertainment, and sacred negotiations. After the first friendly exchanges, the diners get down to business. They swear absolute secrecy, proceed with the assessment of personnel, throw out the names of the candidates for promotion, dictate the course to follow, name the prelates to involve to achieve the desired results, and reveal where to turn for reliable support.

After the meal, the waiter brings the check. Whoever pays it, even if it is exorbitantly expensive, reassures himself contentedly: "My plans were well worth the sum of a mass's collection plate."

Compromises and Pressures

The uninhibited lust for power, megalomaniac promotions, cynical favoritism, and corruption are all found in the Vatican.

The prelates who reach the top are capable of retaining their status even when they are discovered to be inadequate for their office. They inform their superiors that their willingness to accept the dignity and responsibility of such an office is contingent on future consideration for a higher office. A phoenix is continually reborn from its own ashes, ably using its own defeats as a means to new life. Instead of suffering, these prelates manage to secure promotions and approval thanks to the tried-and-true mechanism that we all know too well.

In his simplicity, God knows how to oppose the good and the bad perfectly. Men, with their limited capacity, manage to blend the two, inverting their roles and interchanging them to suit the occasion. They disguise the good with indecent words and slander, and the bad with excellently false ideas. Unable to be judged by God, who would reject them outright, the deceivers are presented to the Pope, who is ignorant to the game and who chooses the bad disguised as good and rejects the good who have been falsely displayed. Once the Pope passes judgment, it is considered the divine work of the Holy Spirit, who of course has had no part in these tricks.

Certain promotional agreements arise through compromises, pressures, and questionable maneuvers. Pascal said that the Church has enough light for those who believe and enough shadow for those who doubt.

THROUGH ONE OF THESE DECEPTIONS, AN AMERICAN prelate managed to secure a position of importance in the Curia. In his few years in that important ministry, he caused a stir over some strange overtime work that he did in the company of some beautiful young man with whom he was locked up in that ministry until late at night.

However, the doormen of both his home and his office expressed that the nightly entertainment was the subject of much conversation. The prelate was offered a large diocese in his country, which he accepted on the condition that it was also a cardinal's office. Soon after, almost by divine consent, the American prelate given to "after-hours" performances was declared a cardinal of the Holy Roman Church.

THE FESTIVAL OF THE CLERGY WAS HELD AT the Vatican as "a gathering on the occasion of the symposium sponsored by the Congregation of the Clergy to celebrate the 30th anniversary of the promulgation of the *Presbyterorum Ordinis*," with the Pope participating in the closing proceedings. The festival took place under the banner of an ill-concealed exhibitionism of the prelate Secretary, an ordinary man who had placed himself in extraordinary circumstances to appear exceptional. He had planned the whole thing to establish a prominent position in his ministry, since the Cardinal Prefect was nearing the canonical age for retirement; but he had just missed his opportunity.

However, the experience from that festival allowed him to organize the following festivities for the fiftieth anniversary of the Pope, which were so successful that he was promoted to the General Secretariat of the Committee for the Festivities of the Jubilee in 2000.

The pompous fiftieth anniversary ceremony was broadcast around the world over several days. The press featured nothing but the anniversary on front pages across the globe. The people in the Horn of Africa, who in those days were busy decimating one another by the hundreds of thousands, were silenced so that they wouldn't distract the world from the papal spectacle that was described as carnivalesque.

Too much of the Church is distracted by material and earthly things and we have become preoccupied with

Presbyterorum Ordinis is the Latin term for "The order of priests."

personal aspirations and physical satisfactions. Even if everyone knows that happiness resides in being and not having, for the prelate with aspirations coursing through his body, it is more fitting to say "give me the superfluous and I will make do without the necessary" (Oscar Wilde).

During those festive days, it was as if we could hear the repudiation of God in the mouth of Malachi: *"Behold I will corrupt your seed, and spread dung upon your faces, even the dung of your solemn feasts; and one shall take you away."*

ANOTHER RECENT EXAMPLE OF A TACTICAL maneuver that appeared in the Roman papers, whose editors were informed by interested prelates, was a report on a changing of the guard "in progress." The office of the Secretary General of the Central Committee for the Holy Year was passing from the outgoing Sergio Sebastiani to his successor, Crescenzio Sepe. These two advancements, two cardinals, and two happy promotions were suddenly intruded upon by an unhappy bishop, Monsignor Liberio Andreatta, who aspired to the heights of the aforementioned committee, and stated that as a logical consequence of accepting Sepe, he also had to be accepted.

Andreatta happened to be the monsignor in charge of the lucrative multibillion-dollar organization that deals with religious tourism and organizing trips to the Holy Land, Lourdes, Fatima, and so on. He also thought of providing each tourist with a colorful scarf as part of the tour package, advising the pilgrims to wear them at all times and to wave them tirelessly at public ceremonies, as if to remind the appropriate individuals of his hidden promotional agenda: "Hey, remember I'm here too!"

He who knows how to read between the lines understands immediately that the choice of Monsignor Sebastiani for that committee was a case of the wrong person for the job—a man without initiative, but full of himself. How should the situation be rectified? With an

Malachi is book of the Bible. Its title means "my messenger," and it is a collection of prophetic oracles dated from 460 BC.

A city in southwestern France, **Lourdes** is famous for its Roman Catholic shrine—reputed to provide miraculous cures for the millions of pilgrims who flock there.

exchange that makes everybody happy, with purple on the horizon! One never knows where Curial favor will begin, but you can predict where it will end up if you follow the ecclesiastical spectacle to the center of town.

One day, prelates such as these will go as wretched mortals to knock on heaven's door: *"Lord, Lord have we not prophesied in thy name? And in thy name have cast out devils? And in thy name done many wonderful things?"* What a blow it will be after so much exhibitionism, so much ranting, and so much bragging to hear the harsh answer: *"I never knew you: depart from me, ye that work iniquity."*

Fraud and Immorality

In ecclesiastical circles, and particularly in the Vatican Curia, homosexuality is either a slander that taints the victim for the rest of his life, or a competition that prelates enter to see how much they can get away with. It is, nevertheless, a dangerous sport played by the less sophisticated.

In some Vatican circles, the phenomenon of homosexuality—a state of being that today is regarded with clemency and understanding—can help a hopeful candidate advance more quickly and cause a rival to lose the desire to present himself for promotion. The intrigues are cruel, and the protagonists are even more so.

In the list of hopefuls for promotion, the one who gives himself from the waist down has a better chance than the one who gives his heart and mind to the service of God and his brothers. In those cases, charm is worth more than merit.

For many prelates in the Curia, the beautiful boy attracts more goodwill and favor than the intelligent one. Subjects can easily detect effeminacy in the tastes of their superior and they will play it to their advantage. The *madonno*, with his masculine attributes yet feminine bearing, often exploits his ambiguity and pleasing features for as long as he is able.

The Competitors

In a diocese in Italy, a young man took his bishop to civil court on charges of sexual abuse. Although the bishop naturally denied everything, the judge ruled against him and ordered a suspended sentence. When asked for his resignation, the monsignor demanded an appointment in the Roman Curia; otherwise he wasn't going anywhere.

In the national civil code, this method of blackmailing is punishable as a crime; in the ecclesiastical code, the demand is justified by that golden rule *promoveatur ut amoveatur*, which means, "let it be moved forward so that it can be put aside." Individuals are promoted to higher offices to remove them from the ones they have tarnished. Confidently and nonchalantly, that bishop was transferred to Rome and appointed to a position in the Curia that was invented especially for him to keep him hidden. Nobody listened to the reluctant head of the ministry who did not want to accept him. In his own show of disapproval, however, he refused to provide the offender with a chair for his desk. However, it didn't matter because the mischievous prelate did not stay long in that office either. Having ably and shamelessly played the head of the ministry, who now found himself in an uncomfortable situation, he was promoted to secretary in another ministry according to the same golden rule.

SOME TIME AGO IN ROME, THE POLICE PULLED up beside a custom-built car parked under the trees by the Circus Maximus. Noticing that the occupants were half-dressed, the officers took them to the precinct for questioning. The next day, the papers published the name of the prelate, whose weakness was well known, along with the name of his special friend.

From that day on, the nasty Curialists started to jokingly twist the Latin aphorism *Si non caste, saltem caute,* which

Built in Rome during the sixth century, the **Circus Maximus** was a stadium and track used for entertainment.

means, "If not chaste, at least be careful," into *Si non caste, saltem castel*, which means, "If not entirely chaste, at least castle." This new aphorism made a reference to both the name of the protagonist and his failure to take proper refuge for his erotic arrangement. Because the prelate was the son of a well-known diplomat, he was destined for promotion despite his lifestyle. He was first promoted to undersecretary, and finally to archbishop and secretary of the ministry. O Lord, you are prodigal even with the wayward!

As punishment, God had Isaiah tell Israel: *"And I will give children to be their princes and the effeminate shall rule over them."*

The prophet **Isaiah** was known for his indictment of the people of God for perpetrating social injustice.

THE STORY OF THE FAT PRELATE WHO PLAGUED the Curia for almost forty years is well known in the Vatican. An only child, he discovered his vocation for the priesthood later in life, which he approached partly out of weariness and partly out of awe for the ministry. He petitioned for office in the Church and immediately landed in the Secretariat of State.

Uncertain as to whether to keep him, he was sent on a trial basis to the deputy Giovanni Battista Montini, who retained him as a personal secretary and, until his death, acted as his ardent defender. The prelate gained the respect of his patron, Montini, with his strict thoroughness. In the Curia, they knew that he was impatiently awaiting his reward.

The prelate was egocentric, rigid, and bitter; he possessed a brilliant mind and behaved as an absolute tyrant. He was brusque and nasty but could also be generous, benevolent, and understanding. He had acquired the defects of his patron; he was erratically partial and partisan to everyone, and would both protect and persecute the same individual. He was a perfect mixture of virtues and vices, and, in the Curia, the flaws of superiors are artfully packaged to pass as virtues. A moral decadence often leads to mental decadence rather than logic.

While in Bern on a diplomatic posting, he had an amorous affair with a young nun, who honestly wanted to marry him. She was transferred elsewhere and he was sent to another nunciature and, of course, given a promotion! There was only one problem. The nun belonged to the same order as Sister Pasqualina, who served Pius XII, and as long as she worked with Pope Pacelli, she managed to keep him from the episcopate. Only after the Pope's death, Sister Pasqualina's retirement, and the election of Pope Roncalli was that prelate made bishop and nuncio.

When Montini became Pope Paul VI, his ex-private secretary contacted him from the Egyptian nunciature to see whether he could return to Rome where he would be better able to serve him. When he arrived in the Curia, the prelate discovered that he had been offered a non-cardinal ministry, which he refused. In the meantime, his effects arrived that he had managed to pack before leaving Egypt. He refused to return and made it clear that he was awaiting orders.

However, the heads of ministries told the Pope that they didn't want him in their offices. But, when he wanted something, Paul VI bore a hole into his interlocutor with his impenetrable eyes, so that the fellow, frozen and helpless, silently accepted his will.

Luckily, the same nuncio who pulled him out of the mess in Bern was now a cardinal in charge of a ministry in the Curia. Only he could help the prelate. His dignified patron told the prelate to visit with him in his villa in Bergamo, where he spent long periods of leisure time. The cardinal took him into his ministry in the name of the Pope. Two days later, the *Osservatore Romano* published the name of Giovanni Scapinelli's successor who, until then, had been living in fear that he would retire without attaining the purple robes of a cardinal. The dignitary continued to do as he pleased in the Curia for more than twenty years, enjoying the boundless support and faith of Pope Montini. All those in the Curia, including the powerful

Benelli, were convinced that he would only leave that office as a cardinal.

The overwhelming power of the promoted dignitary led to his lurid favoritism and questionable friendships that pressed the limits of decency. One afternoon, staggering drunk in the corridor of his office, he was found singing to himself: "What a secretary you have got!" When the porters led him to his adjoining apartment, he reproached them for physically forcing him to leave.

The conclusions of a serious investigation into his affairs were brought to the attention of the Pope, but the Pontiff didn't want to get involved. When Paul VI called for a consistory to name new cardinals, it was made known that his protected ex-secretary was third on the list of possible candidates. Cardinal Dino Staffa, prefect of the highest papal court, the supreme tribunal of the Apostolic Segnatura, tried to corroborate the charges leveled against the archbishop. Once he had confirmed them, disappointed and angry, he declared: "This would have been a good opportunity to get this character out of the Sacred College. He is an insult to every one of its members!" But it is well known that what Man proposes, God deposes.

In 1975, the Italian lira reached its lowest point during a fiscal crisis. Each day the lira fell more dramatically, to the great consternation of those with savings. The lucky ones tried to transfer their currency abroad. Others, however, didn't make it past the Swiss border where they were often imprisoned. The press deliberately documented these instances in an attempt to dissuade others from following suit.

Attempting to preserve his savings, our dignitary decided to transfer his money across the border a few days before his nomination to a cardinal's office. For this citizen of the Vatican, it was to be a routine operation with few possible snags, or so he thought. He was accompanied by a captain of the Revenue Guards Corps, who happened to be a real fop and the brother of a monsignor in his office. The officer appeased the prelate to help advance the career of his brother who, as it turned out, was doing so well in the Secretariat of State that they had given him a visa as an ambassador-at-large in the eastern bloc.

When they arrived at the border town of Pontechiasso, a policeman asked to search the car. Angered by the guard's impudence, the prelate presented his Vatican passport. The border guard, likely a rookie unaccustomed to this diplomatic finesse, excused himself and consulted with his supervisor in the booth. He returned to the car embarrassed but with instructions to search the vehicle nonetheless.

The captain was in a dilemma because he could be criminally charged. Given the inflexibility of the border guards, he told them that he was simply a good friend of the prelate who had agreed to accompany him on the trip, completely oblivious to his ulterior motives. Unfortunately, it was to no avail, and they were both detained.

Confronted with a suitcase overflowing with Italian and foreign currency, the prelate declared that he was transporting the suitcase on behalf of the Vatican. He asked them to contact the deputy of the Secretariat of State, Monsignor Benelli, who, given the late hour, was neither in his office nor at home. The prelate and the captain spent the night and the next day in a holding cell.

The story immediately became a diplomatic scandal. The Vatican, of course, had nothing to do with the suitcase full of money. Benelli was outraged but realized that he couldn't leave the archbishop secretary to suffer in jail and risk a scandal. The Italian and Swiss foreign ministers were summoned, as well as the police and the nunciature. Together, they decided that there was only one acceptable diplomatic solution: the prelate and the captain were immediately released with the money intact, as if the incident had never happened. The prelate was told: "You, Monsignor, have never passed through here. Understood?"

Meanwhile, the third name on the list of potential cardinals was eliminated.

Often, the prelate would ask his superiors to appoint his trusty monsignor to a diocese as a reward for the services he rendered. That was impossible since it had been discovered that a few Boy Scouts in the seminary at Montanina didn't approve of his spiritual direction, which they characterized as very forward and had told their parents about. He was also whisked off to another ministry according to the golden rule that a promotion deals with any embarrassing situation.

The career of this dignitary, whose life read from beginning to end like a cheap novel, was coming to a close, but he was hanging on until the very end. His successor had to be found, and the transition had to be as subtle as possible. Everything in the office had to remain the same, meaning that the ineptitude of his successor would make his predecessor appear intelligent.

Five important prelates, two of whom were from Brisighella, sat together in a secluded room over a sumptuous meal. It was another of the famous working lunches, to decide which candidate would succeed. Given the circumstances this time, the successful candidate had to be the most incompetent and inept of the lot. They settled on a Ukrainian, both clever and cunning, whom the Communist government regarded so highly that they gave him free passage in and out of his country. Another individual had been clad in luxuriant purple by his retiring protector.

In moments of uncertainty and indecision, the one who seems modest finds an easy path to the top, especially if he is unsuited to the task he is assigned. Selected by the five prelates in that remote room, the nomination appeared a few days later, complete with the Pope's consent, who, oblivious to the circumstances, considered it a most inspired and natural succession.

The new secretary, devoid of academic titles, spent the next few years collecting honorary degrees from across

Europe, since a collection of degrees is a good investment for an aspiring cardinal. For many years, he managed to explain to his underlings, with great confidence, things that he knew nothing about.

If the selection agreed upon by this committee occurred at the right time, it was not so for the stagnating dignitary who overstayed his welcome. They wanted to send him to the Church in the Ukraine, but those bishops were opposed to his appointment and thought the Roman Curia should keep him. What difference could an extra cardinal make to the Curia?

The prophet Hosea wrote: *"For they have sown the wind, and they shall reap the whirlwind."*

A False and Deceptive History

Unlike the Renaissance, these times are unable to produce characters on par with Pope Julius II, "the terrible Pope," who was as splendid a patron as he was a daring warrior; or Alexander VI, the Borgia Pope, who commissioned Raphael to paint the loggias, and who was accused of incest. Even though the errors of these men harmed the Church, divine truths were manifest through their patronage and the brilliant minds with which they surrounded themselves. In our day, these petty prelates infest the rooms of the Borgias with their poisonous presence.

Virgil warned that history becomes more favorable with the passage of time: *"Forsam et haec olim meminisse iuvabit,"* which means, "Perhaps this will be a pleasure to look back on one day." But few people are able to fully appreciate the Church's history. The facts must be firmly set against a background of three dimensions: the earthly, the ecclesiastic, and the divine. Against that backdrop, realities appear that history doesn't record. Genuine histories remain concealed in the recesses of reports that record

Serving as Pope between 1503 and 1513, **Julius II** was a warrior who wanted to restore the papal states to the Church. He was the first to suppress nepotism and abate Rome's corruption.

Born Rodrigo Borgia, **Pope Alexander VI** (Pope: 1492-1503) had four illegitimate children—including the infamous Lucrezia. He and his family were widely known for their greed, corruption, and treachery.

only the results, without ever investigating the assumptions and subterfuge that lead to or result from those results. Apart from teaching lessons of life, history can also become a context where lies are presented as truth (Ermanno Olmi). And so, it happens that in the beginning there was the Word, and at the end there is only idle chitchat (Stanislao Lec).

A good example of the selective nature of history appears when the second draft of the previously mentioned Disconcordat of 1984 is compared with the serious spirit of the 1929 Lateran Pacts, which Pope Ratti followed meticulously because of the incompetence of Giuseppe Pizzardo and the meddling of Benito Mussolini. How much more doctrine and experience would be obtained if the historian examined the events thoroughly? Why the truth when it always turns up somewhere else?

History's train doesn't travel on a regular schedule; you must board it when you have the opportunity. An Italian comic, Totò, used to say: "Stop the world, I want to get off!" realizing the futility of the request.

Many individuals, blinded by fame and a lust for power, secretly hide ambitions behind false modesty. The truth is not what it seems but is rigorously hidden from everyone so that the history contained in documents is false and deceptive. Every man is a mystery; but, the more important the man, the harder his mystery is to decipher.

The difficult work for the historian lies in sifting through fact and fiction, and acknowledging that the fantastic is also part of history. Indeed, history moves and grows in the realm of the legend.

To consolidate one's power in the Vatican, one must display prestige, ostentation, and pomp in competition with timeless ancient pagan, Eastern, Renaissance, and Spanish customs. In 2000, these rituals still permeate the papal court as people remain eager to stand out and thirsty for power: in Rome, everything becomes corruptible. *"Then*

Widely known as the Lateran Treaty, the **Lateran Pacts** were signed in 1929, establishing Roman Catholicism as the only state religion of Italy. They state that the person of the Pope is sacred and inviolable, and that the Vatican City is fully sovereign and independent.

shall his mind change, and he shall pass over, and offend, imputing this his power unto his God."

We must reverse the direction of the Church and stand together with Christ at the end of the line. Christ does not guarantee our egocentric choices, especially when they compete with moral interests: *"They always twist my words, they think of nothing but doing ill, they watch my steps so they can take my life."*

In the context of the Curia, loving your neighbor as you love yourself becomes a pretext. Cocteau told us: "The verb to love is among the most difficult to conjugate: its past is not easy; its present is not indicative; its future is always conditional."

XII

Rewards of Corruption

The dependents of the Vatican fall into two categories—those who want it all immediately without giving much of themselves, and those who give everything of themselves without recognition. These are the faceless eighty percent, the ones without fixed rights, destined to perpetual anonymity, wrongfully accused, suffering from arbitrary interference in their private lives, and whose reputations and honor have been sullied. Denied the right to counter the evidence, they are unable to defend themselves, like invalids tried by a third party.

The members of this lot, pariahs of the Curia, aware of their exclusion from unrealistic promotions, resign themselves to positions of inferiority. They spend their lives in shackles, cultivated like bonsai, under controlled growth. Convinced that most positions in the Vatican are like the reserved seating on buses for the elderly and disabled, which is rarely occupied by the deserving people anyway, they remain at the mercy of their superiors who decide if and when these positions will be filled.

In the Vatican, one is classified according to rank. If one is to remain submerged, even if by all accounts he is a genius, he will continue to be ignored until they find some way of removing him, often offering him early retirement with a full pension. The Curia does away with those who ignore the system through exclusion, marginalization, demotion, threats, and even imposed retirement. The stubborn prelate is declared off-limits and ostracized—his colleagues distance themselves, and his friends make themselves scarce.

The discounted ecclesiastic, no matter what he does, appears to be justly discarded. If he doesn't protest his dismissal, his superior will say that his silence is proof that he is unworthy of his office; if he protests, he reveals himself an insubordinate as the charges suggest. The Vatican has adopted, in good conscience, the preventive rule of Don Bosco: "Prevent by punishing."

ON THE OTHER HAND, THE EMERGING PRELATES, who have been chosen for promotion by an earthbound god, enjoy every possible favor and fame while veiling their defects and emphasizing their strengths. They are a team of rogues with a presumed respectability, regardless of their conduct. These promotable prelates enjoy direct access to anywhere—from the refectory to the apartment, from the office to their residence, and especially to positions of prestige. These prelates are entitled to happily bypass apprenticeships and to start immediately in positions of consequence.

Cunning and practice are needed to promote one's favorite. To succeed, one must sing the praises and merits of the promoted one, send the right signals, and direct everything to the appropriate decision-makers. The best tactic is to arrange an invitation to a papal dinner table. The rest will follow as the superior is honored and catered to. When the promoter of injustice imposes his favorite on the others, he tires of explaining to the unruly that remonstration is useless since the promotion is legitimate and has been approved by the powers that be, who, more often than not, know nothing about it.

As founder of the Salesia Society, **Don Bosco** was committed to providing spiritual and material relief to the young and poor. By the time of his death in 1888, there were 250 Salesian Societies in Italy.

The opposite happens to incite suspicion against the individuals who are dismissed. Some plans, even if cruel, are hatched and executed in the name of abuse, subterfuge, and deceit. Aristotle said: "Injustice that has the means to harm is very harmful."

The favored son, even if stupid, will surely succeed. After all, he was promised by his protectors who, in order to place their favorite in a strategic office, work behind the Pope's back who, as we have already seen, acts as their shield.

The temptation for authorities to monopolize the decision-making for promotions is much stronger in the Church than in other societies. The authorities attribute each one of their decisions, especially the discriminatory and unjust ones, to the inspiration of the Holy Spirit, which, as a result, are infallible and incontestable. Without knowing about the methods of the Curia, Einstein stated that it was easier to break down an atom than a prejudice.

The **Universal Declaration of Human Rights** was issued by the United Nations in 1948. It outlined the universal rights that belong to individuals by virtue of their being human.

The privileged individuals live in complete disharmony with the Universal Declaration of Human Rights. Both groups of ecclesiastics, that is, the up-and-coming and the hopeless, sing the same refrain, in dissonance: "Christ made himself in our image, so we could be like him."

The Vatican game is based on snakes and ladders. If you land on the squares of the holy offices, you fall back six squares; if you land on one of those belonging to the Freemasons, you climb a long ladder; if on one of the papal audience squares, you move ahead three spaces; if on one of the promotional demands, you get a warning and return to go; if on the papal dinner table square, you are almost home; if in competition among the emerging, you play with one die. . . . The game continues freely without any referees.

IN AUSCHWITZ, POLAND, AS SOON AS THE DEPORTEES arrived at the concentration camp, a doctor indicated with a stick where each person would be sent. With the subtle movement of that stick, he decided the destination of individual deportees. Some went to the showers—that is, the gas chambers—and others were promoted to the chain gangs. The decisions were so terrifying that they cause dreadful shudders to today's visitors. Some prejudices and promotions in the Curia recall the horrible and macabre oscillation of that evil doctor's stick. The Church must fear its internal threats more than its external persecutors. The Church can convert and sanctify the latter; but, the former will strangle it.

Nothing Comes from Nothing

The Curial system keeps subjects under the heavy hand of a superior who decides everything for them. Those who try to emerge from this power structure without permission must beware. To attempt to escape would mean falling into disgrace, which is an arrogance to be avoided at all costs. Such disgrace can be psychologically traumatic, as expounded by a certain biblical story. Jesus healed a man who had been born blind, and instead of celebrating the event, the man's parents appeared timidly before the members of the Sanhedrin. *"But the Jews did not believe concerning him, that he had been blind, and received his sight, until they called the parents of him that had received his sight. And they asked them, saying, 'Is this your son, who ye say was born blind? How then doth he now see?' His parents answered them and said, 'We know not: he is of age; ask him: he shall speak for himself.' These words spake his parents, because they feared the Jews: for the Jews had agreed already, that if any man did confess that he was Christ, he should be put out of the synagogue. Therefore said his parents, 'He is of age, ask him.'"* Expulsion from the synagogue is tantamount to losing all of your rights and privileges. Just as in the Curia, if you fall from grace, you lose your chance for a career.

Composed of 70 to 72 members, the **Sanhedrin** was the highest ancient Jewish legal and religious council in Jerusalem.

Saint Massimiliano
Kolbe (1894-1941)
was imprisoned in
Auschwitz for his
anti-Nazi publications.
Rather than give up
hope, he ministered to
the other prisoners and
even conducted mass.
He died by lethal
carbonic injection.

Nobody is interested in taking up the cause of a prelate who has had his career cut short, even if he is fully justified. Everybody knows that they would pay dearly for such a stance. Why jeopardize your future to such an extent? There are not many people as generous as Saint Massimiliano Kolbe, who martyred himself for others. The Curial environment paralyzes officials with fear.

In the small chance that a courageous dissenter is supported by a superior, he would be made to understand that his presence was no longer tolerated and that he could be expelled for future disturbances, or at least transferred to a lesser office. Obviously, such a threat is enough to silence everyone. Good sense is useless without luck.

Professional officials who are strict without being arrogant, obliging without being fawning, and united without being sycophantic are disappearing. Considered insubordinate, they make life difficult for the superior who is no longer free to manage the office at his will. While the stars provide guidance, meteors destructively strike the earth. Churchill said that a man of character is always a difficulty because he is not easily maneuvered and manipulated by overbearing individuals. In moments of exhaustion and low spirits, even a morally upright person must compromise to live more peacefully in situations that his conscience would never have previously permitted.

ONE DAY, A GOOD FAMILY MAN AND PRACTICING Catholic well known in the parish visited the parish priest to seek spiritual advice on a curious situation. He was selling an apartment in downtown Rome. A young man, aged nineteen, asked to see the property. The fellow liked the apartment and said he was interested in buying it, so they agreed on a price, a payment schedule, and a down payment. The young man told him he would soon return with a check. Two days later, he returned and presented the owner with two checks. The owner then requested a copy of the checks for verification purposes, which one of his banker friends furnished immediately. The checks were certified but were from the bank account of a cardinal. At that point, the owner asked the young man whether he knew that the holder of the account was an ecclesiastical dignitary. Without batting an eyelid and with great pride, the young man declared that he was a very good friend of the cardinal.

Naively, the owner had come to ask the priest if he should proceed with the sale of the apartment regardless of the strange financial source, or whether it would be wise to find another buyer. The priest reassured him that he should proceed with the sale and that, regardless of the sale, he would never satisfy his suspicions.

IN THE BACK OF THE VATICAN PRESSROOM, A monsignor told a prelate friend that the arrogant bishop Fiore was to be made a cardinal. The prelate asked: "But how? Wasn't he the subject of some serious rumors?" The monsignor replied: "Because he sowed his oats? Don't be so naive!" He then added: "Once you have reached that level, everything is canceled; those things become non-sense. Everything becomes as pure as innocence personified. When you are made a cardinal, you are given your baptismal stole once again. Nobody will speak a word of his past—only merits and honors thanks to his generous contributions to Poland!"

By funneling $50 million to *Solidarnosc* and a hospital, Fiore let the Pope know through a confidant that he expected papal recognition in the form of a cardinal's position. Of course, the Pope rewarded this generous benefactor's cardinal longings.

Meaning "solidarity," **Solidarnosc** is also the name of the Polish labor union that became active in 1956.

A rumor was circulating at the time that the president of the Italian republic, unable to make Fiore a senator for life, made Giulivo one instead; while the Pope, unable to make Giulivo a cardinal, did so for Fiore, out of friendship for the other. This reciprocal arrangement caused considerable distress among many politicians. Since then, in election campaigns, every candidate has wanted his own supporter to sway the voters in his favor, and every careerist prelate has coveted his own Giulivo to back him in government. These perfect symbiotic relationships are executed with courage and impudence.

At every election, chaplains, nuns, and hospital workers expected to be notified by Fiore, who would demand that they vote for that astute president who served as the guarantor of his cardinal's position. The next day, Sunday, the prayer to the faithful went as follows: "O Lord, free your church from class interests, from the privileges of clericalism, and from the positions of prestige that distance it from equality and sharing; defend it from the frenzy of being worth more, of knowing more, of willing more power: we pray of you!" The Communists and Christian Democrats, at their respective masses, without enthusiasm or conviction, mumbled: "Listen to them, O Lord."

Emotional Investments for Long-Term Gain

A young member of the laity was assigned as an usher in a ministry where the staff was already complete. A good fellow, quiet and unassuming, he soon became friends with one of the monsignors in the ministry. He confided in him that he had an embarrassing family situation. For as long as he could remember, he had seen a high-ranking dignitary from the Secretariat of State visiting his home and had subsequently realized that his mother was the dignitary's lover. Now that he was of age, his mother would go to visit the prelate. He asked the monsignor what he should do in this delicate situation.

Given the nature of the facts, the ecclesiastic gave the young man the choice of sharing his account with his superiors. But the young bailiff didn't have the courage to denigrate his mother and the prelate, whom he more or less acknowledged was his father. The matter ended there.

Corruption easily creeps into the inner sanctum of God's sanctuary. Many members and nonmembers of the Curia live double lives, while acting as severe moral critics toward their neighbors.

INSIDE THE WALLS OF A PARTICULAR ROMAN villa, many temporary university professors and young, full-scholarship students shared close relations, all under the supervision of a so-called professor, Ms. Groppelli, and a smiling benefactor cardinal.

Monsignor Domenico Tardini, the author and founder of the institute, wanted that school to favor the elite students, whose intellectual formation would be encouraged by the top university professors in Rome. The boys were forbidden to leave the campus, and their families were not granted easy access to the facilities. Visitors were infrequent, but those who arrived at Tardini's request were almost all notable dignitaries. Until his untimely death, these practices were strictly enforced. Presently, instead of gifted children, the school caters to underdeveloped and disadvantaged students.

However, the revenues from these youths are never sufficient to maintain the program. In an attempt to secure larger donations, it was decided that a publicity campaign, including a television advertisement, was in order. Therefore, the cardinal-protector invited both the Pope and the president of the republic to visit the campus. This venture seems to have been successful, since the money is flowing in.

The Strange Case of Don Mountain Goat

In the early eighties, a young university student from Verona managed to secure the favor of a cardinal-protector. This story reveals how he did it. With lots of pouting and smiles, and a hypocritical sincerity of decorum, dignity, and fairness, the young fop managed to surpass all of his colleagues with a nauseating arrogance. He would do anything to succeed.

The young man's arrival was greatly welcomed by the cardinal, who was depressed after his dismissal from the Secretariat of State and his relegation to the Segnatura. The clever student immediately sensed the poor man's needs and apprehensions, and devoted himself wholeheartedly to the cardinal, catering to him both in public and in private. He organized his affairs, wrote his speeches, prepared homilies, and coached him for interviews with journalists.

He immediately stood out above the others in the villa because of his eagerness to reach the top. His colleagues nicknamed him "Mountain Goat" because of his uncanny climbing abilities. While everyone recognized his intelligence and efficiency, the villa was filled with rumor and insinuation.

"The words of his mouth were smoother than butter, but war was in his heart: his words were softer than oil, yet they were drawn swords." Dangerously, intellect and pride are often lost in flattery and extravagance. In no time, his protector realized how indispensable the young layman had become, and he advised him to take ecclesiastical orders. The Mountain Goat agreed, on the condition that he could avoid the years of religious formation in a seminary and receive private training from his protector. They both agreed on this arrangement. However, since it is still not possible for a cardinal to promote a cleric to cardinal, the ordination of Mountain Goat would require the co-opting of a diocesan bishop or two. That plan was subsequently rejected in favor of a new one.

Now, Mountain Goat was to become a member of one of those communities with very few members and no obligation to a communal life. Like a fraternity with no fixed address, each member chooses his respective home. In no time, the university student became Don Mountain Goat and he became a permanent fixture at the villa.

During this time, the cardinal realized that he would not be promoted to the Secretariat of State and he conspired to leave the Segnatura, which he found too restrictive. He, along with his collaborators in the Curia, wanted to play a greater role in the shadow government of the Vatican, and needed a ministry that would afford him both national and international latitude. He found such influence in the Eastern Congregation.

From his position in the Eastern Congregation, he sent Don Mountain Goat to that office, along with two associates, Rizzi and Bruni, one month before the investiture of the Indian cardinal. Within a few years, the Indian died of a heart attack and was replaced by Mountain Goat's protector. His protégé was immediately given two secretaries to expedite the cardinal's public relations.

Since Don Mountain Goat had the least seniority and stood the least chance of promotion, his protector, always looking out for him, prepared a long- and short-term plan to address this infelicity. Even though Mountain Goat was only a religious man on paper, he called himself monsignor. His protector started sending him around the world on special religious missions and hired five or six new officials to ensure that Mountain Goat was no longer last in the pecking order. He then convinced three officials to take early retirement, promoted two others out of the ministry, and transferred three more to lateral positions with rewards. Mountain Goat was now well placed in the ministry and, with the imminent retirement of three more monsignors, the cardinal decided it was time to take action regarding Mountain Goat's transition from an insignificant employee to a high-ranking superior.

To carry out the plan, it was necessary to vacate the position of undersecretary occupied by the Franciscan Marco Brogi, who longed to be archbishop of that ministry. In a report to the Pope that was forwarded to the Secretariat of State, this Cardinal Prefect recommended that Brogi be

Franciscans are members of the religious order founded by Saint Francis of Assisi in 1209.

sent to Ethiopia as nuncio. The recommendation was refused. A few months later, he prepared another report with the support of several other prelates. This time, there were to be no mistakes. He ordered his colleague from Brisighella, Dino Monduzzi, Prefect of the Papal Chambers, to secure him a thirty-minute audience with the Pope—just enough time for the Pope, misinformed and distracted as always, to sign Father Brogi's nomination as nuncio, this time in Somalia. Guess who was to fill the vacant position of undersecretary? Don Mountain Goat.

During the same period, Mountain Goat's secretary was doing her best to pull together pieces of legal papers for his graduating thesis, which they passed off as an original and inspired work. She submitted the thesis just in time, and it was passed with full marks by the obliging institute. He was awarded a doctorate of lies and false jurisprudence!

Some would be justified in thinking that the two promoters of injustice, the cardinal and his new undersecretary, would have been satisfied with their achievement. But they weren't. Ambition, like greed, is insatiable, which is why the poor Mountain Goat will never know peace.

Also during this period, the cardinal lobbied to ensure that the incompetent Ukrainian archbishop remained in his position. Clearly, this decision was inspired as much by partisanship as by reason: his position, although not yet vacant, was being groomed for the Goat.

Don Mountain Goat, knowing how to resist everything except career ambitions, was seduced by his protector into many dangerous liaisons. His nomination followed shortly and he set about the office, flaunting his many degrees and false knowledge, while his secretary explained the new rules to all of the monsignors who had been detrimentally affected by the newly ordained undersecretary in charge of the ministry. Thanks to his cardinal-protector, we have in our midst a scoundrel from outside who holds favor in the highest circles, even with the Pope.

The ouster of the Ukrainian masterfully gained the Pope's consent in the age-old fashion, and Mountain Goat set out on the road to a cardinal's position. The ways of the Lord are well marked in the Roman Curia!

The expert Vaticanologist of the time observed that the case was more unique than rare. The satisfied protagonist gratefully said to the architect of the Masonic universe: *"Thou liftest me up to the wind; thou causest me to ride upon it."*

Near the end of his days, Cardinal Giuseppe Slipyj, who was saved by John XXIII after eighteen years of a life sentence, confided to his friends: "The time I endured in the Soviet camps and my death sentence are forever ingrained in my thoughts. But in Rome, during my time in the Vatican, I lived my worst moments."

XIII

Climbing the Spire
of St. Peter's Dome

In God's Church, the concept of career success should be completely eliminated. If someone enters ecclesiastical life determined, either openly or secretly, to advance his career, he should never be ordained. If such a power-hungry individual does become a priest, he should be resolutely prevented from advancing, if not sent off to some insignificant parish in the countryside. God doesn't know what to do with the arrogant and the presumptuous, and he rejects them outright. It goes against God's nature to have such people leading his church.

Career ambitions are innate in the aspirant who is willing to thwart God's will to succeed. Ironically, God has always preferred to choose his true candidates from the humble and the poor: *"For do I now persuade men, or God? Or do I seek to please men? For if I yet pleased men, I should not be the servant of Christ."*

The twenty percent of prelates who climb Saint Peter's steeple lack the spirit of resignation that allows them to be satisfied with their current station, and they consider every position not sufficiently dignified for their remarkable credentials. They make the Gospel an auxiliary motor for their human ambitions. With a false religiosity, marked by conceit and lack of interior discipline, they aim for the highest goal. Accession, not ascetic theology, is the rotten fruit that some of the Lord's vines produce today. Only the privileged, intelligent individual overcomes the collective charms of ambition, like a hermit alone in the desert. In fact, a father of the desert delivers this sharp rebuke to the Curialists: *"Our mouths stink of adulation; we know the Scriptures by heart; we mumble all of the canticles of the Psalter; and yet we still do not have what God seeks: charity and humility."*

Experience teaches us that those proud individuals, who the Scriptures state should be last, always find themselves in first place. The enterprising ones secure the key appointments even though they are often not the most qualified. Everyone knows that nothing is more dangerous than having great missions carried out by small minds.

"What was it that ye disputed among yourselves by the way?" If Jesus were to interrogate the Roman Curia today, many prelates would be embarrassed to respond. Absorbed and preoccupied, they continue to discuss who will achieve the most. Mostly from humble origins, they dream of prestigious promotions to the most important ministries and to positions of power.

"If any man desire to be first, the same shall be last of all, and servant of all." When Mother Teresa died, she had a royal funeral because she lived last among the last—a servant to the rejects of our affluent society. The heads of the Church long for positions of control because they are all poor of spirit. It is not poverty that threatens the Church, but the imbalance between the poverty of the masses and the riches of the Vatican leaders.

The careerist travels far but on the wrong path. However, as long as he reaches his destination, he is not concerned with how he got there. He will not accept any obstacle to his advancement, and he will trample whoever threatens his place at the altar. Once one of these careerists has been put on the right path by his patron, he knows how to continue. Archimedes taught: "Give me the proper support and I will

Canticles are religious songs or chants, with words taken from the Bible.

A **psalter** is a text containing the *Book of Psalms*, or a selection or musical setting from it.

raise myself above the world." The patrons and the protected try to convince everyone that the Holy Spirit is the driving force behind what happens in the Vatican; but, today, few can be so easily persuaded.

Jesus warned everyone not to be like the Scribes and Pharisees: *"But all their works they do for to be seen of men: they make broad their phylacteries, and enlarge the borders of their garments, and love the uppermost rooms at feasts, and the chief seats in the synagogues, and greetings in the markets, and to be called of men, 'rabbi, rabbi,'"* (who are so like our present honorable monsignors, excellencies, eminences and the like.) This reproach from the past still applies to today's class of Vatican elite.

IN THE SEVENTIES, SEVERAL PRIESTS ON A PILGRIMAGE took a cruise down the Danube. Four of the priests were from Brescia, and they were all under age forty. On one particular day, the boat crossed three national territories. The priests spent that long, monotonous day observing the lush countryside and the crowds of people gathered on the shore. After lunch and a siesta, one of the Brescians approached the assistant from Rome and, while speaking of nothing in particular, mentioned that he was a classmate of one of his contemporaries, whom we shall refer to as Don Regal. This priest had suddenly left his diocese after a quarrel with his bishop, who had favored someone else in the competition to be appointed parish priest of the cathedral. Magically, Don Regal had found a position in the Secretariat of State, serving the Brescian Pope who had been good to him during his career.

According to the tourist-priest, Don Regal was dim-witted and terribly presumptuous but was quickly able to secure a place beside the ranking prelates in the Vatican. Everyone assured him that he would have a brilliant career. The brother commented: "If these are the individuals that the Vatican chooses to run the Church, we should be truly disappointed."

Two small leather boxes worn on the forehead and left arm during morning prayers by adult male Orthodox and Conservative Jews, the **phylacteries** contain verses from the Scriptures.

From personal secretary to superior, Don Regal was promoted to the command center to replace the assessor, who was undergoing serious surgery to preserve what little sight he had left. The real incident took place when the assessor returned. With the strength of his support, Don Regal assumed the position of assessor, while the convalescing monsignor was designated to relations with the nunciatures, despite knowing nothing about that office.

In the heavenly business of juggling appointments at that level, the fawning Brescian became a prominent figure. Don Regal was offered the See in Genoa, but he declined saying that he preferred to serve the Pope closer to home. *"In the Lord's house there are many duties; I will go and prepare a place for you."* Lord Jesus, allow me to ask, are you perhaps erring in preparing too many places for these people?

"No One Will Know What Happened"

Three prelates met regularly for dinner. The eldest, employed in the Secretariat of State where he held high office, was a walking archive—intelligent, lively, and a witty conversationalist. One afternoon, while walking off a meal, he related anecdotes about Pope Paul VI and those who, because they knew his strengths and weaknesses, were able to blackmail him. "What I am going to tell you is no fairy tale; it is a true story. But, don't repeat it because there," and he pointed to the mosaic wall of the Vatican radio station offices, "morality is only one of the ways to get the backing to reach your goal. You must surely know the reason why Pope Pacelli, Paul VI, sent his close associate, Monsignor Montini, from pro-Secretary of State to Archbishop of Milan." It was clear from the reaction of his two lunch companions that they were either unfamiliar with the story or had heard incomplete or different versions. He related the story with great tact.

After the death of Luigi Maglione, Pius XII no longer wanted to be conditioned by another cardinal as Secretary of State. He allowed Monsignor Giovan Battista Montini to replace Maglione as deputy and, later, as pro-Secretary of State. Nevertheless, the Pope, well acquainted with the untrustworthy Curial environment, hired a secular secret agent to supply special investigative reports that the nuncios were unable to provide, especially on political matters in countries behind the Iron Curtain.

The agent, a colonel by the name of Arnould, reported to the Pope on a monthly basis. In mid-August 1954, the agent personally delivered a package to the Pope from the Lutheran Archbishop of Upsala, Yngue Torgny Brilioth, an admirer of the Pope and a collaborator with the Catholics in Communist countries. His instructions to the colonel had been explicit: the package was not to be passed through Vatican channels, but handed directly to the Pope. The report contained evidence that a high-ranking Vatican official was having relations with the Soviet government. In fact, claims of this nature had been made before, but Pope Paul VI had always rejected the charges, claiming that it would be impossible without his knowledge and consent.

The intrigues of the pro-Secretary, working behind the Pope's back, were dangerous. In complete opposition to the directives of Pius XII, who abhorred Communism, Montini had begun to secretly liaise with the persecutors of the Catholic Church in the Soviet Union. An in-depth investigation revealed that the Jesuit father Tondi, one of Montini's men, had provided the Soviets with lists of the names of bishops and priests sent to or secretly ordained in Communist countries, who, betrayed by the information, were all arrested and killed or sent to die in prison camps. It was also revealed that a serious schism, which had developed and continued to compromise the Chinese bishops, had been withheld from the Pope.

The Pope read the missive in the presence of Arnould and, deeply troubled, fell silent. On August 30, the

Followers of Martin Luther and his religious teachings, Lutherans support the doctrine of justification by faith alone.

Jesuits are members of the Society of Jesus, a Roman Catholic order founded in 1534 by Saint Ignatius Loyola and known for its foreign missionary work.

Archbishop of Milan, Cardinal Ildebrando Schuster, died. At the end of September, Pius XII summoned Montini and told him he would be sending him to Milan as archbishop. Without a doubt, it was a demotion to be moved from the Secretariat of State to a peripheral archbishopric, even if Milan was the largest archdiocese in Italy. Montini submissively replied: "Holy Father, I had thought to finish my modest work here in the Curia serving you!" Pope Paul VI, without another word, stood up and in a severe and authoritative tone stated: "Excellency, accept the first apostolic benediction as Archbishop of Milan! Thank you for the service that you have rendered me!" Montini received all of this on his knees.

On November 1 of that year, Montini took his place in Milan and for four years, until Pope Paul VI died, he was not made a cardinal. This way, the Pope prevented him from becoming a candidate for the papacy. For the rest of his life, Pius XII resigned himself to governing the foreign affairs of the Vatican personally.

As president of the episcopal conference in Lombardy, Archbishop Montini knew all of the bishops in the region, among whom was Monsignor Vicenzo Gilla Gremigni, the bishop of Novara who was highly respected and whose counsel was frequently sought by Pius XII. He was also aware of the previously described events. In 1958, Montini had only one auxiliary bishop in Milan, while Gremigni, in Novara, had two—a sixty-year-old and a forty-four-year-old. Montini observed the discrepancy, which led to more or less secret clashes.

When the Archbishop of Milan decided to dissolve and relocate *Il Popolo d'Italia*, a well-established Catholic newspaper in Lombardy, Monsignor Gilla Gremigni protested that such a decision could not be made unilaterally, without consulting the episcopate. Archbishop Montini's response, which was hand-delivered to the episcopate of Novara late that evening, was so violent that Gremigni, who was already suffering from a heart condition, collapsed over his desk and died while reading it. This happened at eleven o'clock on January 3, 1963.

As soon as he heard the news, Montini, who had since been made a cardinal by Pope Roncalli, set off for Novara. It was one o'clock in the morning when he summoned the young auxiliary bishop, Ugo Poletti, who offered possible explanations for the heart attack. "Perhaps," said Poletti, "the cause was the letter that you sent him, which is still on his desk in his study and which has already been officially sealed." Cardinal Montini demanded the return of the letter to avoid any embarrassing stories in the press. Poletti responded: "Eminency, the seals were put on the letter by the official an hour ago. It is late and we can no longer disturb him at this hour!" Montini rejoined: "Tomorrow will be too late. I came for the letter. No one will know what happened."

Rumors have circulated that the issue of the official seals was a ruse invented by the cunning auxiliary. Nevertheless, Poletti disappeared and, after two fitful hours, returned with the letter and apologized for the delay. Montini and Poletti swore absolute secrecy on the matter and agreed that no one else was ever to know about the letter.

Everyone knew that John XXIII was gravely ill, so it was no surprise when he died on June 3, 1963. The Archbishop of Milan was first on everyone's list for the papacy. He was elected Pope on June 21 and took the name of Paul VI. He was generally good at returning favors, but he had completely forgotten about Monsignor Poletti and Novara. Memory is often jogged by a swift reminder from the past, and when a few short articles started to appear in the papers about a letter sent by Montini to Gremigni on the night of his tragic death, Poletti was immediately made Archbishop of Spoleto. But Spoleto was apparently too boring for Poletti, and he informed the Pope that he wanted to serve him in Rome. Two years later, he was appointed to the Vicariate of

The term "**Vicariate**" refers to the office, authority, or district under the jurisdiction of a vicar.

Rome as second deputy manager to his Excellency Ettore Cunial, ahead of the auxiliaries Luigi Pozzi, Giovanni Canestri, Oscar Zanera, and Priamo Trabalzini.

When Cardinal Vicar Angelo Dell'Acqua died suddenly at Lourdes on August 27, 1972, other articles surfaced in the press. Very quickly, Poletti was appointed pro-vicar of Pope Paul VI in Rome.

At this point in the story, the old prelate tourist paused and added: "And now, by the grace of God and the Holy Mother Church, he is our Cardinal Vicar!" The two monsignors listened incredulously and one of them remarked: "Oh, the power of a single photocopy! Such Renaissance intrigues are played out in the papal court. . . ."

"This story," explained the prelate, "shows that Paul VI is strong with the weak and weak with the strong." Under Pius XII, a prelate like that would have been suspended immediately and sent to some monastery for the rest of his career, just like Cardinal Billot, who was stripped of his cardinal robes. Instead, coerced by blackmail, Poletti served the Pope in Rome until his forced retirement at the appointed age.

Favorable Winds

For decades, the Prefect of the Papal House was a man from Piacenza who had grown old holding that office. His uncle, Archbishop Cardinal of Bologna, had placed him there after failing to secure him a degree from one of the pontifical universities. With great regret, his uncle would comment: "My nephew is bright and cunning; it is a shame he didn't want to study, otherwise he would have easily become a cardinal!"

However, the uncle was mistaken because, without studying, his nephew became a cardinal anyway. In the company of his most trusted prelates from Piacenza, he once boasted about how he secured his promotion. Over forty years, the prelate had moved from being a simple assistant at ceremonies to being the master of ceremonies. During the long apprenticeship at his position, he prepared many consistories for prelates whom the Pope made cardinals. In forty years, he had seen many names promoted.

Once again, the prelate noticed his name was missing from the list of possible candidates that he was preparing for the next consistory. He clearly saw that he would be passed over again and was about to step aside for his successor when he decided instead to take a stand. One day, unannounced, he descended on the Pope who was in his study and declared: "Your Holiness, I have decided to leave tomorrow for my village where I will establish myself in my ancestral castle, since it is clear that here a servant who has given so much of himself to the Church will never be appropriately rewarded." Paul VI glared at him, completely taken aback by his unexpected and disrespectful audacity. After a long silence, he said: "Is that any way to address the Pope?" Without delay, the prelate parried: "And Your Holiness, is this any way to treat one of your faithful servants who has served five Popes? All that remains for me is to return to Conegliano to put the secret papers of my ministry in order, which I guard zealously in a safe." In this way, the prelate alluded to the many secrets that he could share with the public. He then turned and left.

Shortly after arriving home on the other side of the Tiber, his doorbell rang. A prelate had been sent to give him word of his nomination to cardinal. God's will had never been delivered in such record time.

In Christianity, **Lent** is a time of penance and prayer in preparation for the celebration of Easter.

DURING LENT OF 1966, PAUL VI RECEIVED THE bishops of the region of Lucana. One of the most important guests was the Archbishop of Acerenza, Monsignor Corrado Ursi, who knelt to kiss the Pope's hand. While the other bishops formed a circle around them, the Pope said: "Let us praise the new Archbishop of Potenza," indicating

Ursi. But, the Pope saw astonishment and surprise in the face of his appointee and the rest of the group. And yet, Paul VI remembered approving the transfer of Ursi from Acerenza to Potenza, to replace the ninety-year-old archbishop, Augusto Bertazzoni. As it turned out, however, the announcement had not been made and the Pope wanted an explanation from the Cardinal Prefect.

The honorable Emilio Colombo, Italian prime minister, had heard through the grapevine that the venerable Bertazzoni, who had been like a surrogate father to him, was to be removed from the archbishopric of Potenza. Moved by profound filial loyalty, and hoping to save him from an unpleasant situation, the politician asked that the appointment be suspended until the matter could be raised with the Pope in person. Instead, Paul VI, oblivious to these plans, proceeded to make the announcement to the bishops in attendance.

What could they do? On one hand, nothing could be gained from upsetting the honorable Colombo, a fair and respectful fellow, and, on the other hand, the Pope had been embarrassed in front of those bishops by the oversight. Both Colombo and the Pope had to be saved from further embarrassment.

Pope Montini's friendship with Monsignor Ursi dated back to a mission in Milan, where he had summoned the most famous preachers in the country and sent them out to all the parishes and districts of his immense diocese. The press had dubbed it "the mission of a thousand preachers," because of the large number of priests that he had recruited. Ursi, then Bishop of Nardò, had been appointed to preach to the industrialists of Lombardy, who enthusiastically praised him by making generous donations to the Curia. Cardinal Montini had summoned Ursi to preach to his flock on two other occasions. As Pope, his respect for Ursi was unaltered.

After the death of Cardinal Alfonso Castaldo, the See in Naples remained vacant. Without a second thought, Paul

VI transferred Archbishop Ursi from Acerenza to the cardinalate of Naples on May 23. This man of the church had done little to warrant such a prestigious office in southern Italy, but an unexpected felicity favored him and he is still remembered with sympathy and affection by the priests and faithful of that archdiocese, who are quite demanding of their archbishops.

There was a big difference between Ursi and his successor, Cardinal Michele Giordano, who has been investigated for loan-sharking—for which his brother has already been arrested—and embezzling on behalf of the Neapolitan Curia. In interviews, the Curia complained of the crimes perpetrated against the Church by Giordano, while the Neapolitan mafia asks: "What sort of expression of the Church is he?" With the whole world watching, why doesn't the Vatican ask Cardinal Giordano to step aside and let the authorities discover the hidden truth of those Church offices?

X I V

The Cardinal Rules

I t isn't easy to write about the vain men of the Church who covet honorary or prestigious titles, and who yearn for, chase, and obtain high-ranking positions. Placing oneself ahead of more deserving brothers is evidence of a self-serving faith, since it is written: *"Look not every man on his own things, but every man also on the things of others."*

In the Roman Catholic Church, the danger of a not-so-veiled new Pharisaism is emerging. The power games among ecclesiastics are similar to tribal wars composed of mafia-Masonic intrigues. The Church has become a gaudy festival of red, as the powerful want to be revered as much as the underlings want to venerate them. The one who graduates to a higher office secretly notices the movements of his distracted inferior who, forgetting to pay his respects, becomes the target of his wrath. These narcissistic prelates derive immense pleasure before, during, and after these high-level papal meetings. Ghika wrote that Narcissus is farther from God than Cain.

Monsignors in full trim, dressed smartly in their prelate's cassocks, supercilious and smiling, make a point of paying their respects to the cardinals and prelates in the reserved seats of the first two rows. Jesus said: *"The Scribes and the Pharisees sit in Moses' seat: all therefore whatsoever they bid you observe, that observe and do; but do not ye after*

Pharisaism refers to the doctrines and practices of the Pharisees—or the hypocritical observance of the letter of religious or moral law without regard for the spirit.

their works: for they say, and do not. For they bind heavy burdens and grievous to be borne, and lay them on men's shoulders; but they themselves will not move them with one of their fingers. But all their works they do for to be seen of men: they make broad their phylacteries, and enlarge the borders of their garments, and love the uppermost rooms at feasts, and the chief seats in the synagogues, and greetings in the markets and to be called 'rabbi, rabbi.' But he that is greatest among you shall be your servant."

If a seat remains vacant in the front row, a prelate will find some excuse to warmly greet an acquaintance in that row and sit down comfortably beside him. Just like that, he jumps ahead of his colleagues and moves much closer to the Pope, of course out of pure veneration. Later, he will also act this way in life, impeding those who are less adept. *"Woe unto you Pharisees, for ye love the uppermost seats in the synagogues and greetings in the markets."*

EVERY YEAR, ON THE VIGIL OF SAINTS PETER and Paul, the Polish Pope meets with all of his collaborators in the ministries of the Roman Curia and the Vicariate. Obviously, this is the best time to be seen resplendently dressed in full finery.

However, there was an ill-mannered monsignor with a sharp mind, who showed up regularly for this papal function *in nigris*, that is, in a simple black cassock, and not even a new one! His appearance so annoyed one of the guests that he instructed a security guard to move the poorly dressed intruder at least four or five rows back. The guard showed him to another seat, explaining: "Monsignor, excuse me, you should move from here because that seat is already taken."

Accustomed to this kind of treatment, and without hesitation, the monsignor left his friends dressed in red in their appointed seats and took his place toward the back. But, he didn't stay there very long. The same guard approached him again, embarrassed, and asked him to move back:

"Excuse me, Monsignor, it isn't up to me where you sit, they demand it!" The simple priest tried to cheer up the kindly layman by saying: "Don't worry about me, I am used to the method of San Giuseppe Cottolongo." "What method is that, Monsignor?" the guard asked. The priest replied: "San Giuseppe used to tell the disabled children who were systematically moved from one place to another because they were undesirable: 'Don't trouble yourselves too much, because, in order to be truly tasty, cabbages have to be planted twice.'" The peal of laughter from the guard drew the attention of the other prelates.

A few minutes later, the security guard approached the prelate smiling and said: "Monsignor, there is a place in the very first row; if it weren't for that allusion to the cabbages, I would have taken you there in front of everyone, because you deserve to be there by right. But, I swear to you, Monsignor, from now on I will be very careful before moving reverends without finery!"

GOD DOESN'T MAKE DISTINCTIONS BETWEEN people; he isn't partial; and he doesn't have preferences. But, here, we are not talking about God in heaven, who is far from our miserable little problems of colors, tricks, and deceptions.

However, humans make distinctions to reach their goals. The proverb confirms: "Help yourselves and God will help you!" This notion is lost on the ecclesiastics, particularly members of the Curia.

Contrary to what was said during the twenty-year dictatorship in Italy, having friends in the Curia is equivalent to having honor, which varies according to the colors of the Curia members' robes. A mother of a young priest once told her son: "We all have a guardian in heaven; blessed is he who also has one on earth!" He later learned that she was absolutely right.

In this parade of cardinal red, nobody likes to recall the Lord's reproach to the Pharisees: *"How can ye believe, which receive honor one of another, and seek not the honor that cometh from God only?"* Perhaps, they believe that God is blind to their brilliant red robes. Anyway, they certainly haven't learned that true greatness comes from above, not below, and from the inside, not outside.

At these papal ceremonies, nuns of every shape and size inevitably gather. They also appear impeccably dressed with curly locks carelessly peaking out from their veils, or without a veil and sporting a fresh perm from a stylist in town, who has also given them a manicure.

Purple Showmen

Simon Peter never wanted to be the leader of the budding Church. Yet, from their first meeting, Jesus declared him just that: *"Thou art Peter, and upon this rock I will build my Church; follow me and I will make you a fisherman of men."* But Peter, on more than one occasion, revealed himself a failure: *"Get thee behind me Satan; thou art an offense unto me."* He had yielded to the pressures of the Jews to the point of having one attitude with them and another with the pagans, regarding ancient law. Paul intervened to free him from his errant ways. Yet, Peter was the first vicar of Christ, the first Pope who, while despising his errors, admitted them and demanded that Mark record them in his Gospel for the edification of the Church.

A Christian apostle and author of the second Gospel of the New Testament, **Mark** is the patron of Venice.

History has chronicled more than one Curial dignitary who elected himself to lead the Church, or at least command its shadow government. One, however, stands out above the others, and the usual toady broadcaster of "Telepeace" never fails to praisingly mention him at every opportunity. This dignitary attributes to himself such a presence that he brazenly glorifies his leadership abilities and behaves in such a way that others in Vatican and ecclesiastical circles, as well as the social and political spheres, also see it.

Convinced that he is the measure of all things wise and wonderful, this fellow plays to the media, flaunting his brilliant purple robes. With false modesty, he accepts the title of Foreign Minister of the Church to the Middle East. Presumptuously, he grants interviews on the future government of the Church, makes so-called pastoral visits to foreign churches and governments, receives all sorts of politicians, never misses a papal ceremony, is invited to every high-ranking meeting, celebrates the weddings of high-profile individuals, and presides over the funerals of the great directors, actors, or politicians who, at the end of their lives, want us all to believe they were good Christians. He will do anything to make himself look good.

This purple-robed phoney tries to convince others that he is the most powerful Vatican dignitary of his time. He shows the political world that he can select the candidates and nominees for bishops and cardinals, and that he can favorably propose them to the ailing Pope, all to benefit his gang from Emilia Romagna. The onlookers take note of this star and try to make him their friend and protector. Because of his ability to attract such positive publicity, the president and other members of state clamor to visit with him, even before they visit the Pope and the Secretary of State.

In 1994, a spectacle arose between the cardinal's ego and the prime minister, the Honorable Catholic Silvio Berlusconi. The meeting of the two had been quite congenial. The cardinal was not embarrassed to be seen shaking the hand of the politician, who was a veteran of Masonic associations, the founder of three morally questionable television networks, a rich mogul whose wealthy origins were shady, and who had proclaimed himself as Anointed by the Lord. This last point may explain why Berlusconi has two wives and two families. It is rumored that, at some point, the cardinal had secured a private family chapel for the Anointed Berlusconi where he could attend mass in the utmost domestic bliss. Someone once asked which one of his families would attend with him.

In 1997, Italian business executive and politican **Silvio Berlusconi** was convicted of financial crimes.

In a world of daring self-promotion, modesty is of little use; indeed, it has the opposite effect. The ambitious have no need of modesty. The pride of knowing how to rise to enormous heights inebriates them and they remain convinced that power is pleasure and that pleasure is their duty. Their thirst for power emphasizes the otherness of God and the similarities of their collaborators. The Lord continues in vain to suggest that they should descend from their heights: *"Learn from my example for I am meek and humble of heart."* Lucifer was an angel of light who ascended too high and fell into darkness. Ghika noted that pride is the splendor of stupidity, and Padre Pio maintained that love of self, the first-born son of pride, is more ambitious and malicious than its mother. Even a pagan emperor, Marcus Aurelius, said the following about these powerful imbeciles: "This is how they are: they eat, they sleep, they defecate like the others, but once they are made shepherds of a human flock, they become difficult and, from their heights, become beyond reproach. A moment ago they were slaves to innumerable human passions and, in a few moments, they will be again."

In the Curia, where feudalism runs rampant, the superior bastardizes authority and persists with an excessive authoritarianism: *"Let favor be showed to the wicked, yet will he not learn righteousness: in the land of uprightness will he deal unjustly, and will not behold the majesty of the Lord."* Winston Churchill once said of Richard the Lionheart: "His life was a magnificent parade. But when the procession passed, there was nothing behind him but empty fields."

Obsessed with appearing young, our purple leader appears in public surrounded by hand-selected prelates whom he shamelessly appoints to offices. *"The show of their countenance doth witness against them; and they declare their sin as Sodom, they hide it not. Woe unto their souls, for they have rewarded evil unto themselves. O my people, they which lead thee cause thee to err, and destroy the way of thy paths."*

Elected Roman Emperor in AD 161, **Marcus Aurelius'** reign ended the *Pax Romana,* and Rome found itself threatened by barbarians.

But even worse than an old imbecile is a young imbecile, prostrate at the feet of his old, purple protector. Saint Bernard's warning to Eugene III about the vices and whims of the prelacy is worth repeating: "Your brothers, the cardinals, must learn by your example not to keep young, long-haired boys and seductive men in their midst."

WHETHER PROMOTING THE SPIRITUALITY OF Mother Teresa or prostrating themselves at the grave of Padre Pio, these actors of the clergy perform best in the presence of the appointed media, where they always appear suffering and pious. They reinvent themselves tirelessly for fashionably worthy causes.

Saint Augustine said: "Love the sinner, hate the sin." Gregory the Great echoed this sentiment when he said: "Arrogant individuals do not know how to teach with humility, and even the good things they know, they are unable to communicate well. When they teach, they give the impression that they are well above and looking down on their listeners, to whom they appear as domineering commanders rather than counselors."

X V

The Power of Silence

The Roman Curia is a house of mirrors where everyone spies on each other. Divided in two, one half controls the other, and each believes the other half is teeming with spies, sneaks, and deceivers, so they follow the warning: "Quiet, your friend is listening!"

Secret misunderstandings envelop this jealous court that is as powerful as it is ruthless. In this environment, rumors are kept in reserve and spread so that the subject of the gossip never finds out. Seneca advised: "What you want to keep hidden, don't tell anyone." In this passage, the "anyone" refers exclusively to the subject of the rumor. If he were to inquire about the gossip, they would deny everything to his face using bureaucratic jargon, whether it was true or false.

In Machiavellian terms, the end justifies the means when someone is promoted to someone else's rightly deserved position. This administrative secret is kept even if it destroys the interpersonal loyalty that is indispensable to any peaceful and fraternal relationship.

Numerous examples of this practice are at work among the Pope's collaborators today. In these enormous abuses of power, the dependants lack the ability to champion their natural or divine rights, since it is written that the worker is worthy of his reward, especially if it is a promotion. The power of papal secret favors the slanderer and punishes the innocent, who is denied any recourse to justice or truth.

This power has become prevalent in administrative circles where it should, by right, be absent.

The stance on secrets in the Vatican differs according to the situation. For example, to avoid a worldwide scandal over the Virgin's revelations at Fatima about the ecclesiastics at the head of the Church, the hierarchy's policy would have been to maintain, if they had ever entered the public domain, that the Virgin's revelations were foolish and false. But, when it comes to spreading slander and insults in order to sideline a possible candidate, then it is permissible to perpetrate such iniquity.

Saint Bernard once again instructs us on this matter: "I would like you [Eugene III] to establish a general rule that states that whoever is afraid to say in public what they whisper in secret is suspicious. If he refuses to repeat his words in public, consider him a slanderer, not an accuser."

Secrecy and Secretaries

During the seventies, the rector of the pontifical Lateran University drew attention to himself by organizing many trips around Italy and abroad. From a distance, the counterintelligence agents monitored him, and he became suspicious and paranoid. Halfway through the academic year in 1974, the rector fired a Slovak professor, a Franciscan friar, for having denounced him to the Rota. Following the investigation of this matter, the Rota issued a Solomonic response asserting that the Franciscan was partially right. Nevertheless, the monk-professor refused to remain silent about the Masonic maneuvers of the rector. Out of spite, he was dismissed for his persistence and insubordination.

The **Rota** is the tribunal of the papal Curia that presides over cases, especially matrimonial cases, appealed from diocesan courts.

This next episode was related by the Franciscan himself. On a summer's day in 1974, the same Masonic rector was arranging to book a hotel in Genoa, in the vicinity of the railroad station. He arrived late that evening and rather than walking to the hotel, because he suspected that he was being followed, he opted for a long, winding taxi ride. He showed up at the hotel's reception desk in plain clothes and presented false identification papers. He then made a reservation for the following morning for a working breakfast with two associates, a married couple who turned out not to be married after all. The next day, a secret-service agent prepared a table for them in the corner of the dining room, but they decided to sit at another one. The waiter quickly set the new table as close as possible to the one that had been wired, so that the agents could successfully follow what turned out to be a rather circumspect and whispered conversation. The agents discerned a reference to February 1975, the death of Paul VI, the conclave, and the names of Baggio, Poletti, and Villot as possible candidates. However, at the time, Paul VI was not suffering from anything that would suggest the end of his papacy.

February came and went uneventfully. Paul VI was alive and well, and the conversation attributed to the rector and his cohorts seemed to have been misinterpreted. However, an article appeared in the weekly magazine *Il Tempo* confirming the gist of that conversation. The article stated that a plot against the Pope had been thwarted, because a typewritten note had been placed in his quarters alerting him to the danger. Interestingly, the names of Cardinal Baggio and Monsignor Annibale Bugnini were mentioned as possible perpetrators. The article described the Pope's bitter surprise, and the many difficulties associated with removing Baggio from his important position as secretary of the Congregation for the Divine Cult. He vanished into thin air and then resurfaced as nuncio in Iran on January 4, 1976. The story, which was never denied, caused a stir throughout the world and shed light on the shady machinations of Masonic organizations within the Vatican.

SOME TIME AGO, A CARDINAL WAS NOMINATED as visiting inspector to a religious community that had fallen under the control of unscrupulous individuals. In Italy, extortion was rampant at the highest levels. The inept cardinal chose the untrustworthy Monsignor Franco Lesarno to contact the superiors of the concerned ministry. Lesarno immediately decided to have the monsignor in charge removed, so that the inspection could proceed without supervision. He arranged for a secret meeting with the superiors and related an incredible, utterly false accusation against the monsignor: "Yesterday I picked up the phone and happened to overhear a conversation between your official and Mrs. Ortensia from Venice, whom the religious community owed money. The monsignor revealed these detailed instructions that were given to the visiting cardinal. . . ." Lesarno then listed, item by item, all of the suggestions made to the visiting cardinal from a letter that he had obviously prepared.

Overjoyed by his discovery, the superiors asked Lesarno to document the whole affair. A report was submitted to their office that afternoon. To ensure that the slandered monsignor wouldn't refute the accusations if deposed by his superiors, Lesarno called him and brazenly accused him of the facts he had related to the superiors and tried to convince him they were true.

How did his superiors respond to this disclosure? As is customary in these Curial matters, they accepted the signed documents and immediately placed them in the slandered monsignor's file, without considering the validity of the assertions. Because of practices such as these, transgressors of norms rest assured with consciences that constrict and expand according to the circumstance.

The next morning, the slandered monsignor found the drawer empty where he kept his voluminous file of reports. In response to his protests, the hypocrites assured him, invoking a circular logic, that the move was wise and necessary. Jesus said: *"Woe unto you, scribes and Pharisees, hypocrites, for ye are like whited sepulchres, which indeed appear beautiful outward, but are within full of dead men's bones, and uncleanness. Even so ye also outwardly appear righteous unto men, but within ye are full of hypocrisy and iniquity."*

The so-called inspection-visit lasted four years, until both the cardinal and his monsignor were driven away. It was an utter disaster that cost the Vatican millions of dollars in mortgages and sales of real estate properties. But, not surprisingly, Lesarno was ordained a bishop by the Pope in 1998. In the Vatican, anyone can become victim to nefarious conspiracies and unscrupulous behavior.

Secrets and Lies

A monsignor, well advanced in years and with plenty of seniority, was to be promoted to a vacant position at the tenth rank. The promotion had been delayed by his superiors in the hope that he would go away on holidays, at which time they had planned to propose a careerist monk for the position. The prelate had paid dearly for his sincere dissension and the vigor with which he confronted unpleasant situations, and had been denied a promotion every time he was entitled to one. He was known throughout the office for the bitter and sarcastic pasquinades he wrote.

Satirical writings posted in a public place, **pasquinades** take their name from a statue in Rome on which critical passages about specific individuals were posted.

Suffering from Alzheimer's disease, the Cardinal Prefect was not responsible for the following events. His two subordinates secretly promoted the monk instead of the prelate, even though the latter had been in the ministry for fifteen years. Upon returning from his holidays, the shocked monsignor asked why he had been overlooked. In response, they quoted the operative regulation that stated: "Officials cannot invoke rights, including superiority, in order to secure a promotion." With this, the malicious scoundrels managed to silence the monsignor, and felt justified in doing so.

The monsignor, however, insisted on knowing the reasons for this arbitrary decision. The primary motivator of this action, the undersecretary, hid behind the shield of office secrecy and, with false concern, alluded to the existence of some serious reasons for his exclusion. He encouraged the disconsolate monsignor not to pursue the matter, leaving him to suffer in a vague, nameless suspicion, since he could not recall anything in his past that would justify his exclusion from promotion and further loyal service.

Doubt now colored his life, and he found little peace and comfort. He lived for another ten years with this question mark of doubt over his head. In the meantime, another vacancy at the tenth level transpired due to the retirement of a pensioner. The monsignor was obviously in line for the promotion, but everything fell silent around him once again. The principal motivator during the earlier fiasco had since been promoted to nuncio, but the others were still around. To promote the aged monsignor now would reflect badly on them since they had bypassed him earlier when a promotion would have been appropriate and fair. What were they to do? What scheme could they fabricate? The issue was put aside and sealed in utmost secrecy for a year.

The letter of promotion to be sent to the Secretariat of State was already drafted. This time, it bore the name of the rejected monsignor who should have been promoted to head clerk ten years earlier. The official request had been signed by the new Cardinal Prefect and was ready to be sent to the Secretariat of State. Those who wield power sow dissent among ecclesiastics in the same office so that they will fight among themselves. The powerful employ this tactic since united forces can defend themselves against a despot. This diabolical trap is set to ensure that group members distrust one another.

Since everything was still under lock and key, the champions of the plot to undermine the promotion had little time in which to work. Once again, they set about vigorously slandering the elderly deacon and they submitted another name for the position, which they expeditiously sent to the Secretariat. This time, they told him that his nomination had been rejected by higher-ranking officials, for reasons that they were unwilling to share. Again, a thorough and successful operation left the old man psychologically and morally beaten: *"The wicked in his pride doth persecute the poor: let them be taken in the devices that they have imagined."*

Once the letter had arrived and the announcement had been made, the slandered monsignor visited the cardinal to ask why his name had been removed when it had already been established that he had been unjustly overlooked ten years earlier. He told the cardinal that his right to defend himself against the malicious plot that had sullied his reputation and railroaded his career for a second time had been denied. Shaking and mumbling, the ailing cardinal inveighed against him for presuming to break the code of secrecy and threatened to expel him: "You, Monsignor, should not have known about all this! You must tell me who told you these things, otherwise you run the risk of being disciplined!" The impassive monsignor replied: "Cardinal, I am sorry for what has happened to your brain, but I must inform you that you don't have to ask who revealed the secret; instead, Your Eminence should ask who perpetrated this pitiless injustice." For the little purple man, the injustice was that the code of secrecy had been violated. The promotion business could have been dealt with, but the breach of the code was the true sacrilege.

The monsignor was finally promoted, but never restored in reputation or granted the material benefits that would have accompanied his office had he received the position years earlier. The fellow who first replaced him reached the level of undersecretary and later, to remove him from that office, he was made archbishop and nuncio in Somalia. Those promoted late are like dying men who are graciously spared at the eleventh hour. Pyrrhic victories, with equal measures of victories and defeats, are like the glass that is half full or half empty, but always bitter. God, to preserve the dignity of the individual, forbids calumny and the defamation of a good name.

Spying and Inquisitions

The Inquisition hasn't altogether ended. It has been perfected, but not ended. In the Vatican, there remain traces of
an inquisitorial state that spies and keeps dossiers on its
personnel. The inquisitors, at the beck and call of their
powerful superior, have mastered the old art of sabotaging
a victim who never knows how and why he was targeted.

One of the time-worn instruments of this ancient revived
art is the Vatican telephone system. Although it is illegal to
invade someone's private life, it is perfectly acceptable and
normal for a superior to ask that one of his subordinates'
phones be tapped without any authorization from or warning to the interested party, who, from that moment on, will
have all of his incoming and outgoing calls recorded. This
arbitrary abuse of power undeniably exists, but it is so common that all concerned parties—the superiors, the employees, and the spies themselves—have clear consciences.

All Vatican employees know that their personal telephone could be tapped at any time, if it isn't already. The
more prestigious the prelate, the greater the chances that
his telephone will be wired. Obviously, none of the
recorded conversations will ever be played back to the interested party. The most prudent prelates prefer to make
important calls from home rather than from their offices,
but home phones have also been known to be monitored.

MANY POLICE-LIKE INSPECTIONS OCCUR IN THE
office filing cabinets and desks of the "suspect," who never
knows of these events. These practices are common and
considered standard procedure for the most zealous superiors in search of a crime.

On Friday, November 9, 1990, at approximately 12:15, a
monsignor was summoned by his Cardinal Prefect. In the
cardinal's studio, a secretary of a nuncio of a country deci-
mated by civil war was lamenting the fact that secret docu-

ments were being leaked from the ministry. The prefect had no doubts about the loyalty and confidentiality of his collaborator, but he wasn't as sure about the foreign monsignor.

The monsignor responsible for the department swore that he had never revealed any office secrets, but he couldn't speak for the others who worked in the office. Unexpectedly, the Cardinal Prefect told him to lock his door whenever he left his office, even if he were leaving for just a moment. The official responded that if he followed that instruction, he would likely offend his colleagues. The prefect repeated the instruction and, to the surprise of the two men in his studio, revealed: "You shouldn't be surprised. You should know that your room, as I found out when I arrived, was carefully and thoroughly searched with particular focus on where you keep your personal effects and private papers." The collaborator thanked him for his warning and noted: "Whoever lowers themselves to such tactics is capable of finding things that are not even there to begin with. They would simply bring something along with them and say, 'Well, look what we have here!'" The investigative methods used by the Vatican were perfected by the Gestapo and the KGB.

At that moment, the monsignor remembered an inexplicable warning from an aging monsignor who had advised him to keep personal papers that could be easily photocopied in a safe place, away from the office. Later, he learned more about these inquisitorial techniques. To avoid leaving evidence or raising suspicion during these searches, the desk drawers are carefully opened by experts with a special device, who then take instant photographs of the contents so that, when they have finished rummaging, they can restore the contents of the drawer to its exact original state. This technique was borrowed from secret agents from around the world.

Such accounts of control and monitoring inside and outside the Vatican are intriguing, but for those who sacrifice themselves on the funeral pyre of the true Church, enduring these practices becomes a silent martyrdom.

X V I

Justice and the Liturgy

I n the Vatican ministries, as in all respectable offices, appropriate qualifications or university degrees are obligatory to accede to certain positions. Every protector understands this and should not propose his favorites for important appointments if they lack the qualifications. Yet, hoping for the best, the superior often proposes his candidate for a position, knowing full well that he is unqualified. If the committee responsible for promoting the employees doesn't notice the lack of credentials, all the better. This trick is played on the poor unsuspecting officials who conduct themselves fairly and correctly. If the promotion is later rejected because of obvious deficiencies in the applicant's dossier, some candidates even manage to overcome that.

In civilized countries, the crime of falsifying degrees and doctoring qualifications is punishable in a court of law. A guilty verdict carries the following punishment: the degree is considered null and void; all of those implicated in the corruption, whether willing participants or not, are condemned; and the professors involved are dismissed for forgery of a public document. The doctored theses and fraudulent degrees in Vatican universities, often tailored to specific promotions, deserve special investigation by a body independent of the papal courts. The individual with the courage to denounce that caste of professors must be prepared for the fiercest persecution from the entourage of the guilty, including the protectors, the protected, the readers and examiners, the authors of the fraudulent theses, and so on.

Everyone in the Vatican knows about these practices, yet nobody dares to expose them to the Pope or the corps of professors. No inquiry commission will ever be able to conduct a serious inspection of the corruption and the corrupt prelates with their newly conferred degrees. In their opinion, it is better to avoid a scandal than to sink a scalpel into a festering wound to heal it.

Not long ago, another well-known cardinal at the head of a ministry wanted to promote his personal secretary to head clerk without the requisite qualifications. Rightly rejected, he promptly nominated him for an archbishopric, while also procuring a degree for him from a professor-friend. The cardinal later rewarded the professor with a consultant position to his ministry.

Aside from being criminal, these illegal and despicable operations that flood the Vatican are representative of those superiors who, in the delirium of their omnipotence, confer promotions, titles, and miters to their personal secretaries and clan members, or remove them from those they don't like. Instead of working hard in classes and libraries, these protected students are awarded their degrees with full honors, to the satisfaction of their examiners. The convocation of the degree is followed immediately by the graduate's promotion to a preordained position and the supervising professor is rewarded in the presence of all the department members.

IN HIS DESIRE TO INSTITUTE SERIOUS ACADEMIC reform in the pontifical universities, Leo XII (1823–29), recalling Sixtus V, quoted the following: "The cities and kingdoms are governed best when the wise and intelligent are in power." Never has a remark so aptly suited the anomalies of the pontifical universities, where academic freedom mysteriously and enigmatically envelops the real learning of professors and students.

As Pope from 1585 to 1590, **Sixtus V** brought order to the papal states, and constructed and rebuilt many buildings and churches in Rome.

The pontifical institutes require thorough and immediate reform. In these universities, he who studies theology
loses the faith; he who studies morality lacks it; he who
closely examines the Holy Scriptures doubts the
Revelation; and he who studies the law transgresses it.
Without scruples, they all recite the divine words in the breviary: *"They speak vanity every one with his neighbor: with flat-
tering lips and with a double heart do they speak,"* and *"His
mouth is full of cursing and deceit and fraud: under his tongue
is mischief and vanity."* Yet, these warnings do not apply to
them, for they believe themselves to be above such rebukes.

The Ill-Balanced Scales of Justice

The most serious blow to justice is the suspicion that the
court uses varying scales to administer it. A Curial court
presiding over a matter involving a superior, such as the
head of a ministry, often simultaneously acts as judge,
plaintiff, and defendant. For friends, the law is interpreted;
for the powerless, it is applied.

Juridical constrictions at some times seem rigid, and at
other times seem elastic. The standards established for
laws are based entirely on convention. However, laws can
be changed by subsequent interpretations.

It is important to allow the law to develop naturally,
without obstacles. The Romans called this *aequitas*, meaning fair and impartial justice. Thankfully, this justice has
endured in every society as a living, growing, and changing
force. If subjects are free to express themselves, then they
will determine its course. The legislators may guide it, suggest the appropriate paths to follow, and describe its limitations, but without becoming despotic.

In the Vatican, the law favors the interests of the authorities who impose it on everyone. Everything proceeds
according to a well-detailed agenda. Mark Twain said: "We
should always leave ideas in the sky; there isn't one that,

coming down to earth, doesn't stop in at a brothel." This notion that humanity corrupts what is ideal certainly applies to the law.

Judgment changes with its environment, just as materials take the shape of their container. Ecclesiastical judgments are not immune to this principle. Unproven facts are taken for granted, and injustices become disconcerting legal matters. The accused doesn't stand a chance. The blessed Federico Ozanam said: "Justice without charity becomes petrified; charity without justice begins to rot."

"Therefore the law is slacked, and judgment doth never go forth: for the wicked doth compass about the righteous; therefore wrong judgment proceedeth." In the Vatican, ideas and terms that express important juridical concepts assume nuances in meaning that are quite different, and that span the conceptual spectrum. The judge invariably becomes an inquisitor, no longer an impartial witness to the arguments for the defense and the prosecution, but an investigator rummaging undisturbed for clues and evidence.

In the Vatican, the scales of justice are balanced acrobatically by a careful play of weights and counterweights, depending on the circumstance.

Justice is not equal to the law, because justice precedes the law. If you must choose between the two, choose justice, since every era has laws that desecrate the equity of justice. Preferably, questionable and mistaken positions held by the superiors are defended by impartial men, since it is dangerous for irreverent and partial men to defend just positions.

THE VATICAN INSTITUTION MOST MALIGNED BY outsiders, particularly journalists, is the court of the Roman Rota with its college comprising prelate judges, and which broke away from the Apostolic Chancellery under Innocent III. The Rota is the supreme court for both ecclesiastical and secular causes, and its judges are appointed by the Pope. In the past, some nations enjoyed

In the nineteenth century, scholar **Federico Ozanam** helped found the Saint Vincent de Paul Society, a charitable organization.

The ecclesiastical doctrine of **Innocent III** (Pope: 1198-1216) stated that the spiritual takes precedence over the physical, and that all earthly things are subject to the spiritual authority of the Pope.

the privilege of nominating judges, but that no longer happens. In 1870, the Rota's activities ceased, but it was reconvened under Pius X, and on February 1, 1994, John Paul II revamped it. For most people, the Rota is known as the arm of the court that dissolves marriages. It does this, but it is primarily a court of second and third appeals.

A famous actor once asked a religious judge: "Father, I know that the Rota dissolves the marriages of the wealthy and powerful: how much would I have to spend to get a judgment like that?" The judge responded: "For you, sir, there would be a real discount, because if you married with this kind of superficiality, I would feel authorized to tell you, with great probability, that you have never fulfilled your contractual obligation."

"Hate the evil, and love the good, and establish judgment in the gate. But let judgment run down as waters, and righteousness as a mighty stream."

As Pope from 1903 to 1914, Saint **Pius X** found himself in conflict with the French government over the separation of church and state.

The Manipulated Liturgy

In the Church, the Word remains immutable, but there are external forms that clothe the Word. Like fashions, these forms change over time. We must not confuse the term "ancient" with the term "old" when referring to the Scriptures, prayer, the liturgy, and the sacraments, since it implies a different meaning.

What we express on the subject of the liturgy draws heavily on an article written by the Archbishop of Brussels, Godfried Danneels. He defined the liturgy as "God's work which works in us, for us. Therefore, I enter into the liturgy, I don't create it." The liturgy derives from the Bible and tradition, and has become engraved in the Church over centuries. The liturgy serves as it is; it need not be manipulated.

The reform of Vatican II put the emphasis on the catchword "participation," meaning the active role of the

The **liturgy** is the prescribed form of public worship for ceremonies and rites such as the celebration of the Eucharist.

congregation in the liturgy. Before the pronouncement of that council, we were guests in the house of God, listening to him as he made us understand his teachings. We passively experienced the mysteries of Christ through the symbolic actions of the liturgy. The liturgy, however, must be lived. It must be entered with all of one's mind, body, and soul. Therefore, the liturgy is dialogic. It moves toward the mystery of the individual, and we allow it to touch us. It is an invitation to Christ, through participation.

Since the reform, in complete transition, humanity has become the lead actor, the director who manipulates the liturgy to make it conform to our needs: *"Let us go and celebrate that which we have prepared for Christ."* Reduced to this, the liturgy is nothing more than a container of pedagogic and humanitarian concerns with teachings professed by didactic masters. The liturgy has become a laughing-stock where all we do is listen. They claim that dialogue damages the intelligence of the celebration more than it fosters it, but nothing could be more devastating to the liturgy than treating it as a lesson to be lectured.

The liturgy, as part of the theological truth, should have been better respected and protected. Instead, it has been completely destroyed. A professor, employing the crudest language, called the reform a liturgical rape committed before the whole world.

The new liturgy lies marginalized and prey to the abuse of any liturgical manipulator. The guardian of eternal truths, rich in art and thought, the liturgy is subject to the contemporary master of ceremonies who bastardizes the liturgy and pompously imposes it on the whole assembly, from the Pope to the altar boy. *"Wherefore the Lord said, Forasmuch as this people draw near to me with their mouth, and with their lips do honor me, but have removed their heart far from me, and their fear toward me is taught by the precept of men."*

Never in the history of religion have people been stripped of their traditions as they have in the Roman Catholic Church with respect to the ancient liturgy, whose reintroduction, in whole or in part, is still forbidden. From the true liturgy that was bolstered with elegiac Latin and Gregorian chant, we have been given compositions without lyricism and aestheticism—two-bit poems with little theological content, devoid of meaning and lacking any literary flourish. We are left with only primitive conceptual art without ideals, vigor, poetry, or music.

The anonymous music of Gregorian chant was the result of centuries of prayer and the search for realities that bring us closer to God. Whoever felt authorized to apply liturgical reform by excluding Gregorian chant took his responsibilities too far along the road to secularization. There is nothing left to do but watch the parades and dancing that the television broadcasts from the papal ceremonies—events produced and directed by individuals who know nothing and care little about the liturgy.

Inspired by that immortal motto of Christ *"nova et vetera"* (the new and the ancient), the ancient is rejuvenated in the new and the new is consecrated in the ancient. Lavoisier's observation: "Nothing is created; nothing is made; everything is transformed," applies to Church reform when it is inspired by divine tradition. When he founded his Church, the Divine Teacher knew it would be a turbulent reign, so he warned: *"Again, the kingdom of heaven is like unto a net, that was cast into the sea, and gathered of every kind; or unto a man that is a householder, which bringeth forth out of his treasure things new and old."*

In this spiritual context, we hear that the traditionalists fought for the observance of tradition and ancient customs. The others, the progressive ones, championed the creative and the new. The powers that be must keep watch over this conflict, which has become an indispensable source of progress. He who accepts new choices accepts the risk of losing what is discarded.

AT THE TIME OF VATICAN II, MANY WORKED diligently at establishing who was issuing the orders to reject the ancient liturgical traditions. The customs are the untouchable patrimony of the Church, whose secular roots originate at the time of the Apostles who, in turn, descend from the Chosen People of the Old Testament. As it turned out, the culprit was none other than the Secretary of the papal Department for the Divine Cult, Archbishop Annibale Bugnini.

After following him for some time and observing his residence, the secret service followed him to the Masonic headquarters of the Great Orient of Italy. It seems that Bugnini was working for the grand master who was paying him handsome monthly sums for his services. One of his paychecks was even photocopied and published in a well-known magazine in 1975. The following October, newspaper articles indicated that Bugnini had vanished from the Curia and that nobody knew his whereabouts. The dispatch with which Monsignor Bugnini was dismissed was intended to be a diplomatic and political lesson.

The Masonic prelates of the Curia ensured that the two members of their confraternity, Bugnini and Baggio, were spared the wrath of Paul VI who had been informed of a plot against him by the secret service under the command of Enrico Mino. Enraged, the Pope had Bugnini sent to Iran as nuncio, where he remained until his death in 1982.

Defenders of the Faith

In 1563, the Venetian ambassador to Rome, Alvise Contarini, wrote: "Here adulation disguises itself as honesty, intrigue as shrewdness. Every vice appears in costume: all honesty, all honorable, all that is necessary to profit, the only deity that they adorn. Simulation is the soul of the Roman court." On the eve of 2000, nothing has changed.

XVII

Communism in the Vatican

L enin believed that the Secretary of a Communist Party in a Catholic state must dress himself in a Franciscan robe to succeed.

In 1935, the secret service indicated that, during those years, approximately 100 Communist students had infiltrated the seminaries and novitiates of Western Europe where, feigning a true religious vocation, they prepared to become priests. Once ordained, the party intended to place them in the most important and sensitive positions in their respective national churches. During the sixties and seventies, the phenomenon became so serious that there were conflicts and protests over the many Communist priests in the seminaries and novitiates.

In the 1920s, under the pseudonym of Caesar, Antonio Gramsci made the following prophetic observation in his *New Order*: "Christ's red tunic blazes more brightly today, more red, more Bolshevik. There is a strip of that tunic in the innumerable red flags of the Communists who are storming the bourgeois fortresses around the world, in order to restore the kingdom of the spirit on the material, and to ensure peace on earth for all men of good will."

Devastating Effects

During the 1970s, the Slovak bishop Monsignor Pavel Hnilica was expelled from the Soviet Union, where he had been detained. The Vatican assured the Russians that he would be persuaded to transfer to the United States. But, as soon as he was released, the prelate revealed his intentions to serve the faithful behind the Iron Curtain from Rome. Occasionally, an official from the Secretariat would invite him to go to the United States to better fulfill his apostolate. The Slovak monsignor promised to move, but always postponed his transfer.

Once, returning by plane from one of the East Bloc countries, Hnilica asked the flight attendant to bring him a copy of *Pravda*, the Russian newspaper, so that he could remain informed on what was happening in the communist countries. To his surprise, he found an article stating that he, the bishop, had requested and been granted a transfer to the United States. The prelate, knowing how things work in those countries, folded the paper and put it away. Three days later, he was summoned to the Secretariat of State to be received by a high-ranking official who informed him, in no uncertain terms, that he was to be transferred to the States. He was given only a few days to make the necessary arrangements. Monsignor Hnilica had brought along the copy of *Pravda* and, with composure, found the article. He showed it to the official and translated it for him. Then, in an impressive manner, he said: "Monsignor, what game are we playing at?"

As it happened, nothing came of the incident, and Hnilica stayed in Rome where he resides today. Obviously, they couldn't outsmart him, but he didn't escape completely unscathed. Some time later, he was implicated in a money-laundering scam, perhaps as retribution for his refusal to leave.

IN 1956, DON PASQUALE UVA, FOUNDER OF THE House of Divine Providence in Bisceglie, somewhat belatedly invited a young aspiring priest from Basilicata into his new fraternity. He told the directors of the regional seminary that he was willing to vouch for the young priest whose name was Sanomonte. He was intelligent and exemplary in every respect, though he was somewhat withdrawn. In his personal notes, the prefect of his dormitory remarked: "More or less cautious and not too talkative, but kind to all."

Meanwhile, the academic year was coming to an end. One muggy afternoon, about thirty members of his dormitory went for a walk through the town. Generally, Sanomonte preferred to be last in line, and this day was no exception. Suddenly, he bent down to pull up his socks, keeping an eye on the group as they turned the corner. He looked angrily at the shuttered door of the local Communist party offices. An obese fellow with his hands behind his back was leaning against the shutter as if he were waiting for it to open. With a little trepidation, thinking about his classmates who had disappeared from sight, he mustered the courage to approach the stranger, and said: "Comrade, give this sealed package to the comrade secretary . . . Don't forget: deliver it sealed!" But, he had made a terrible mistake. The fellow hanging around the party office was the most fervent Christian Democrat in town, named Peruzzi. Sneakily, Peruzzi had followed Sanomonte's every move and now, with the package in his possession, he asked himself what he should do.

He spent three days deciding whether to turn it over to the Communist secretary. Perhaps Sanomonte had a relative there. Should he destroy the package? Should he leave it closed, or read the contents? Should he take up the matter with the rector of the seminary? What would he say? He remained puzzled until he prodded the corner of the envelope with a letter opener and it opened. He proceeded to read: "Dear comrade secretary, I find myself a long way from home studying in this regional seminary. I urgently need to see you to work out a plan for the immediate future. Family visits are permitted on Thursdays from four o'clock on, in the parlor on the ground floor. You should visit and pose as my uncle. All the best, Andrea Sanomonte."

Peruzzi, who delighted in gossip, couldn't believe his luck. He arranged for a meeting with the rector in absolute secrecy. He related precisely what had transpired and then handed over the letter in the open envelope. That evening, with the vice-rector and the prefect of the dormitory, he carefully searched Sanomonte's desk and personal effects. It appeared to the three of them that they were unsuccessful. They had uncovered some suspicious notes, some Communist writings, his day planner with indecipherable scribblings, but nothing of any real consequence.

This was the first time that something like this had happened, and they were unsure of how to proceed. They consulted the police, who had them bring the letter to the precinct for a detailed examination. In consultation with Don Uva, they decided that Sanomonte should be sent home until the matter was settled. When the whole incident was over, the rector received a reprimand from the appropriate ministry in Rome, which was annoyed at not having been immediately informed of the case.

Among the apparently harmless figures transcribed in Sanomonte's day planner were some secret codes that revealed the cargo and destination of an Italian warship in the Pacific Ocean—information that only high-ranking military and naval personnel were privy to. The military department was located in a tunnel beneath the Santa Rosa barracks near La Storta, a suburb of Rome, and was a top-secret location that extended over eighteen kilometres underground. A shroud of utter secrecy descended on the matter and it was never raised again.

SINCE THE MID-THIRTIES, HOW MANY OF THOSE false seminarians became priests? How many became bishops and cardinals? Everyone remembers the demise of Cardinal Alfredo Ottaviani who, in a post-conciliar article, addressed a number of ecclesiastics as "little Communists of the sacristy."

The Communist current in the Roman Curia adopted a policy of *ostpolitik* toward the Communist bloc and its leaders. Among the many martyrs of this policy was the

Hungarian primate Cardinal Josiph Mindszenty, who was condemned to death for high treason against the atheist ideology of his country. His sentence was later commuted to life imprisonment, first by the Communists and then by the ostpoliticians from the Vatican. The Vatican also expelled him as primate, citing the historical compromises with the atheist Magyars.

The Secretary of State, Agostino Casaroli, who died in June 1988, gave a television interview in which he boasted of having forged ahead with the Communist governments through his policy of *ostpolitik*, and of having achieved significant and dazzling results. But, the next day, the press asked rhetorically: "If men of the Church, such as Montini and Casaroli, hadn't fueled their love affair with the countries behind the Iron Curtain, how much earlier would the Berlin Wall have fallen?" Unfortunately, we will never know the answer.

While Christ and his faithful suffered in lunatic asylums, prisons, and labor camps in the East, atheism was alive and well in the Vatican, proclaiming that God was finally dead. The priests and bishops in the asylums and camps were shown photographs and newsreels documenting cordial meetings between ranking prelates and Communist government officials. They were presented with these images so that they would realize they were the last of a stubborn breed that refused to sign that insignificant little document renouncing the Catholic Church and aligning themselves with the Communist regime, thereby regaining their freedom.

WHEN STALIN, WHO FEARED THE POPE'S ARMY more than any other, realized that the Bolshevik persecution of the Church had yielded only small results, he decided to change tactics: he had to corrupt it from within to do the most damage.

The fruits of that policy were so abundant that other organizations, which continue to propagate and spread social atheism around the world, have adopted his model.

The term "**ostpoliticians**" is a reference to the policy of Communists adopting trade and diplomatic relations with non-Communist nations.

A **primate** is a bishop of the highest rank in a province or country.

Between 1903 and 1917, **Bolsheviks** (radical members of Russia's Social Democratic party), advocated immediate and forceful seizure of power by the proletariat, and attempted to usurp all established powers, including those of the Church.

Inside the Confessional

Satan, the Prince of Darkness, cunningly plots the moves of his followers. Today, his attack is a frontal one, and he boldly appears in the open. He wants everyone to know that he commands an infernal strategy, assisted by rapidly growing satanic sects.

The **beatitudes** are the nine blessings spoken by Jesus in the Gospel of Mark.

Satan's logic states that you don't have to go against God when you can go without him. The world models this principle by permitting human egoism in churchly affairs and by promoting an irreligious materialism. Satan encourages men to fulfill the exact opposite of the beatitudes.

ONE EVENING, IN THE POPULAR PILGRIMAGE destination of the Roman sanctuary of Divine Love, a penitent approached the confessional. He was particularly upset and embarrassed, and the confessor encouraged him to open his soul.

"Father, I don't know where to begin or whether you will be able to absolve me. I have a great weight on my conscience; I even fear that you may be shocked and surprised by what I have to say."

"My son, don't worry yourself about that. At the end of the day, we liken ourselves to dumps where everyone unloads their burdens. Where would we dump our bundle of guilt if not here in confession? That's what we are here for."

"Father, I am part of a satanic sect where I play an important role. I have enlisted many others."

"How long has this been going on?"

"Father, I have been actively involved for about ten years."

"And why have you come here today? You are not confessing yourself: you are only sharing your worry, which is not enough to be absolved. You need to provide details in order to be absolved. What sins have you committed?"

"I convinced others to take part in black masses and other satanic rituals. The other day, though, I was invited to attend a black mass in a place where I never thought such a ritual could be celebrated."

"Where?" asked the priest from behind the grille.

"At the Vatican."

"Is that possible? What you are saying is incredible! Are you certain? Who else was present?"

"Believe me, Father, I am not here to tell you lies. I'm a mess. I'm no longer at peace with myself. I don't know what is happening to me. I had always derided the act of religious confession. I even passed that derision on to others. I am now ashamed to take a step backward, but I can no longer go forward after this experience. I am overwhelmed by grief!"

"Who else was present? Did you know them?"

"It wasn't possible to see them because we were all hooded from head to toe. For satanic rituals, you are naked underneath, but hooded from head to toe. The voices were deep and unrecognizable. I felt honored to be invited; but, now I curse the day that I accepted to go. Father, what does one do in a case like this? What must I do in the future?"

It was late and the church was packed with believers from a charismatic group that was busy singing, praying, and displaying their praise for the Trinity and the Holy Virgin. It was almost midnight when the penitent left the confessional and merged with the others.

JOHN WROTE, "AND IT WAS NIGHT," TO EMPHASIZE the time when Judas chose to leave the Last Supper and make his way to the place where he was to betray Christ. *"And the Lord says: Woe to the contaminated and arrogant city; I will eliminate the braggarts from your midst and you will cease to be proud."*

Saint **John** was the author of the fourth Gospel, three letters in the New Testament, and the book of Revelation.

XVIII

Freemasonry
in the Vatican

Inspired by deism and rationalism, Freemasonry is religious in its own way. It posits a great architect of the universe that every individual in the order can call whatever he or she wants. There is only one creator of the existing reality in the universe who is constantly building. Each Mason works toward contributing to the great architect's project. This belief promotes both rationalism and faith through rites and prayers directed toward a deified universal reality.

Every secret association that depends on the Masonic order must help and collaborate with other members of the order. The Masonic organism intends to expand its dominion over economic, political, military, and religious organizations to create one world government obtained through either consensus or conquest. For the Freemasons, Satan is also part of this reality. They accept Satan since reverence for the architect encompasses his whole creation, including Satan, who participates in the universal reality.

Whoever is invited to join the Masonic family must undergo a rigorous initiation, including a three-year apprenticeship during which one receives three degrees—apprentice, guild member, and, finally, master of the lodge. All promotions are confirmed by secret vote. The title of master confers upon the member the right to speak in the temple.

The Masonic brothers reveal their identity to one another through secret handshakes. If one wants to identify himself, he taps lightly three times with the right thumb on the back of the other's thumb. If the other is complicit, he responds with the same gesture either immediately or at their next meeting. This ceremonial handshake is practiced by the Masonic laymen as a sort of identity card. Some even greet their ecclesiastical counterparts this way. But, among themselves, the ecclesiastics are much more prudent and avoid this blatant gesture.

The Masonic Octopus

The Roman culture is extremely exclusive, and noble and aristocratic titles are not enough to break into it. The Church is even more exclusive. However, the Freemasons have waltzed into it from servants' quarters without so much as a word. Freemasonry generally doesn't attempt to change the environment that it infiltrates. In the Vatican, the bastion of the Catholic Church, Freemasonry arms itself with diabolical patience and waits. It waits until it can accede to the most powerful positions and infiltrate the command structure. Such sects have systematically infiltrated central organizations throughout history because they realize that these groups are the beacons that transmit and receive the most important messages. The ability to transmit messages so diffusely is tantamount to destroying the immune defenses of the human mind. In response, Giuseppe De Mestre proposed: "Believe as little as possible without being a heretic, so that you can obey as little as possible without being a rebel."

The fact that the invisible hand of the Masons exists at the highest level in the Vatican is not a fabrication. It is evident in the hiring, firing, and promoting of candidates. This center that should, by divine mandate, be a lighthouse is instead a tumor that poisons the Church from within.

If someone were to damage the painting of the Universal Judgment in the Sistine Chapel, the world would protest, but the infiltration of the Vatican by the Masons is a more serious violation since it twists the minds and sacredness of the Christian heart. Believers are disoriented by contradictory and ambiguous realities, and cannot stop and control fluid and dynamic events.

Today, the octopus of Freemasonry is rampant in the Vatican. Its long, opaque tentacles are everywhere, but hidden. It surfaces in secret agents placed in offices and sinister mercenaries who enjoy the vile and noble organized underworld. It strikes with precision and forethought, and its blow is so severe that one realizes one's own impotence and understands that retaliation would be more damaging to the self than the beast.

Many magazines and newspapers have written about the Masonic infiltration of the Vatican. For two centuries, the Freemasons have continued to thwart the true Church in Rome. Clement XII imposed an excommunication on the Freemasons in 1738 with a Papal Bull. This lasted until 1974, when Jesuit father Giovanni Caprile, in a conciliatory article called "Catholic Civility," reassured the Catholics affiliated with Freemasonry: "If your faith as a Catholic doesn't detect anything systematically hostile and organized in the Masonic group to which you belong, against the Church and its principle doctrines and morality, you can remain in the organization. You should no longer feel yourself excommunicated, and therefore like all other believers, you are entitled to share in the sacraments and participate fully in the life of the Church. You do not need a special absolution from the excommunication."

In reality, a large number of Catholics and Masonic prelates had been "participating fully in the life of the church" for years. As soon as Monsignor Montini arrived as the Archbishop of Milan, he appointed the most Catholic Mason, Michele Sindona, as his financial adviser. Later, as Pope, he placed the financial fate of the Institute for the

When he took the papal seat in 1730, **Clement XII** confronted poor finances, a large deficit, and an exasperated public. He encouraged the arts and manufacturing, and modernized commerce laws.

A **Papal Bull** is a pronouncement that is more solemn than a papal brief or an encyclical.

Work of Religion in the undisputed criminal and thieving hands of Sindona and his partner, Roberto Calvi, who employed the services of two other Masons of the Propaganda 2 (P2) Lodge, Licio Gelli and Umberto Ortolani.

In 1987, the Masonic journalist Pier Carpi confirmed the recruitment of "brother" Fulberto Lauro, who claimed that the P2 Lodge included cardinals and bishops among its members. He indicated that it was called the "Ecclesia Lodge" and that it was in direct contact with the grand master of the United Lodge of England, Michael, the Duke of Kent. That particular lodge had been in place in the Vatican since 1971. More than 100 cardinals, bishops, and monsignors are among its members. They manage to maintain the utmost secrecy, but not enough to escape every investigation.

The Catholic Mexican magazine *Trial* (no. 832, October 12, 1992) reported that Masonry had divided the Vatican into eight territories, four of which were Masonic lodges of the Scottish rite whose members were all high-ranking officials in the Vatican. Because these groups are independent of one another, the members are unknown to each other even if they tap three times with their thumb. When necessary, these lodges forge contacts with the Masonic lodges of other countries. In those places where the Church operates clandestinely because of the Koran, relations with the local church run secretly through sectarian lines that perform a religious service for their brothers in the Vatican Stanzas.

While maintaining relations with the Apostolic See, countries in the Islamic bloc, in accordance with the Koran, continue to forbid any form of Catholic proselytizing. The respective governments appoint the most zealous Masonic brothers as ambassadors to the Vatican. They are instructed on how to interact differently with the hated ecclesiastics and their own spiritual "brothers" inclined toward Masonry, many of whom occupy high-ranking positions in the Vatican. Together, they try to steer the ailing John Paul II, who walks slowly and suffers from amnesia.

The **Vatican Stanzas** are the halls, rooms, and abodes of the Vatican.

The press continues to identify cardinals and high-level dignitaries, along with other prelates who are affiliated with Masonic lodges within, and associated with, the Vatican. However, none of them are fazed by the accusations. On occasion, one or two will deny the charges or demand a retraction out of concern for their good name or, perhaps, in deference to the office or department they serve. Their silence doesn't honor the axiom "that which is asserted gratuitously, is denied gratuitously," because, in the Vatican, he who remains silent consents.

False Apostles and Fraudulent Workers

How does a Freemason infiltrate the Vatican offices? Or, how does an ecclesiastic of the Curia become a Freemason? These questions were posed to a prelate in the Curia by a young priest who was working in an Islamic country and who was distressed by the constant anti-Catholic propaganda shown on television there.

The young priest stated: "When it is convenient, our nation pretends to ignore the Catholic Church, the Pope, and the hierarchy; but, when a scandal is rumored, it is presented to the public in detail, to denigrate it altogether. The entire press corps is mobilized to report the deeds and misdeeds, armed with facts. They speak of this Cardinal Secretary of State, or that bishop, and still many more prelates affiliated with the Masons. They have the first names and family names of some of them, the date of their initiation, the positions they occupy in the Vatican, and even their lodge affiliations. Our small Catholic communities in these countries are left literally dumbfounded by these reports, and the authorities turn to us for explanations on the authenticity of these developments and how to respond to them. You, Monsignor, what do you think? Is it possible for a cardinal or a prelate in the Curia to join a Masonic lodge and collaborate with the grand master? It seems incredible that such a thing could happen. If it isn't true, why doesn't the accused sue the slanderers in national and international courts? Why doesn't the Vatican intervene through its apostolic nuncio and officially deny so many scandalous assertions?"

The young priest was equally concerned about the rumors surrounding the death of Pope John Paul I, which was shrouded in mystery. Claims were circulating that he had been murdered, but these rumors were fueled almost entirely by circumstantial evidence. During another scandal, the Vatican bank was accused of having an enormous amount of dirty money that had been laundered and deposited in foreign banks. Referring to these two events, the young priest commented: "They are naming high-ranking Vatican dignitaries as accomplices of the leaders of the Italian Freemasons. There is talk of murders, suicides, and arrest warrants being issued by the Italian government for members of the Institute for the Work of Religion. They are talking about the dismissal of Monsignor Marcinkus and of the promotion of Donato De Bonis to the Order of Malta. I will give you another example: after the attempt on the Pope's life, the newspapers published a photograph of him seated beside the pool at his summer residence at Castelgandolfo. They further claimed that it had been taken by a Vatican employee, unbeknownst to security officials, and that it had been found in Ali Agca's possession on the day of the botched assassination, May 13, 1981. The photo was apparently bought for three hundred thousand dollars by the P2 member, Licio Gelli, who is reported to have told his 'brother,' Vanni Nisticò: 'It was worth it; if these photos can be taken of the Pope, imagine how easy it will be to shoot him!' For those of us surrounded by enemies of the faith, these assertions are particularly disruptive and they threaten to undermine us."

As he concluded these remarks, the monsignor noticed that his colleague was profoundly dismayed. He knew that the young priest was tirelessly devoted to the young in his country, and that he had to provide him with a serious answer.

The **Institute for the Work of Religion** is the papal bank.

A religious and military brotherhood, the **Order of Malta**'s leaders must take religious vows of celibacy, poverty, and obedience.

Ali Agca is a Turkish national who shot and seriously wounded Pope John Paul II in 1981.

"You see, my dear brother, yours is a question that we all ask ourselves. The photograph of the shirtless Pope was taken from inside his summer residence by an insider whose identity everyone wants to know. Personally, I do not side with those who want to deny everything at any cost, as if, for example, the attempt on Pope John Paul II was nothing but a simple hunting accident. The ostrich that buries its head in the sand as the storm approaches to avoid its wrath becomes its victim. This is how I see it.

"I consider the idea impossible that a Freemason would leave his lodge, find himself a prelate or cardinal of consequence, and propose that he join the Masons. That this dignitary should then, as if nothing were the matter, immediately agree and join the side that destroys the very God he has taken vows to serve is equally unthinkable. On the other hand, it is difficult to contest that Freemasons exist among the ecclesiastics and have penetrated the upper levels of the Roman Curia.

"You alluded to the dirty money that the self-declared Masons funneled out of the country with the cooperation of high-ranking ecclesiastical dignitaries of the bank, whose story broke during the 1994 trial on the Enimont scandal. During these proceedings, it was revealed that more than $100 million had been laundered through the Vatican for ignoble Masonic ends, and that the curious death of the son of one of the principal actors, Roberto Calvi, who was found hanged under Blackfriars Bridge in London, was likely a casualty of criminal activities. So you see, Freemasons are definitely at work in the Vatican, even if its headquarters is elsewhere. Pope John Paul I should have known immediately when journalist Paolo Panerai, on August 31, 1978, suddenly addressed a mournful open letter to the Pope in the influential economic weekly *Il Mondo*: 'Holiness, is it right that the Vatican operates in the stock market like a speculator? Is it right that the bank intervenes in the illegal transfer of capital from Italy to other countries? Is it fair that the bank helps Italians avoid paying taxes?' The Pope hadn't even recovered from the shocking questions directed at him when, on September 12, the weekly publication directed by Mino Pecorelli, a Mason who was later murdered, published a list of 121 names of Vatican representatives and important prelates affiliated with the Masons.

"'And the Lord said unto Moses, stretch out thine hand toward heaven, that there may be darkness over the land of Egypt, even a darkness that may be felt.' By touch, a blind man can tell a table from a chair, even though he cannot see it; the Masons in the Vatican operate in much the same way: you can feel them, but you can't see them. Paul VI realized the Masonic presence in the Vatican, and told the world about it, calling it Satan's smoke. He knew that the smoke had penetrated and darkened the temple of the Lord from that Masonic crack. Last century, the Masonic strategy favored a frontal attack on the Catholic Church, but it didn't work. This century, it changed its approach, understanding that it was much more profitable to infiltrate its ranks. This tactic required patience, and enough time to select and train the best candidates for the task. Supported by unlimited resources, the most competent individuals are prepared to penetrate the upper echelons of the hierarchy, and to select and co-opt ecclesiastics in order to gain bright futures in the Church's administration."

AT THE END OF THE 1940S, POPE PIUS XII WAS already disturbed and terrified by the thought that atheism, very much in vogue under the guises of Freemasonry and Communism, would infiltrate the Church. In July 1949, a small village was celebrating the ordination of a young priest, Don Francesco, the only son of extremely poor parents who had lived sparingly for years in order to send him to the seminary. The newly ordained priest decided to take his parents to Rome, a city they would never have been able to visit, as a way of thanking them for their kindness. He planned to pay for the trip and their lodgings with the donations he had received. They set off in their Sunday best and didn't sleep at all during the entire trip. At dawn, the mother gazed out upon the houses of the suburbs as if she were in a dream. In her lifetime, she had never imagined that she would visit Rome—the Pope's city and the capital of Christianity.

Their small hotel was near the Vatican, and they began their tour by visiting the basilicas and other notable monuments of ancient Rome. At Saint Peter's, the visit was more detailed, with Don Francesco acting as a guide and translating the Latin inscriptions as best he could. In the square, he pointed out the Pope's studio apartment. Pius XII wasn't in the habit of greeting believers from his balcony as his successor John XXIII started to do.

The mere mention of the Pope filled his mother with the desire to see him. Don Francesco told her: "Mother, only heads of state, ambassadors and, from time to time, cardinals can visit with the Pope."

A few days later, near the end of their stay, they tried to contact some distant relatives and old acquaintances. Among these friends was a captain in the police force who had enjoyed a marvelous career in the service. He was the pride of the village and revered by all. When Don Francesco contacted him, he was delighted to hear from them and eager to meet.

The captain took great interest in their Roman sojourn and in everything they were able to accomplish. Don Francesco spoke for his parents, listing all the monuments that they had seen and expressing their amazement. He also related his mother's impossible desire to get close to the Pope. "Do you want to see the Pope?" asked the captain. "But no, Captain," replied Don Francesco, "I have already explained the matter to my mother. We have seen so much already and have so much to tell our relatives." But the captain, with that proposal fixed in his mind, asked the priest to give him the address and telephone number of the hotel where they were staying, and told them, as he accompanied them to the door, that he would be in touch.

At dinner that evening, a waiter approached their table and told Don Francesco that a police captain wanted a word with him on the telephone. He rushed up the stairs and listened to the following instructions: "Be at the Arch of the Bells to the left of Saint Peter's Basilica tomorrow at 9:30. You will be accompanied by car to the private elevator and then to the Pope's apartment. At 10:00, you will be received for a private audience with His Holiness. Obviously, you should dress appropriately and be punctual and, above all, I beg you to exercise the utmost discretion." Don Francesco wasn't able to respond before the phone went dead at the other end.

The audience with the Pope lasted twenty minutes and went off exactly as planned.

In the village, nobody believed that such a poor family could have had a private audience with the Pope. They thought that the young priest was boasting, eager to make a name for himself. Truthfully, not even Don Francesco understood what had happened.

After a year, that captain, who had since been promoted to major, died of a sudden heart attack. From the papers, Don Francesco learned that the officer had been master of the Masonic lodge in Palazzo Giustiniani, in Rome, for the last eighteen months. Perhaps his securing of the audience for three of his townsfolk had been part of an initiation test—a way of proving just how much influence he had on the other side of the Tiber. With the goodwill of John XXIII, he was able to orchestrate the whole affair.

A SPECIFIC DEPARTMENT EXISTS IN THE MASONIC order whose sole responsibility is to recruit young collaborators from among the ecclesiastics. Qualified recruits must possess a strong intellect, lively intuition, ambition, lust for power, good communication skills, the ability to understand and to pretend not to understand, and, finally, a good form and good looks. Once these qualities are identified in an ecclesiastic, the process of winning him over begins. It is of the utmost importance that, during the first phase, the subject remains oblivious to the trap that is being set. Masonic techniques employ a gradual progression so that the candidate gradually learns the sect's goal, as the superiors see fit.

The ways of co-opting recruits are many, and they vary from person to person. The first phase may involve techniques as simple as an invitation to an embassy to celebrate a national day, an unexpected meeting with someone who says he is delighted to have made his acquaintance, or a prelate who asks for something and says that he is indebted. Then comes the praising and cajoling stage: "What a marvelous and kind person you are; what intelligence; what manners; what exquisiteness! How is it possible? You deserve better; you are wasted where you are. Shall we go on a first-name basis? Let's think of a better placement for you!" We then enter the prospect phase: "I know this prelate, that cardinal, that ambassador, or such and such a minister. If you wanted, or were not opposed, I could put in a word for you. I will tell them that you deserve a higher office; for example, undersecretary of a ministry, bishop in . . ., nuncio in . . ., private secretary to . . .," and so on.

At this point, the agent realizes immediately whether the ecclesiastic has swallowed the hook, even if he modestly claims: "I am not worthy. I am not up to it. I am a simple man. Others are better than me," and so on. The agent is well trained, and knows that prudence is the virtue of the strong, and that false modesty is the virtue of the ambitious.

Slowly, promises are kept and the candidate begins to feel a debt of gratitude toward his sponsor-friend, whom he considers his benefactor. Meanwhile, his career is progressing smoothly, and the possibilities seem endless. Now, as the subject falls prey to ambition and vanity, he enters the phase where he is informed of the motivating factor behind his rise through the ranks. The revelation usually goes something like this: "Monsignor, Excellency, you must know that your rapid rise is due more to the

Masonic order, and all of its friends in and outside the Vatican, than to me. They have orchestrated your prestigious rise to important positions in the Church. As you can see, you don't have to worry because many influential people already hold you in high regard. You are now free to decide whether to remain where you are and collaborate with our organization in the future, or not."

In this delicate phase, the prelate, in a state of crisis, must decide which road to travel. His ambition craves greater advancement, but he is bewildered by the introduction to the Masonic order. He fears being exposed if he doesn't join, and imagines the emptiness around him if he does. The fraternal advice of an older dignitary who stayed in the Masonic order and continued his career success convinces the prelate, in spite of himself, to remain on the path he has started.

Ensconced in the ecclesiastical environment, the first duty of the new Mason is to appear as credible as possible to those around him. He must keep his promises and, where possible, cast aspersions on and falsely characterize the best and most noble prelates in his office, becoming yet another pawn to that secret fraternity with infinite potential for advancement. Satan's realm relishes positioning the false in place of the true, so that right can be made to appear wrong. Voltaire convinced his followers: "If you believe that God made you in his image and likeness, try turning the tables. Make yourselves a God in your image, with your evils and defects—powerful, vindictive, dominant, ambitious, and hungry for power. The more you are convinced by him, the more you will believe that he suits you to a 'T,' discoloring and eventually extinguishing the other God in you, the real one." This is exactly what the Freemasons do with their illustrious young novices and how, with the assistance of important individuals such as Licio Gelli, Michele Sindona, Roberto Calvi, Umberto Ortolani, and the rest of the Propaganda 2 Lodge, they undermine the true Church of Christ.

AT THIS POINT, THE YOUNG PRIEST SAID: "Monsignor, your analysis brings to mind something that happened to me about four years ago that went exactly as you have described.

The **sacristan** is the person in charge of the room in a Church that stores the sacred vessels and vestments, as well as the ceremonial equipment.

"One morning, right after mass, the sacristan approached me and told me that there was a distinguished visitor who wanted to meet with me. He was apparently the Great Rabbi of Jerusalem. I asked him if he was sure that it was me that he wanted to see, and not my brother, the Vicar General. It was me! I decided to accompany him on a tour of the historical monuments of the city.

"When we had finished, he spoke to me in the precise way that you just described, saying that I should have a better position, perhaps in Rome or another diocese. I told him that I wasn't interested, but he insisted that I think it over. He told me to meet him the following day with my decision. In the morning, he had a meeting with the Secretary of State at a convent in Via delle Mura Aureliane, but he said that he would meet me there after mass. He said it was better to meet there than the third loggia where there were many indiscreet eyes and ears. If I wanted, he said he would talk to the Secretary, with whom he was very close, on my behalf.

"After so many years, I now realize that he was trying to recruit me, and I subsequently discovered that he frequented ecclesiastical circles for the Masons."

"For such are false apostles, deceitful workers, transforming themselves into the apostles of Christ. And no marvel; for Satan himself is transformed into an angel of light."

True and False Masonic Prelates

When the press broke the story, the powerful P2 Lodge was headed by master Licio Gelli in conjunction with Michele Sindona, Roberto Calvi, and Umberto Ortolani, who were all Catholics and Masons implicated in the Ambrosian Bank scandal. The press also alluded to a list of 121 names of prelates, alphabetically arranged and including the dates of their initiation and their lodge affiliation. The list had apparently been in circulation for a few years. The reports resonated inside and outside of the Vatican because many of the names were high-ranking dignitaries of the Curia.

At the same time, the Masons circulated another list that included many more prelates and laymen in order to confuse the true members with false ones. It was very difficult for members of either group to plead their innocence and the groundless nature of the charges. Those in the Vatican knew that the second list was a ruse. For some time, they had been compiling a list of ecclesiastics and prelates who were suspected of collaborating with the Masons. They decided, however, that a policy of silence was best.

Any reader who wants to know the truth can check the Index of the Papal Yearbook for the nineties and compare it with the names on the initial list of 121 names. Most of the names on that list have enjoyed splendid careers in the Vatican. More than two-thirds of them, some are now dead, occupy positions in the upper echelons of the Roman Curia.

"Righteous art thou, O Lord, when I plead with thee: yet let me talk with thee of thy judgments: wherefore doth the way of the wicked prosper? Wherefore are all they happy that deal very treacherously?"

FOR THOSE ECCLESIASTICS NOT FORTUNATE enough to be chosen, but who are still interested in joining the Masons, the "brothers" start them off by sending them to give lectures at the Rotary or Lions Club in their district. These are cultural clubs where future Masonic members are molded.

The Jesuit magazine *Catholic Civilization* has clearly shown that these associations maintain close contacts with

The Church was accused of laundering money through the Institute for the Work of Religion and the **Ambrosian Bank**. In 1992, investigations showed the bank was missing $1.3 billion. The money was traced to accounts owned by the Vatican.

the Masonic sect. There was quite a fuss over these assertions until Grand Master Giordano Gamberini, in an article
that appeared in the Masonic magazine *Hiram* on February
1, 1981, officially claimed that both the Rotary and the Lions
derive from and converge in the Masonic organization. He
wrote: "Melvin Jones, master Mason of Chicago, was one of
the founders of the Lions. He became General Secretary
and Treasurer in 1917. In the Lions, the Masonic origins are
evident in the first coat of arms that they chose. The Rotary
has had almost identical relations with the Masons."

In 1982, Jesuit Federico Weber became governor of
the Rotary district of Sicily-Malta for the first time, without
any comment from his superiors. In fact, many well-
remunerated cardinals encouraged by Cardinal Baggio,
who is now thankfully deceased, consider it an honor to
accept an invitation from a Rotary dignitary to inaugurate a
new office or a new social year.

A PROPHETIC CONFIRMATION OF THIS WILLINGNESS
ness to associate with the Masons comes from an apparition of Jesus to Padre Pio, which he described to his
confessor on April 7, 1913: "Friday morning, I was still in
bed when Jesus appeared to me. He was extremely disconsolate and disfigured. He showed me a great multitude of
priests among whom were church dignitaries. Some were
celebrating mass and others were decorating the church
and removing their holy vestments. The sight of Jesus in
such pain caused me greater pain and I asked him what
grieved him. He didn't reply. However, his gaze settled on
those priests and then, almost in horror, he turned away
and looked back at me. To my great horror there were two
tears streaming down his face. He walked away from that
crowd of priests in disgust, shouting: 'Butchers!' Then,
turning to me, he said: 'My son, the ingratitude and the
sleep of my ministers makes my agony more intense . . .
they are indifferent, full of contempt, and faithless.' Sadly,

Jesus was right to lament our ingratitude! How many of our brothers reciprocate Jesus' love by giving themselves freely to the vile Masonic sect! Let us pray for them."

Jesus revealed this to Padre Pio four years before the revelation at Fatima. The fact that many Church dignitaries have collaborated with the Masons has never been a mystery.

To those who consider themselves indispensable to the government of the Church, while risking scandal at every turn, the Holy Spirit through the prophet Malachi warns: *"And now, O ye priests this commandment is for you. If you will not hear, and if you will not lay it to heart, to give glory unto my name, I will even send a curse upon you, and I will curse your blessings. For the priest's lips should keep knowledge, and they should seek the law at his mouth: for he is the messenger of the Lord of hosts. But ye are departed out of the way; ye have caused many to stumble at the law. Therefore have I also made you contemptible and base before all the people."*

Jesus is much more severe with these people: *"Woe unto you scribes and Pharisees, hypocrites! For ye have omitted the weightier matters of the law, judgment, mercy and faith. Ye blind guides, which strain at a gnat, and swallow a camel."* Lord, stay clear of the men who occupy your Church and act as its owners and who claim that they are doing your will on earth, repeating to everyone the refrain: *"The temple of the Lord, the temple of the Lord, the temple of the Lord, are these."*

The mistakes that have been made in these ecclesiastical environments are the price we must pay for the enormous privilege of profiting from the blood of Christ the Redeemer. We are all guilty of indifference for leaving Christ's love in the care of the profane and the wicked. We are responsible for having destroyed that love with cold, human calculations.

As we approach the millennium and prepare for the Jubilee Year, the great powers of light and darkness battle in the most secret rooms of the Vatican, and it is unclear whether Satan will be victorious.

X I X

Power and Celibacy

Manzoni wrote, "If we admit that the morality of the Scriptures issues from God, we must admit the Church's absolute obligation to adopt it to the exclusion of all others."

It is unlikely that all those who hold positions of authority possess responsibility and impartial morality in equal measures. In the Vatican, the monopoly of dictatorial power is incompatible with the dignity and liberty of man. Today, nobody is surprised by the nepotism of the Middle Ages and Renaissance, since our times are a revival of that much deprecated practice of the Popes. However, our modern form is more harmful and less forgivable. In the past, Popes were forced to defer to the people around them who were masters of deception and assassinations. They trusted in the closest members of their extended families, hoping their instructions would be carried out in the interest of the Church. Today's neo-nepotism between the protectors and the protected is not punishable because no legislation exists to curb the excesses.

IN GENERAL, SOCIETY HAS FOUGHT STRINGENTLY against all forms of discrimination and in favor of human rights. To govern their constituents under auspices of compassion, the men of the Church have developed their own set of laws and conventions that disregard equality and justice. Conforming to the principle that the superior is beyond reproach, defending and exercising one's rights is considered an unwarranted affront to the superior. In the Curia, the worth of the entire ecclesiastical office is not based on the sum of its employees, but on the will of its ranking member. The success or failure of individual members of this ecclesiastical team depends on one man's benevolence. Unlike a decathlon, where the fittest athlete wins, the Vatican doesn't permit progression or victory based on merit. Each person's rights and responsibilities are arbitrarily invoked and withdrawn by the superior and his influential lackey who survive unscathed through both good and bad times. In short, everything is imposed from above.

The ideal employee for this sort of supervisor must be just virtuous enough, that is, insensitive, passive, spineless, and indifferent to the things that happen to him. The best dependents allow themselves to be programmed and deprogrammed by their superior, like simple cogs in a wheel that are worn and replaced. A medieval belief states that the subject isn't owed anything and that everything is a gift for which he should be grateful and indebted. The best and most competent prelates are forced to endure a debilitating solitude. Unable to help one another, they drift further apart. But, our Lord has immense respect for all of the sheep in his flock, and if one of them should get lost in the anonymity of the herd, he prefers that it go its own way. The sheep will eventually leave the flock and follow its own path. The individuality of the sheep that strays gives Jesus more satisfaction than those that remain lost in the ecclesiastic crowd.

The greatest paradox, however, is that the morally subjugated prelate is convinced that he is not deserving, and that he must accept his superior's extravagant behavior.

In the Vatican, things work backward: the environment reacts to the crowd, and the Lord speaks to the individual. To reach the masses, the Church ignores the individual and his needs, since quantity and numbers are what matter most. God loves every man, especially if he is marginalized. He seeks out those who have been cast aside and cries with them.

In the absence of democracy and debate, the Curia is a collection of anonymous individuals whose conscious expression is encapsulated in Ugo Ojetti's statement: "If the conscience is a mirror, at least let it stay still. The more you focus on it, the more it shakes."

EVEN IN THIS VATICAN WORLD, SOME FORM OF morality must exist, but no one embraces its cause. Everything in the Vatican is hierarchical, and nobody investigates from the ground up, only vice versa. Espionage and decisive orders are regulated from above. The barrage of accusations from the bottom, from the lower class, never reaches the top.

The Curia's Gospel is distorted. The first and the last in their version don't correspond to the first and the last indicated by our Lord. In the Vatican, the first are the careerist prelates who are protected to the bitter end—the devil's corruptors and collaborators. All of these firsts—the twenty percent of Curial employees who climb the ladder—are shrewd, swift, ruthless, and lacking scruples. They are ambivalent toadies who prudently discern and patiently wait their turn. They advance in their careers and are rewarded with the positions that they longed for.

Clearly, making progress in their careers changes their strategy: "*We are ordered by him as something base, and he avoids our ways as unclean; he calls the last end of the righteous happy, and boasts that God is his father. Let us see if his words are true, and let us test what will happen at the end of his life; for if the righteous man is God's son, he will help him, and will deliver him from the hand of the adversaries. Let us test him with insults and torture.*"

Cardinal Newman wrote: "In Rome the view is clear from the Vatican hill, but the part below is full of malarial bogs."

According to the Curial code, the ones that come last are the demoted, the deprived, the suppressed, the nonaligned, and the slandered who are devoid of hope and opportunity. They are owed and deserve nothing except the most humiliating silence, indifference, and psychological torture that produces an exaggerated sense of guilt. If they try to fight, appealing for rightly deserved promotions, they are either locked up or sent to a psychological hospital to recover from an alienating schizophrenia that they never had. The French psychologists who examined Bernadette Soubiroux, the clairvoyant at Lourdes, wrote: "She is entirely sound of mind, her faculties are normal; but, since she continues with these affirmations, perhaps she is dazed."

In 1858, a French peasant girl named **Bernadette Soubiroux** claimed to see the Virgin Mary in apparitions at a grotto near Lourdes.

The Sentence of Forced Retirement

As members of the Vatican reach the appointed age, they gradually begin to lose power and consideration in their offices and with anyone else they come into contact with. When they reach retirement, like dead souls, they are released to wander in the isolation and shadow of a Dantesque limbo. They fall into a category of deaf and mute ex-members who, like the other marginalized or ostracized prelates, are entitled to nothing. The pensioners feel helpless, and any concession granted to them from above is considered a gift of grace. They are a voiceless group, like the disabled and handicapped who require others to arbitrarily decide their every move, with no chance to appeal.

If one of these aged prelates appeals to a higher authority, he is immediately informed that a commission of cardinals has refused to hear the case, whether or not such a group exists. In the Vatican, when any ecclesiastic or layperson takes a stand to claim a rightful position, a cherubic busybody invokes inaccessible or nonexistent commissions, and the matter is avoided.

From the day that this layman or monsignor is left languishing in inactivity, he realizes that he has also lost the right to eat in the company of his colleagues, in the common refectory. Another dining hall is set aside for these rejects. The day before, he could fill his car at the usual gas station around the corner from the Vatican; but now, with his computerized pass deactivated, he must travel to another service station several kilometers away, to his surprise. Those who commanded an office, a section, or even an entire intercontinental area, just one day before, are assimilated with the mentally disabled.

Pensioners from the top ranks, cardinals, bishops, and dignitaries of note are not far behind this group. For many of them, the saying *solitudo eminentium amarissima* (the solitude of the most eminent is the most bitter) fits perfectly. The sanctuary of choice for these retiring luminaries is located a few hundred meters behind the Vatican and is called the Madonna of Forced Retirement. Didn't Sophocles compose *Oedipus* at age 100, and wasn't Michelangelo eighty-nine when Pope Paul III commissioned him to paint the "Universal Judgment," the masterpiece of the Sistine Chapel?

Paul III (Pope: 1534-49) was an astute Church diplomat who was a patron to the newly founded Jesuits, founded the Farnese Palace, continued Michelangelo's decoration of the Sistine Chapel, and rebuilt and repaved many streets in Rome.

Post-conciliar canon law demands that any bishop in charge of a diocese, or cardinal, must submit his resignation to the Pope in his seventy-fifth year. In reality, however, most bishops reject this canonical imposition. While deferring to the Pope's dictate, these cardinals express to the Pope in their letters of resignation that they feel better than ever and are willing to extend their mandate if the Pope will defer their retirement. The canonical norm presents a problem for every ecclesiastic, since it doesn't address each case fairly and adequately. Not everyone suffers dementia and senility at age seventy-five. Many seventy-five-year-olds are among the best teachers of life and science, while others show marked signs of mental deterioration before that age.

Imagine the ramifications of having a cardinal in charge of a ministry in that condition. There have been some extreme cases of senility, particularly cases of Alzheimer's disease. For example, a cardinal prefect, who was incapable of understanding or functioning, was known for his documents that carried his signature in exaggerated, shaky letters.

DURING THE EPISCOPAL MEETINGS OF VATICAN II, one bishop was particularly critical of the many aged brothers who dragged themselves, rickety and slobbering, throughout the event. Without pretense, he encouraged them to have the decency to submit their resignations, but to no avail. In the end, he too was aging. From one year to another, his step faltered and his memory faded. Many people reminded him of his entreaty to the others: "Excellency, do you remember asking your colleagues to submit their resignations once they started to become decrepit?"

"Of course I remember! I continue to maintain that position!"

"Now, Excellency, don't you think it would be right for you to submit yours?"

"What do I have to do with it? I am still useful and in perfect health. When I realize that I no longer am, it will be my duty to do so, but not now!"

A FEW YEARS AGO, THERE WAS A DRAMATIC coup. A number of retired bishops decided to hold a national conference to denounce the Vatican's abandonment of this group of wandering shepherds without a flock. Monsignor Ismaele Castellano, Archbishop Emeritus of Siena, then eighty-one years old, explained how the curious assembly was brought about: "The idea came to one of my angry brothers. One day he telephoned me and said: 'why don't we get everyone together in Rome and present our concerns to the Curia?'"

Discontent was rising among the ranks and John Paul II was alerted. Before the scheduled assembly, another was quickly convened. A plenary assembly of the College of Cardinals met to examine the matter of the retired bishops. As usual, the most combative delegate was Cardinal Silvio Oddi: "The norm that requires bishops to submit their resignations at seventy-five is a violation of human rights. It has no basis in the Church, and could be applied to the Bishop of Rome, the Pope. But a bishop is a father, not an employee, and fathers don't retire, they dedicate themselves to their families until the end. It is the same for eighty-year-old cardinals barred from the conclaves. Today, I believe that the majority of cardinals would agree to repeal that norm." Monsignor Alessandro Maria Gottardi, who considered the norm appropriate, emphasized: "The problem is a psychological one. The retired clergymen experience a sense of uselessness from one day to the next, after years of intense pastoral service to the diocese."

Everyone lives longer today, and the number of idle bishops is increasing. There are 226 Italian dioceses and, by 2000, approximately 200 bishops will be on pension. The tentative remedy for this situation suggested that bishops be integrated into advisory committees in their dioceses and respective conferences. However, this decision did not placate the mounting dissatisfaction.

No sooner had the law been passed than a loophole was discovered. To avoid retirement, prelates have invented very creative strategies. For example, those who find themselves at the head of a diocese call a diocesan synod precisely on the vigil of their seventy-fifth birthday and drag out the pastoral initiative to ensure a lengthy postponement of their retirement. The seventy-five-year-old cardinal in charge of a ministry makes it known that he intends to convene a plenary of cardinals, to whom he will pose the most important juridical and theological questions. Ill as he is, Pope John Paul II remains silent and leaves these cheats alone. In his present state, it is best if he pretends that he doesn't know what is happening.

A Burning Question

The canonical law on ecclesiastical celibacy interests all Latin priests of the diocesan clergy belonging to the Latin rite of the Western Church.

Since the time of the Apostles, the Catholic and Orthodox Eastern Churches have allowed their ministers to fulfill their pastoral ministry either married or celibate. The tradition is so conciliatory that the hierarchy and congregation consider both types of priests to be equal. They appreciate them for what they accomplish, not for their civil status.

In the West, the law on celibacy is entrenched in the historical-political context of the first millennium, through the revival of the Holy Roman Empire by Charlemagne and his successors. The idea was that this empire would remain one and indivisible, like the Church. Experience had shown Charlemagne that principalities governed by bishop monarchs reverted back to the emperor upon the monarch's death. The emperor would then appoint a successor, as opposed to those princes with progeny who would divide and subdivide their territory into counties and duchies, according to the number of their descendents. The diocesan duchy needed to be entrusted and unified in the hands of the bishop. To have bishops without progeny, there had to be a presbytery of celibate priests from which to choose these bishops. To this political end, the ruling Longbards and Merovingians imposed dictates on monks and clergy regarding priestly life and celibacy. During those years, various regional or national councils and synods unanimously respected the rulings of the secular wing, assimilating them slowly into the canonical tradition of the Church.

A loosely federated European political entity, the **Holy Roman Empire** began with the papal coronation of King Otto I in 962 and continued until Francis II's renunciation in 1806.

THE SECOND VATICAN COUNCIL DEALT WITH everything except the inherent rights of the priests of the Latin Church. When it came to an end, a worrisome identity crisis developed in the priesthood that precipitated a mass exodus of priests no longer convinced of their faith. Statistics suggested that 15,000 to 20,000 priests resigned and married. Paul VI was frightened and demanded that Cardinal Giovanni Villot, the Secretary of State, study the matter so something could be done about it.

Of the defrocked priests, the most combative and corrosive formed an association and convened a conference to be held in Rome. But the police would only consent to it if it were held outside Rome. The meeting took place a considerable distance from the city and was well attended. Among the participants were spies from the Curia. A Franciscan, who worked for the Congregation of the Clergy, was sent there in plain clothes and submitted a report on the points that arose from the various expositions and discussions. His report included, among other things, the following statements.

The first Christian communities chose married men as their priests; the Apostles chosen by Jesus had wives and children. For Saint Paul, a bishop could be married only once. Christ's true teachings were love of God and the other, a shunning of worldly riches, and humility. These teachings are in complete contradiction with the behavior of the Vatican hierarchy, which oppresses the priest with celibacy as if it were the Lord's will. The Vatican prelates strive for more important, more honorable, and more remunerative positions even when they're wealthy: *"For laying aside the commandment of God, ye hold the tradition of men."* The Vicar of Christ lives in the most sumptuous palace in the world while thousands of families live in hovels and slums not far away. The following are examples of corruptly wealthy priests.

Cardinal Tedeschini left his family an inheritance of almost $2 million and is attributed with saying: "We are all overtaken by the same plague of gold, but we are celibate."

Cardinal Canali, a prelate who was as celibate as they come and the person in charge of disciplining indecent priests, left $6 million to his nephews.

Cardinal Dell'Acqua, alias Vanda Osiris, requested $5,000 from the donations for the poor to refurbish his bedroom.

Many other entire orders and congregations of brothers and sisters are swimming in a sea of money of dubious origin.

The Pope proclaimed that everyone agreed on the conclusions reached by the Synod of Bishops on the sacred celibacy of the priesthood. But the priests were never seriously or honestly polled on the matter. The proposal to have a referendum on the issue among priests was rejected, but the Vatican says the Latin clergy remains tied to sacred celibacy because it was chosen freely by all. This claim is a hypocritical lie and a betrayal! The position of the Church elite has caused many unpleasant situations to arise that are steeped in sin, scandal, and sacrilege. Priests of the Latin rite are not allowed to marry and are supposed to content themselves with ecclesiastical celibacy, which some people feel is an oxymoronic concept.

ONE OF THE MOST AGITATED PRIESTS AT THAT meeting had been legally married, with papal dispensation, to the sister of three monsignors who were already well placed in the Secretariat of State. As a simple priest, he was boastful of having three monsignors in the Vatican as brothers-in-law. From time to time, he managed to learn a state secret from one of them. In an effort to show off, he would tell the stories to anyone who would listen. In absolute confidentiality, he would whisper the latest gossip to several colleagues. Following a breakdown of the apostolic delegate in Jerusalem, the speedy intervention of the Vatican managed to promote the delegate and send him to Argentina as apostolic nuncio, within twenty-four hours. Why did this incident occur so hurriedly?

The very efficient Israeli secret service had warned the delegate in Jerusalem that a journalist was about to publish a story about his cordial relationship with a nun in the delegation, which had spread as a result of the indiscreet priest. He was told that the scandal could be deferred for no more than one day. Something had to be done quickly. He was to be transferred immediately, since this action would soothe everything, including the press. The delegate called the foreign minister, also from Brisighella, and told him of the rumors. In order for him to remain in the infamous white book of candidates destined for great things, the matter had to be dealt with in twenty-four hours. So, the Pope was asked to sign the nomination of the delegate in Jerusalem to nuncio of Argentina.

At the end of that anecdote the ex-priests said: "Soon this fellow will be in charge of the Vatican and, who knows, they may even make him Pope." Today, as a cardinal, he is being considered for the next conclave. Since he is about the same age as Roncalli was when he was called, it may happen.

X X

A Union for Employees
with No Rights

The Pope sends many social encyclicals, starting with the *Rerum Novarum,* to every country so that they can standardly apply Church doctrine. The governments of those countries conform with these addresses, some sooner than others.

In the Vatican State, however, these same encyclicals are placed in a sealed box and are overlooked by all of the dependants of the Vatican. The content of these encyclicals is like an apocalypse of abstruse language and symbolism that continually reaches toward the future. Presently, they are not understood and, therefore, are not applied. Apparently, the acclaimed declarations on human rights apply only beyond the walls of the Vatican.

An ancient Chinese history book says: "The people must be nourished; the people must not be oppressed. The people have their roots in the country; if the root is strong, the country will be peaceful." In the Vatican, ecclesiastics are denied an organization to protect and defend their interests. A *Solidarnosc,* which takes to heart the personal vindication of these ecclesiastics, would threaten the intrigues of the high-ranking careerists on their road to the top.

Today, with so much social doctrine and respect for intellectual achievements, nobody presumes that God will perform miracles protecting the rights that the Vatican

An **encyclical** is a solemn papal letter that informs the Church about an important matter.

systematically disregards and violates. There is an obligation to uniformly enforce these laws everywhere, just as they are enforced on the individual and social conscience through trade-union organizations.

We need to create a community in which the Pope's coworkers live in peaceful harmony, a world opposed to the coexistence of isolated individuals. Many types of solitude exist, but the worst is the kind that makes you feel alone in a world where everyone turns their back on you. The Church must subject itself to scrutiny so that it can move forward.

The protection of human rights, even in the Church, presumes a sound relationship with the sociological reality. The relationship between the individual and society hinges on the intersection of rights and obligations. God never endorsed Cain's arrogant reproach: *"I am not my brother's keeper."*

Solidarity is based on the principle that every individual must be aware of the dutiful relationship that binds him to the other and to society. Ecclesiastics can no longer treat their less fortunate and unjustly marginalized brethren indifferently. Rejection and disinterest are today's social and personal evils.

After developing over a century's worth of social doctrine, the Church has done nothing for its ecclesiastics. On the eve of the year 2000, we must help the Vatican Curia open itself to the freedom and democracy that the Church teaches in its encyclicals, yet which it aggressively and categorically discourages. Toward the end of the millennium, the evangelic and papal message on social work must consider church members as well, if only in the form of mutual love and understanding.

To sin by discretion rather than indiscretion is a sublime virtue, but no state, big or small, can lay its social foundations on oppression and assume that no one will contest it. *"Severe judgments fall on those in high places."*

If a valid organization were in place to defend the dependants of the Curia, then a denunciation such as this one would be superfluous. An ecclesiastical *Solidarnosc* would have forced the Curia to adopt the principles that the Popes of this century have suggested to other countries and have forgotten to apply to their own little state.

THE WHOLE WORLD WAS SHOCKED BY THE tragedy that occurred in the Vatican on May 4, 1998. After writing a letter to his mother begging forgiveness, a young corporal in the Swiss Guards, Cedric Tornay, knocked on his newly promoted commander's door, Alois Estermann, and murdered him and his wife, Gladys Meza Romero, before killing himself.

The **Swiss Guard** was founded in 1505 by Julius II to serve as the personal military guards of the pope.

Tornay believed that his superior, Estermann, had been oppressive and persecutorial toward him. When he discovered, on May 4, that the rest of his military career would be spent under his tyrannical command, he wrote a letter to his mother outlining the plan that he executed that same night, in cold blood.

At first, this incident was dubbed as the rash act of a madman and talk of the incident was soon hushed. Eight months later, in an attempt to alert the public and gauge their response, it was rumored in all the papers that the case of the three deaths was likely to be closed.

Some sociologists and psychologists question whether that young man would have chosen to act differently if a forum had existed where his grievances would have been fairly reviewed. Nobody will know whether Tornay would have ignored such a forum anyway, opting instead for the tragic alternative that he knew would upset his mother. If Julius II could have predicted such an appalling tragedy within those walls, he would have surely created the institution of a Swiss Papal Union.

Make No Mistake

An organization of ecclesiastics is desperately needed that is in constant consultation with the superiors, in a spirit of reciprocal respect and openness.

In secular offices, a superior assesses each employee's progress in terms of his strengths and weaknesses. If the employee is satisfied with the report, he signs it in agreement. If, on the other hand, he disagrees with the assessment, he can refuse to sign it and contest the report through the appropriate channels.

In the Vatican, however, this procedure is carried out in the secrecy of the department, unbeknownst to the employee who never receives access to the report. The reports are stored in a secret cabinet, accessible only to those with authorization. Only employees who prepare the files on others have the right to see their own assessments and evaluations.

Because records are so strictly maintained and cataloged, ecclesiastical employees in the Vatican are never able to verify anything in their personnel files. Their superior is not obliged to disclose their reviews; they only draft and edit them, in great secrecy, and submit them to the party responsible for promotion or demotion. The Curial employee knows that his personal evaluations will be public knowledge to everyone except him.

The Vatican is stuck in the Middle Ages, and shows no sign of immediate progress. The notorious secret commissions of nameless prelates continue to decide the fate of others without consulting them. These commissioners follow their superiors' opinions and accusations to either scold or praise the individuals in question.

The Curia ignores public opinion and takes refuge in altered realities and truths.

THE OFFICE OF WORK OF THE HOLY SEE, THE body responsible for defending Curia members' interests, is a board of magnates whose meetings are in continuous session. The discussions that interpret the accusations made by the superiors occur behind closed doors. No defense is admitted for the simple reason that there is no debate, since the superiors who issue the directives enjoy the presumption of being right. The defendant is summoned only when the "wise men" have reached an unequivocal and irrevocable decision.

The powerful commissioners side with their superiors and agree on how to best silence the inferior dependent, leaving him suspended in isolation or demoting him outright. If the subject seeks recourse against the prejudice of his superiors, his action becomes a mark against him and a wall of silence is built up between the accused and the rest of his office.

AS MENTIONED PREVIOUSLY, THE SUPERIORS are not expressions of perfect justice. Often, they are capable of making anything happen, even the impossible. The management of their offices is a curious mixture of mediocrity, hypocrisy, cruelty, corruption, and favoritism.

True honesty is an ideal that is not incarnated in the ecclesiastical superior. Since the Curia lacks an entity mandated to protect the interests of its members, justice is often lost if the superior is not constantly guided, disciplined, and corrected from both vertical and horizontal levels.

One cannot expect the regime to police itself on these matters. The judge in these cases often presumes that the superior is both a good man and incapable of injustice. Therefore, a case against him is unnecessary. For the defendant, this principle is inverted and the presumption starts from the contrary. If his superior is against him, he is generally wrong and must prove his innocence.

Many Curialists live with this injustice on a daily basis. They are treated as unruly schoolboys and suffer constant accusations. The virtue of modesty that is demanded of the dependents is an incentive for the superiors to hide the merits of those they dislike.

An Organization to Stop the Abuses

The institution of a trade-union organization for all clerics and religious men and women is needed immediately in the Vatican, the dioceses, and all other religious jurisdictions. Otherwise, the flood of petitions filed by ecclesiastics in civil courts will continue to multiply.

All religious individuals feel the need and the urgency for an egalitarian body that can end the excesses of the superiors, reevaluating the top-heavy bureaucratic power structure and developing protection for the dependents. For the monks, the matter is somewhat easier, particularly if an important superior supports them. But the regular clergy is rarely granted an opportunity to petition on its own behalf at the diocesan level; theirs is a desperate situation. Moreover, if they are dependent on the Curia, and are in poor standing with their immediate superiors, they are treated like damaged merchandise and left to gather dust.

THE TWO CONGREGATIONS FOR THE MONKS AND the clergy, although concerned with legal matters, must not and should not be substituted for an association elected by the base members, since they are expressions of the hierarchical authority. The congregations are in opposition to the individual members, and lose the capacity to judge fairly.

Instead, the organization that stands for the rights of all ecclesiastics must operate on the basis of mutual love and fraternal care, and must be the product and expression of all of its members. Justice in the hands of the authorities is often wielded without equanimity. Another organization is needed to remind it of its duty, one that represents its members and that champions equality and charity. There should be no opposition to the institution of such a positive organization.

When the law is deficient and the State disinterested, plans for such a project are postponed. We must act, since this is an issue for the base members that must not be contingent on the whims of the authorities.

IN A UNION THAT SUBORDINATES AND DOMINATES, adulation, obsequiousness, and subjection prevail. These qualities do not conform to Catholic social doctrine. Our Lord's Church will acquire dignity when it allows its ecclesiastics to organize freely on a basic level and to collaborate with the authorities in granting justice to the oppressed and freedom of expression to every member of the community.

Fifty years after the triumph of the Declaration of Human Rights, the world must recognize the equity of its principles. In his first encyclical, *Redemptor Hominis* (The Savior of Humanity), the Polish Pope declared: "In sharing the joy of this achievement with all men of good will, with all men who truly love justice and peace, the Church, aware that the 'letter' alone has the power to kill, while only the 'spirit gives life,' must, together with these men, continually ask whether the Declaration of Human Rights and the acceptance of their 'letter' mean everywhere also the realization of their 'spirit.' There are often fears that we are far from this realization, and that the spirit of social and public life is in opposition to the 'letter' of the rights of man. This harmful state of affairs would make those who continue to determine and enforce it particularly responsible to these communities and the history of man. This sense will not be realized if, in the place of the exercise of power with the moral participation of the people, we allow the imposition of power by one particular group (clan, faction, family, etc.) on all members of society. These, then, are problems of primary importance from the point of view of the progress of man and the global development of his humanity."

In the same encyclical, John Paul II states: "The Church has always taught the duty to strive for the common good, teaching that the fundamental duty of power is the concern for the common good of society, from which its fundamental rights derive. That common good, which the authorities serve in the State, is only fully realized when all of the citizens are secure in their rights. Without this, there is a total breakdown of society, with citizens in opposition to the authorities, or worse, a situation where oppression, intimidation, violence, and terrorism prevail. This century, the totalitarian regimes have given us a good example of this."

These words demand that everyone reflect on the central place of humanity, dignity, and human rights. No authority can avoid these responsibilities, not even the Roman Curia.

PRESENTLY IN THE VATICAN MINI-STATE, ONLY one such organization exists and it is exclusively for secular employees. It managed to emerge despite the underhanded opposition of the employers. The organization's members and directors lament the systematic and concerted efforts of the authorities who are determined to discourage their initiatives. Until now, nobody has seen fit to unite priests, monks, and nuns at the base level into an organization in which they feel themselves, and their rights, better guaranteed and represented, without cultivating class struggles and conflict.

The matter is disarmingly simple; professional ethics must be aligned with the principles of human and ecclesiastical dignity, which are both equally sacred. The Pope has expressed himself in favor of organizations that protect the rights of all and has encouraged constructive and open dialogue with the powers that be, in the true spirit of the Church. On November 20, 1982, the Pope wrote: "I have confidence that associations of this nature, drawing on the social doctrine of the Church, will carry out a fruitful function in the community."

If secular Vatican employees can form a union that defends and promotes their economic and social concerns, and if the Pope exhorts the civic authorities to assist them in this task, then it is unacceptable that the same Vatican State, even if in a veiled and indirect way, forbids the ecclesiastics from creating such a movement. The right of free association is natural to humans and the ecclesiastics are no exception: *"Naturalia non sunt unquam turpia"* (That which is natural is never shameful). With the Pope's blessing, it is time to act on behalf of the thousands of ecclesiastics who no longer have faith in the ministries and ecclesiastical courts, and who want to entrust the defense of their human and religious rights to an organization whose leadership is democratically elected and dismissed by its members.

X X I

The End of an Era

Without unduly emphasizing the imminence of the Holy Year 2000 and its epochal significance, or creating a psychosis of great expectations, something will change in the Church in the new millennium.

This heartfelt book begins now that an end is in sight. As Saint Augustine says, the tongue has expressed itself as well as it can, but the rest must be imagined with the mind. A period of reflection is necessary to decode the original facts. Knowing that we have been on the wrong course is enough incentive to find the right and dutiful path that is in each one of us. These are the concerns that preoccupy us in this new millenium.

Poverty and moral evil have never defeated the Church, but its desire for power and its passion for ostentation have cheapened it. It must be returned to the Church of the Beatitudes, and eschew this world of excess. It must be stripped of power so that the powerful ones follow the poor and the meek, the inheritors of the earth. Saint Augustine said: "Perhaps Rome won't perish, if the Romans don't want to perish. But they will not escape from their downfall if they praise God."

To appreciate the *perestroika* of the Gospel, the Church must wage a battle against the enemy of Vaticanism and Masonic corruption. Leaving Christ's structure intact, the poor and meek must aspire to a true and decent *glasnost*—a

The term **"perestroika"** is an allusion to the Soviet economic and social policy of the late 1980s that transformed the Soviet Union into a decentralized market-oriented economy.

Meaning "openness," **glasnost** was the Soviet cultural and social policy of the late 1980s promoted by Mikhail Gorbachev.

unanimous decision regarding the direction that the Church should take in the third millennium.

IT MUST BECOME, AGAIN, THE CHURCH OF THE Crucified Lord and renounce material things and ambition, or risk expulsion from the kingdom of heaven. Saint Vincent de Paul said: "Pray to God so that the poor forgive you the humiliation they experienced at your hands."

Sertillanges wrote: "The word has resonance when you hear the silence in it, when it hides and leaves you to guess its treasure, which it releases bit by bit, without haste and frivolous agitation. Silence is the secret ingredient in the words that count. The value of a soul is found in its silences." A silence that restructures is required, not one that encourages passivity. Victor Hugo says: "Written words are the mysterious passers-by of the spirit, because, before being released, they solicit the soul for input."

The Church has experienced everything, is it not time for it to also experience the truth? In the praetorium, Pilate asked Christ: *"What is the truth?"* when, silently, he found it embodied in front of him. In this Curial world, the truth often conforms to the interests of those in power. Manzoni says: "Man, at times, must champion the truth; but he doesn't always see it triumph." The purpose of this book is to see that the truth triumphs.

The **praetorium** was a castle built by Herod that Pilate occupied when Christ was captured and brought before him for trial.

Facts are facts, and they cannot be undone by prejudice. The officials of the Curia, however respectable, will not eliminate the gross errors cataloged in this book with the same indignation of the officer who, after striking Christ, said: *"Answerest thou the high priest so?"* With God, he answered the rebuke: *"If I have spoken evil, bear witness of the evil: but if I have spoken well, why smitest thou me?"*

This book was conceived as an act of love toward the Church of Jesus as it enters the third millennium. It would be shameful to ignore the love that abounds in the Church to vilify the accused.

Paul loved the early Church when he confronted the hardships of the journey toward Jerusalem to get Peter, the first Pope, who had erred in his discrimination against the circumcised and formerly pagan believers. Paul had loved this duty even more than his apostolic travels where he announced the crucifixion and resurrection of Christ.

We, the Church, are the continual incarnation of divine love: *"Deus caritas est"* (God is love). The omnipresence of this fact echoes God's expression of his eternal existence: *"I am."* The form of his utterance, *"I am,"* means that he always exists and loves us in the present moment. *"Understand, ye brutish among the people: and ye fools: when will ye be wise?"*

Even if this book were placed on the Index of Prohibited Books, the Church's wound would become deeper and scarred like the five wounds revealed by Rosmini and by the martyr Savonarola. The Index does not reveal the truth that will eventually free itself and appear to all.

The authorities at every level must impartially examine how to respond to those seeking justice. Optimism isn't believing that all is well with the Church, but is believing that it will always be well, despite everything.

In his plan for redemption, God punishes his children to save them from eternal damnation; he undermines the Church to raise it again; he cuts off the useless branches to bring life; he grounds his pride for it to triumph in humility. The correction of one's own errors, and those of others, grants wisdom. The Church's humility is its descent into the divinity of its founder—a man who questioned the certainties of the scribes and Pharisees and who wants to delimit the extravagant power of the ecclesiastics.

We need a moment's silence to ask the Lord to give us, the Church, the grace to doubt our current practices and to make us willing and open to receive the divine truths. We, the Church, cannot remain forever embroiled in troubles,

The **Index of Prohibited Books** is the list of books that the Vatican bans on the premise of being heretical or of questionable character.

213

since our intellects are not appeased by their discovery, but rejoice in their solutions.

Some episodes in the Church cause us discomfort and confusion. However, a religion does not become corrupted when we denounce its corrupt practices. Instead of discriminating against our brothers, we must conform to Jesus' attitude in the face of the confused and shaken adulteress: he bent down to the ground, to look into her eyes. We wish that the Church were composed only of saints, but there is also an unhealthy side in need of thoughtful sympathy, in which we often recognize ourselves.

We must not forget these considerations, or everything will return to a treacherous calm and the victims and despots will fade into the distance. A small amount of rhetoric will not appease those waiting for radical justice and reform.

Those who plan to emerge victorious from the next conclave, which has been imminent for years, should institute a thorough Church reform, beginning with themselves, so that the missing is found and the defective is corrected. However, those who carefully choose the right opportunity to secure their place in the new conclave will attempt to hide that which would bring them shame if disclosed.

The Church is the fruit of recovered fragments and of mysteries in progress. It must learn to encourage a society of believers that is free and less dependent on absolutism, so that it will no longer suffer abuses and distortions.

These are the days of patience, tenacious hope, and unshakeable pauses. President Johnson said: "We have discovered that every boy that learns, every man that finds work, every sick individual who is healed, like a candle placed on the altar, makes the hope of all of the faithful more resplendent." In writing this book, we hope to shine this light of hope on the Church of the third millennium.

Lyndon B. **Johnson** was president of the United States from 1963 to 1968.

The Lord must eliminate the prejudices that represent the history and politics of ecclesiastical life and all of its broken-down ethical values. Too much waste has built up and become doctrine over the past 2,000 years of sedimentation.

The martyred **Saint Clement I** (Pope: 88-97 AD) was one of the Apostolic Fathers and author of the first epistle to the Corinthians.

Saint Clement I tells us: "Now, instead, listen to the nobodies, to people who pervert you and cast dispersions on that fraternal cohesion, which has made you justly famous. It is a dishonor that we must eliminate as soon as possible. Let us throw ourselves at the Lord's feet and beseech him with tears, so that he restores to us his friendship, and reestablishes us in a magnificent and chaste fraternity of love. In thought and deed, the wise man must be as humble as he is esteemed and must search for what is useful to all, not his own well-being."

Peter's ship is still in distress in the tempest of the Curia. *"And when evening was come, the ship was in the midst of the sea, and he alone on the land. And he saw them toiling in rowing; for the wind was contrary unto them: and about the fourth watch of the night he cometh unto them, walking upon the sea .... And immediately he talked with them, and saith unto them, 'Be of good cheer: It is I, be not afraid.' And he went up to them into the ship; and the wind ceased."*

We, the patients of the Divine One, are given one of two options: self-realization or the realization of Christ. If we choose the former, the whole world and we will remain in a state of contingency. If we choose the latter, we will become essential aides to Christ the Redeemer.

The Courageous Voice of a Simple Priest

The present state of the Vatican is only a poor representation of the true Church of Christ in the third millennium, which is poor, plain, humble, and contemptuous of the corrupt and powerful.

To imagine the Church of the future, let us use words of Don Francesco Emmanueli, who was expelled by his bishop, Monsignor Enrico Manfredini from Piacenza.

"While subscribing to the appeal for unity, which I feel is a duty of conscience, I am taking the liberty of making a few specific observations which seem necessary to me.

"Like the Mystery of the Trinity, the unity of the ecclesiastical body is profound, vital, and indispensable to the Church. *Ut unum sint* (That all may become one) is the supreme wish of the Lord. This said, one cannot ignore that, on a psychological and existential plane, such a mystical and metaphysical unity occurs in a unanimity that is logically postulated and presupposed. This is how the disciples were unified, according to the *Acts of the Apostles*. Unity, then, is manifest in belief—in accepting the Truth that God revealed and that the Church professes. Unity is also manifest in the acceptance of the rule of Christian ethics, which has an authentic and incontrovertible interpretation. There is no room for reservations or pedantry. And, I am with you all. I am with you because I am with the Church, which is the way that the founder wanted it, constitutionally hierarchical: 'The Holy Spirit has chosen you, bishops, to rule the Church.' Even the most elastic and malleable material of the pastoral ministry demands a certain discipline and a singular voice, if only for a greater efficacy in its initiatives and a greater incisiveness in its acts. This all means that I am for unity.

"But, we have reached a limit that has to be recognized. The individual conscience also has a voice, just as the individual has dignity. We cannot simply reduce every form of dissent to a subversive action even if, in certain situations, it may be convenient. In fact, the invoked unity, the one that constitutes the Church, cannot be reduced to conformism, nor can it be lowered to a level of practical calculation. It can't be reduced to a 'meeting of the minds' for the use of the hierarchy, with the result of a collective conscience and ecclesiastical standardization. No, everyone must be themselves. I seek nothing less: I will defend no other position.

"During my lifetime, I have already lived through a dictatorship. I was told then that power came from God and it

> Written in Greek around AD 65, the **Acts of the Apostles** is a book in the New Testament that chronicles the expansion of Christianity in its early days.

must be accepted and obeyed. It was dictated. After a war, in which I fought and was imprisoned for four years, I returned bitter and deluded to be told by the same people that I had got it all wrong, that I shouldn't have believed, and that I had been naive. Since then, I have no longer accepted dictatorships, regardless of their appearance and claim, so that I will never make that mistake again. Is this wrong?

"What is more, I know that the Church is hierarchical, but it is not a legitimate dictatorship and it is not in the service of personal ambition. I know that it exercises a legitimate power, but it is a power of love and service. Am I mistaken in drawing these logical and practical conclusions?

"When a tyrannical priest takes questionable initiatives that, to the naked eye, lack good taste, a sense of opportunity and proportion, if not simple common sense, he cannot in any way presume a unanimity in the name of God. Particularly, when many of these priests abuse public funds behind the back of the overtaxed contributors. You, the hierarchy, have the right to see it differently, but you are also convinced that the public condemns a waste of money that it cannot morally justify, while it condemns at the same time the people that projects like this promote, favor, and accept. We are in the realm of a superfluous collapse. We are on the verge of a scandal.

"It pains me that all this must be brought to the attention of you, the hierarchy, which is, for the most part, made up of individuals from working-class roots that you have denied with foolish and princely ambitions. Here too, it is a question of authenticity.

"There is no shortage of valid reasons that often pit the hierarchy against the political class, which have brought us to the brink of corruption. But what sense and what purpose can all of this have if, on the pragmatic level, we cooperate in their intrigues by compromising and allowing ourselves to be conditioned by them? The ecclesiastical identity crisis, with its overwhelming burden squarely placed on the shoulders of the poor, the workers, the unemployed, and the homeless, demands a change of course and style. It also imposes a limit on what is legitimate. It gives voice to an imperative of conscience that says, 'Enough is enough!'

"We are the followers of the one authentic Christ who was crucified and who is the thrust of our message and the only model for our lives. We bear witness by our visible, controllable, and systematic acceptance of Christ's sacrifice, not with hollow words and meaningless actions.

"How can the demonic genie of business and money figure into this logic? According to the Gospel, every Pope, cardinal, bishop, and prelate is synonymous to friend, brother, father, and shepherd, but never businessman! Things must become clear. The Crucifixion is the only measure of our authentication.

"Let us have unity then. We need it. A society that doesn't see the need for solidarity and the importance of defending itself against its enemies is lost. Let's have unity, but unity has its price, even for the hierarchy. To be unified, we must eliminate discrimination against the clergy that is perpetuated and methodically imposed by bishops in their dioceses and cardinals in the Curia. We should not listen exclusively to the co-opted and self-interested adulators, but also to the dissenters who have consciences. In fact, we should listen more to the latter than the former.

"Power should not be concentrated in the hands of the few, nor should the few enjoy the trust and confidence due to us all, by creating a privileged class. So that we remain united, we must put an end to marginalizing priests and abandoning ecclesiastics to isolation and despair. In short, we need a standardization of affection that demands, in prelates, bishops, cardinals, and the Pope, a heart capable of loving the other without belittling him. But, not everyone knows how to impose on himself the unity of Christ.

"Today, the Church isn't suffering a division, but a disintegration that is the last stage before ruin. We are not even friends. Regardless, the celebrations continue even in the Church's downfall, which is a sure sign that their significance has not been understood. The liturgy is more often an empty theatrical performance than a rite.

"It is true, they will say, that I am consumed by arterial sclerosis. But that which I am I have offered to the Church, even if it didn't know what to do with me. But, don't count on my silence. This letter could become an open letter for ecclesiastical inspection and an examination from above. I am waiting and remain obedient to Christ.

"Francesco Emmanueli, simple priest."

In the face of such a brilliant witness, the whole Church, bent over in prayer, must ask itself why this man was cast aside while seven of his brothers, all linked to the gang from Piacenza, were promoted to cardinal.

Vultures around the Pope

Most people hoped for a radical change in the Roman Curia when Pope John Paul II became the head of the Church. Instead of an earth-shattering change, a wall of isolation formed around him. Today, everything around him is at a dangerous standstill, except for his travels, which make him distant, distracted, and scatterbrained. Like a sickly watchman at the lighthouse, he continues to reflect the constant divine light.

At the end of the televised extravagance that marked the celebration of the twentieth anniversary of his papacy, the focus was on the event organizers who, every once in a while, allowed the Pope to appear in the distance like a meteor sideshow. In front of the world, with tears streaming down his cheeks, John Paul II asked whether he had carried out his duties as Pope as well and as thoroughly as the faithful had expected. Perhaps he was thinking of that gang of meddlesome bishops who, sending him to the four corners of the earth, had deceived him for twenty years and had co-opted his duties at the helm of Peter's ship.

"When the supreme judge arrives," wrote John VIII to the empress Engleberg, "he will ask whether we have left the Church in better condition than we found it. Is it freer, more peaceful, more prosperous?" This is the calling of every Pope and Curial dignitary as they pass on the Church to future generations.

The strongest Pope (872-82) of the ninth century, Pope **John VIII** temporarily reconciled the differences between east and west.

AS HE APPROACHES HIS EARTHLY DEPARTURE, the world anxiously watches the Pope's health almost as closely as the cardinals and prelates in the Curia. To be present at the final passage of the Pontiff, the gang leaders and department heads monitor him with constant supervision. The ailing Pope allows duties to be prolonged until the next order, so that the new Pope will be responsible for them.

In the twilight of the twentieth century, the sun, lowering behind the hills on the horizon, reddens in embarrassment at all it has witnessed this century.

X X I I

The Church of
the Millennium

his is the hour of God who rouses his Church with a
cock's crow because the alarm no longer works.
Dismantled carelessly, piece by piece, it lies on the
table to be examined in detail. However, they have no idea
how to put it back together. God asks us to repair it, before it's
too late and before the cock crows a second and third time.

This is the hour of Mary, the prophetess who, at Fatima,
declared the triumph of the Church in the year 2000—a
time when her Immaculate Heart would usurp the devil's
reign that clouds God's holy place with Satan's blackening
smoke. As the mother of God, she is invincible and will be
victorious. She is not the God of the temple, but is the temple of God and will lead the Church, by the hand, to Christ
(Saint Ambrose).

The **Immaculate
Heart** is a reference
to Mary's purity and
the fact that she was
freed from sin by a
special grace of God.

This is also the hour of the Church: "We are the harp
that you play with your plectrum: that sweet lament does-
n't issue from us, it is you who produce it. We are the
flute, and you are the sound within us: we are an impass-
able mountain, and the echo in us is the sound of your
voice. When you hide, I believe in nothing: when you
reveal yourself, I am a believer. I possess only what you
grant me! What do you seek in me?" (Gialal ad-Din
Rumi). At the end of this book, the Church of Christ and
the apostle Paul conclude:

"I have fought the noble battle; I have finished the race; I have kept the faith." Lord, if you want to save your church today, you must use all of your omnipotent mercy; if you wish to abandon it, you need simply apply your implacable justice. Do as you see fit.

But it is also, and above all, the hour of Satan during the final confrontation of the Apocalypse: "And when the thousand years are expired, Satan will be loosed out of his prison . . . . And will go out to deceive the nations in the four corners of the earth . . . and infest the camp of the saints and the beloved city." Emissaries of Satan besiege the beloved city of Christ, the Church.

A Meeting with the Divine

"I know that thou canst do everything, and that no thought can be withholden from thee. Who is he that hideth counsel without knowledge? Therefore have I uttered that I understood not things too wonderful for me, which I knew not. Hear, I beseech thee, and I will speak: I will demand of thee, and declare thou unto me. I have heard of thee by the hearing of the ear: but now mine eye seeth thee. Wherefore I abhor myself, and repent in dust and ashes.

"I, Jesus, have sent mine angel to testify unto thee things in the churches. I am the root and the offspring of David, and the bright and morning star. And the Spirit and the bride say, come. And let him that is athirst come. He which testifieth these things saith: Surely I come quickly. Amen."

Afterword

FROM THE EDITORS OF *VIA COL VENTO IN VATICANO*

Via col vento in Vaticano was published in Italy by Kaos Editions in February 1999. The book's release gave the public—Catholic and non-Catholic—its first look at the direct testimony of a group of high-ranking Vatican prelates (known by the collective pseudonym of the "Millenari" regarding the vices, corruption, and intrigues of the Roman Curia.

Via col vento in Vaticano has a strong religious imprint—formal and fundamental—and is marked throughout by a constant profession of love for the Church. However, it also has a hard critical purpose: To denounce the corruption that afflicts the Church and to promote a radical renewal based on morality and disclosure. The Millenari avoid excessive scandalizing, sometimes using allusions and elusions and often writing with irony and sarcasm. Yet the denunciation is strongly communicated. At the start of the third millennium, the Roman Catholic Church is plagued by a fierce internal power struggle. Many Vatican clerics are not turned towards God but rather are consumed by their own career ambitions and living with an "ends justify the means" attitude. This same ecclesiastical summit is also infiltrated by a Masonic faction.

Via col vento in Vaticano is a shocking book and its publication was rigorously censored by the Italian print media. The only exceptions were the weekly *L'Expresso* (March 18) and the small daily *Il Foglio* (March 19), which minimized the value and content of the book by maintaining that it was a mediocre gossip pamphlet written in expectation of the next Conclave's election of a new Pontiff.

Despite the Italian mass media's silence, *Via col vento in Vaticano* spread, especially in the Catholic ambit. During the first two weeks after publication, religious bookstores of Rome situated close to the Vatican sold 3,000 copies. In the Vatican, the book became *the* topic of conversation and was passed from person to person. The high-ranking curia were reading it, including the Holy Pontiff's secretary Monsignor Stanislaw Dziwisz. In the meantime, the hunt to discover the identities of the authors was on—with the Vatican using any means, including inferences and threats.

On March 23, 1999, through Kaos Editions, the Millenari released the following statement to the press:

The thousands of readers, mostly religious, who are critical of the success of our book *Via col vento in Vaticano*, are the best answer to the threats that will filtrate from the top of the ecclesiastical hierarchy, and they are testimony that the "conspiracy of silence" and intimidation will not win.

Via col vento in Vaticano is not a book against the Church, but for the Church. It denounces the deformities that are thriving inside the Roman Curia like a bad plant infecting the Holy Seat of Peter. We denounced the unscrupulous career advancement, the pernicious method of selecting bishops and cardinals (methods that have given the clerics of Anglo-Saxon countries great reservations to the point of breaking with Rome). We denounced the infiltration of the Masonic movement within the highest ranks of the clerical command: An intolerable pagan power, the Masons seek to limit the Holy Father's will. We reported the internal events, episodes and circumstances that everyone in the Vatican knows should not have been hidden. The Holy Seat should be like glass, nothing should be hidden from the eyes of the faithful. We called for the necessity of a religious "Solidarnosc" to protect the ecclesiastics who are exposed each day to tyrannies and injustices by their superiors in authority—superiors strong and absolute in power.

In front of our denunciations—which are, we repeat, for the Church and in the Church—the religious and lay mass media remain connivingly silent, or they minimize them as gossip, silencing the essence of the problems that we listed above. But the Lord warned: *". . . you hypocrites . . . . You leave the commandment of God, and hold fast the tradition of men."* (Mark 7:8) And again: *"If I have spoken wrongly, bear witness to the wrong; but if I have spoken rightly, why do you strike me?"* (John 18:22-3)

No Italian newspaper took up the Millenari's message. No one in the Vatican mentioned the book that everyone in the Curia talked about. The Holy Seat's strategy of silence was as strong as iron.

On April 12, 1999, the Roman daily *Il Messagero* published a false piece of news, initiated by "the waters of the Vatican." The paper reported that a brawl would occur, "under the Pope's very windows," between one of the authors of *Via col vento in Vaticano* and one of the prelates named in the book. The prompt denial of this piece by the Millenari (the presumed fight was completely invented, aimed at ridiculing the book) was ignored by the same newspaper.

The shroud of secrecy adopted by the Italian mass media was torn by the international press, particularly the German media. During the second half of April 1999, *Via col vento in Vaticano* was discussed by two German radio stations in Catholic areas, and covered by the daily *Suddeutsche Zeitung* and the press agency KNA.

Vatican news is covered by the English language journal *Inside the Vatican*. In its April 1999 issue, this paper published a long and scathing article that defined the Millenari's book as being "written by one Monsignor Frustrated . . . a paper-pusher who has written a sad and claustrophobic book." The article, penned by Desmond O'Grady, raised the opinion—circulated at the top of the Curia—that the main author of *Via col vento in Vaticano* was an elderly retired official of the Congregation for Oriental Churches named Monsignor Luigi Marinelli. With its first guilty party, The Holy Seat continued its search for the identity of the other authors.

In the meantime, *Via col vento in Vaticano* continued to leave its mark within the Roman Curia. In May 1999, the Catholic monthly, *30 Giorni*, published an interview with Cardinal Bernadin Gantin (deacon of the College of Cardinals and the prefect of the Bishop's Congregation from 1984 to 1998). Cardinal Gantin condemned the limitless corruption of many bishops and expressed how disturbed he was by the frequent requests for promotion that came his way when he was responsible for the Congregation. This was authoritative confirmation of the accusations of career-climbing corruption contained in the pages of *Via col vento in Vaticano*.

A few days later, in the columns of the *Osservatore Romano*, one of the most important Vatican jurists, Cardinal Vincenzo Fagiolo (President Emeritus of the Papal Council for the Interpretation of Legislative Texts and of the Disciplinary Commission of the Roman Curia) wrote: "A bishop is not an official or a temporary bureaucrat that is simply preparing for more prestigious positions." He proposed the re-establishment of the religious and moral authority of the Church, an end to the political corruption, and a return to stability. A bishop, elected to a determined seat, must always maintain an indissoluble rapport with his diocese. This was yet another confirmation that the problems outlined by the Millenari in their book were very real—and recognized even at the highest level of the Church.

IN THE MEANTIME, BEHIND THE SCENES, THE Vatican's witch-hunt named its scapegoat. On June 23, 1999, Monsignor Luigi Marinelli was notified by the Tribunal of the Sacred Roman Rota (the religious tribunal of the Vatican state) that he was to stand trial as the author of *Via col vento in Vaticano*. The Sacred Rota asked him to be present, as the defendant, at a hearing fixed for July 16, 1999, accompanied by a defense lawyer or advocate selected from those accredited by the Sacred Rota. In addition, the Vatican Tribunal ordered Monsignor Marinelli "to recall the book from distribution" and further forbade "its translation in other languages."

The Sacred Rota's action is extremely serious, mainly because this form of censorship has long since been abandoned. Analyzed legally, the charges against Monsignor Marinelli are even more arbitrary. The action purports to recall the book from territory outside the Vatican City State—that is, Italian territory—and assumes the legal right to restrict the translations and distribution of the book outside Italy.

The Sacred Rota's notice to Monsignor Marinelli was sent by Kaos Editions to the principal press agencies on June 26, 1999, and the news spread around the world. The wall of silence crumbled even in Italy. The Catholic intellectual Vittorio Messori, an author close to high-ranking names in the Vatican, declared:

I flipped through the book, laughing and becoming bored. These things, which are beyond verification, exist and have been noted since the time of Constantine, because men, even those who are part of the ecclesiastical hierarchy, are not up to being a testimony of the Bible. The faithful are not scandalized by these things . . . . The history of the ecclesiastic machine is also a story about limits, errors and darkness: but this is normal and has nothing to do with the power of Christ's mystery. . . . I am surprised that the Sacred Rota took this pamphlet so seriously thereby making more of it for the public. We would not be talking about it today if the Vatican had not intervened.

A group of Italian lay intellectuals—Giorgio Bocca, Alessandro Galante Garrone, Vito Laterza, Paolo Sylos Labini, Federico Coen, Franco Grillini, and Maria Luisa La Malfa—signed the following release:

The decree of the Papal Tribunal, in addition to being devoid of any jurisdiction—given the lack of jurisdiction over the Republic of Italy—is more disturbing when ethically analyzed or profiled. In addition to being a provision that goes against fundamental rights of liberty, such as freedom of expression and of the press, it is evident demonstration of the anti-libertarian and censoring vocation of the ecclesiastical hierarchy and shows in fact a return to the times of the L'Indice. We wish that Monsignor Marinelli not suffer the same treatment as Salman Rushdie.

THE ITALIAN PRESS BECAME ABSORBED BY THE scandal of *Via col vento in Vaticano*. It was even talked about in the House of Deputies. The Honorable Giuliano Pisapia, a former Secretary of Justice, turned Parliament's attention to the issue, asking the government: "If it was aware of the facts . . . and if so, was it informed ahead of time about the banning and what is its opinion; if the Holy Seat protested formally or informally against the publication of the book, and if so, what was the government's response; if the government was aware of the ban within the Italian judicial authority?" The Italian government did not respond.

The first hearing against Monsignor Marinelli took place on July 16, 1999, with the defendant absent. His reasons were listed just before the hearing in a press release by Kaos Editions:

> On Friday, July 16, 1999, the Sacred Rota will begin proceedings against the book *Via col vento in Vaticano* accusing Monsignor Luigi Marinelli, a presumed author of the book. . . . Internally, the Vatican has put in motion a search to discover the identities of the "Millenari"—the other authors of the book. It is like a witch-hunt, conducted in turns by inferences, oaths and inquisitions. This is a police-state type of practice as confirmed in Chapter XV. Those in the Vatican, meanwhile, made malicious accusations against Monsignor Marinelli including accusing him of being psychologically unfit. In addition, a bishop mentioned in the book has uttered verbal threats against Monsignor Marinelli. The Rota proceedings against Monsignor Marinelli are a sham. It shows an unheard-of pretence in banning *Via col vento in Vaticano* and preventing its translation in other languages when the supposed defamation in the book has not been ascertained and the rights for the book are the property of a small publishing house. In voicing its solid support of Monsignor Marinelli, Kaos Editions wishes to report a significant situation: Despite *Via col vento in Vaticano* having been listed as banned by the Ecclesiastical Tribunal, the Catholic bookstores in all of Italy continue to sell thousands of copies.

The Vatican Tribunal began proceedings without Monsignor Marinelli and assigned him a public defender. A second hearing in the Rota proceedings was held behind closed doors in mid-September 1999, and a third on March

23, 2000. Monsignor Marinelli was absent from both, maintaining that the proceedings were illegal in method and merit.

N EVERTHELESS, THE CASE OF *V IA COL VENTO* *in Vaticano* has had international resonance. Publishers from around the world are clamoring to print editions in the languages of their respective countries, and the book has become a bestseller in Italy, France, Germany, and Spain. It has earned prestigious recognition in the Catholic world. including the Swiss Herbert Haag prize for liberty in the Church. This was presented to Monsignor Marinelli (representing the Millenari) by the noted theologian Hans Küng on January 21, 2000.

At the time of writing, in mid-May 2000, no further news of the Rota proceedings was available. Gravely ill, Monsignor Marinelli has left Rome, refusing to meet with the defense council assigned to him by the office of the Vatican Tribunal.

Glossary

Acernza: Situated in the Apennine mountain range, Acernza is one of Italy's oldest cities in Italy.

Adamello: A ski resort town in northern Italy.

Agca, Mehmet Ali: On May 13, 1981, Turkish national Mehmet Ali Agca shot and seriously wounded Pope John Paul II in an assassination attempt in St. Peter's Square. Agca's attack is believed to have been the result of the Pope's support of the Solidarity movement in Poland. Other conspirators were acquitted for lack of proof. The pope later met with Agca and pardoned him.

Alba: A town in northwestern Italy with Roman origins, Alba is located on the Tanaro River. During the fourth century, it had close ties with Milan.

Alexander VI (1431-1503, Pope 1492-1503): A Spaniard born Rodrigo (de) Borgia, Alexander VI was elected Pope by a corrupt conclave. He spent papal resources to support his illegitimate son, Cesare, and was known for his unscrupulous political methods, his irreligious materialism, and his nepotism.

Alighieri, Dante (1265-1321): An Italian poet and author of *The Divine Comedy*. Recounting a journey through Hell, Purgatory, and Heaven, the work is a religious dialogue that deals with the revelation of God to a pilgrim and addresses sin, piety, predestination, and classical philosophy. It is believed to be an accurate portrait of the medieval worldview.

Alvarez, Louis (1911-88): An American physicist who was awarded the 1968 Nobel Prize for Physics. He played an important role in the Manhattan project when he suggested the technique for detonating the implosion-type atom bomb.

Ambrosian Bank Scandal: The Church, under the auspices of Licio Gelli, was accused of laundering money through the Institute for the Work of Religion and the Ambrosian Bank. Rumors abounded when Pope John Paul I, who had vowed to end Vatican corruption, was found dead in his bed after serving only one month as Pope. After the unexplained death of bank president Roberto Calvi in 1982, investigations showed the Ambrosian Bank was missing $1.3 billion. The money was traced to accounts owned by the Vatican.

Antioch: The Turkish city of Antioch is a thriving trade center for grains, olives, grapes, cotton, and more. Under Pompey, the city was an important Roman military, commercial, and cultural center. Antioch was a center for early Christianity; Peter and Paul both preached there, and followers of Jesus were first called Christians there.

Apocalypse: A Jewish and Christian writing dating from 200 BC to AD 150. It is marked by pseudonymity, symbolic imagery, and the expectation of an imminent cosmic cataclysm in which God destroys the ruling powers of evil and raises the righteous to life in a messianic kingdom.

Archbishop: A bishop at the head of an ecclesiastical province.

Archimedes (287-12 BC): A Greek mathematician, physicist, and inventor known for his work in geometry, physics, mechanics, and hydrostatics. He famously exclaimed: "Eureka!" when he discovered that the amount of water an object displaced was dependent on its mass. He is also credited with discovering the principles of the lever.

Aristotle (384-22 BC): A Greek philosopher who studied under Plato. His works—including *Organum, Rhetoric, Physics*—are generally written versions of his lectures. He placed great emphasis on the direct observation of nature and believed that theory should follow fact. He defined philosophy as the discerning of self-evident principles that form the basis of all knowledge. Lost to the West after the decline of Rome, Aristotle's work was preserved by Arab scholars. It was reintroduced to the West during the ninth century. Aristotle has influenced much of Roman Catholic theology through the writings of Saint Thomas Aquinas.

Arlington National Cemetery: Located in suburb of Washington, D.C., Arlington National Cemetery is the burial ground for more than 60,000 American war dead, as well as notable Americans including presidents William Howard Taft and John F. Kennedy. Burial in Arlington is limited to active, retired, and former members of the armed forces, Medal of Honor recipients, high-ranking federal government officials, and their dependents.

Augustoni, Gilberto: Born in Sciaffusa, Switzerland, Augustoni was ordained in 1946 and made the Cardinal Deacon of Saint Urbanot and Lorenzo at Prima Porta in 1994. He is Prefect Emeritus of the Supreme

Tribunal of the Apostolic Segnatura, and served as Prelate Auditor for the Church Court until 1986.

Aurelius, Marcus (121-80 AD): At an early age, Marcus Aurelius benefited from the friendship and patronage of the Roman Emperor Hadrian. He became Roman Emperor himself in AD 161 and held the position until his death. His reign ended the *Pax Romana*—the golden age of the Empire—and Rome found itself threatened by barbarians. Although many have called him one of the best men of pagan antiquity, he was more concerned with acheiving stoic perfection in his own life than in performing the duties of his office. He was consumed with superstition and sanctioned the active persecution of Christians.

Avignon: Located in southeastern France on the Rhone river, Avignon was the papal city from 1309 to 1378.

Bacci, Antonio (1885-1971): Born in Guignola, Italy, Bacci was ordained in 1909 and became a cardinal deacon in 1960. He held many positions within the Church, including Archbishop of Colonia de Cappadocia in 1962. He attended Vatican II and participated in the conclave of 1963.

Bacon, Francis (1561-1616): An English philosopher who believed that philosophy and experience illuminated each other. He thought humanity should seek the discovery of the truth, welfare of the state, and religious reform.

Baggio, Sebastiano (1913-93): Born in Rosa, Italy, Baggio was ordained in 1935 and entered the diplomatic service of the Holy See. He was made a cardinal in 1969, and participated in the conclaves of August and October 1978. He was made President of the Pontifical Commission for the State of Vatican City in 1984 and resigned in 1990.

Baptism by desire: The act of officially declaring people baptized to save their souls. In Catholicism, only baptized souls will enter the kingdom of heaven.

Baptism: Usually performed soon after birth, baptism admits members to the Church through a ritual use of water. Through the pouring or sprinkling water, the baptized is purified of sins, blessed by the Father, Son, and Holy Spirit, and marked with an indelible character that requires him or her to worship regularly.

Baptismal stole: A religious garment that consists of a symbolic, white band of material worn over the shoulders and around the neck of the person being baptized. Priests also receive a stole when they are ordained, and wear them while celebrating mass.

Beatitudes: In the Gospel of Matthew, the beatitudes are the nine blessings spoken by Jesus at the beginning of the Sermon on the Mount: *"Blessed are the poor in spirit, for theirs is the kingdom of heaven. Blessed are those who mourn, for they shall be comforted. Blessed are the meek, for they shall inherit the earth. Blessed are those who hunger and thirst for righteousness, for they shall be satisfied. Blessed are the merciful, for they shall obtain mercy. Blessed are the pure in heart, for they shall see God. Blessed are the peacemakers, for they shall be called sons of God. Blessed are those who are persecuted for righteousness' sake, for theirs is the kingdom of heaven. Blessed are you when men revile you and persecute you and utter all kinds of evil against you falsely on my account."* (Matthew 5:3-11)

Benelli, Giovanni (1921-82): Born in Poggiole di Vernio, Italy, Benelli was ordained in 1943 and became a cardinal in 1977. He participated in the August and October conclaves of 1978.

Bergson, Henri (1859-1941): A French philosopher, Bergson won the Nobel Prize for Literature in 1927 for his brilliant and imaginative works, including *Two Sources of Morality and Religion*. He had a dualistic philosophical approach and believed that the world was composed of two opposing tendencies—a life force and a resistance to the material world.

Berlusconi, Silvio (1936–): An Italian business executive and politician who made his fortune in real estate in the 1960s. In the 1980s, he founded commercial TV networks. He established the conservative Forza Italia party in 1994, which became prominent through the denunciation of the other corrupt and overpublicized parties. In 1994, he became premier in a three-party, right-wing coalition, but it collapsed by the end of the year and he resigned. In 1997 and 1998, he was convicted of financial crimes, proving that he was just as corrupt as the parties he condemned.

Biondi, Pietro Fumasoni (1872-1960): Born in Rome, Biondi was ordained in 1897 and became a cardinal in 1933. He participated in the conclaves of 1939 and 1958.

Biretta: A stiff, square cap with three or four ridges across the crown. It is traditionally worn by the Roman Catholic clergy: priests wear black, bishops wear purple, and cardinals wear red.

Bisceglie: A city in southern Italy on the Adriatic Sea. A thriving seaport, resort, and commercial center, the city has several churches and historical buildings, and is known for its prosperous merchant and military fleet.

Bishop: A clergyman ranking above a priest. Bishops have the authority to ordain priests and confirm parishioners, and typically govern a diocese.

Bloch, Ernest (1880-1959): A composer whose music reflects Jewish cultural and liturgical themes as well as European post-romantic traditions. His famous works are the *Israel Symphony* (1916), *Trois Poems Juifs* (1913), and *Shelomo* (1916).

Borgias: Originally from Aragon, the Borgias were an Italian-Spanish noble family whose name has become synonymous with greed, corruption, and treachery. Its more notable members included Cesare and Lucrezia, the illegitimate children of the Borgia Pope, Alexander VI.

Brescia: A city in Lombardy in Northern Italy where Roman remains have been found. It had a flourishing painting school headed by Moroni and his pupil Moretto. It was a Roman stronghold and, much later, a revolutionary center.

Brindisi: A port on the Adriatic Sea that has traded with eastern Mediterranean countries since ancient times. It was a Roman naval station and an embarkation point for Crusaders during the twelfth and thirteenth centuries.

Brisighella: A city in Italy's Lamone Valley, located near Faenza and famous for its olive oil. Ruled by Cesare Borgia in 1500, and by Venice until 1509, it was eventually annexed to the Papal State.

Calvary: The hilly area outside the wall of Jerusalem where Jesus was crucified.

Calvi, Roberto: Calvi was head of the Ambrosian Bank—the largest privately owned financial institution in Italy. On June 17, 1982, his body was found hanging from Blackfriar's Bridge in London, dangling by a rope, weighed down with bricks, with his hands tied behind his back. The coroner pronounced his death a suicide.

Cardinal Prefect: The head of a group of cardinals.

Cardinal Secretary of State: The head of the Secretariat of State.

Cardinal: Appointed by the Pope to serve as his principal assistants and advisors, cardinals are members of the highest body of the Roman Catholic Church, ranked just below the Pope.

Casaroli, Agostino (d. 1998): Born in Italy, Casaroli was sub-dean of the College of Cardinals. He was also a former Vatican Secretary of State.

Cassandra of Troy: In Roman mythology, Cassandra was daughter to Priam, King of Troy. She was endowed with the gift of prophecy, but fated by Apollo never to be believed.

Castaldo, Alfonso (1890-1966): Born in Casoria, Italy, Castaldo was ordained in 1913

and made a cardinal in 1958. He attended Vatican II and participated in the 1963 conclave.

Charlemagne (768-814): King of the Franks and founder of the first empire in western Europe after the fall of Rome. His court at Aix-la-Chapelle became a center of cultural rebirth in Europe known as the Carolingian Renaissance. He regulated existing administrations, permitted conquered peoples to retain their own laws, stimulated foreign trade, and educated the clergy. He became a figure of romance and legend pictures him as a champion of Christianity.

Chesterton, Gilbert Keith (1874-1936): A conservative English author who converted to Roman Catholicism in 1922 and became a champion of the religion. Called the Prince of Paradox, his dogma was often hidden in a light, energetic, and whimsical writing style. His novels include *The Napoleon of Notting Hill* (1904) and *The Man Who Was Thursday* (1908). His essays include *Tremendous Trifles* (1909) and *Come to Think of It* (1930).

Churchill, Winston (1874-1965): A British statesman, soldier, and author elected to Parliament as a Conservative in 1900. While out of office from 1929 to 1939, he remained a public figure. In 1940, during World War II, he became Prime Minister. A great orator, he refused to make peace with Hitler. After the war, he became the leader of the opposition and then Prime Minister again from 1951 to 1955. In 1953, he was knighted and received the Nobel Prize for Literature.

Cicognani, Amelto (1883-1973): Born in Brisighella, Italy, Cicognani was ordained in 1905, became a cardinal in 1958, and attended Vatican II. He was elected by the cardinal bishops and confirmed by Paul VI as dean of the Sacred College of Cardinals. He was appointed Cardinal Bishop of the suburbicarian of Ostia in 1972.

Ciriaci, Pietro (1885-1966): Born in Rome, Ciriaci was ordained in 1909 and became a cardinal in 1953. He attended Vatican II and participated in the conclave of 1963.

Glossary

Cistercians: A religious order of monks founded in 1098 by Saint Robert, abbot of Molesme in Citeaux. The order practiced strict asceticism and a life of poverty in an effort to emulate the ideals of the Benedictines. Influenced by Saint Bernard's writings, the Cistercians focused on farming and abbey life. It was the first order to use lay brothers.

Clemenceau, Georges (1841-1929): Called "the Tiger," Clemenceau was twice premier of France. Although trained as a doctor, he was well known for his journalism, socialism, and republicanism. His political career was stormy and punctuated by verbal and physical duels. During World War I, Clemenceau renewed the dispirited morale of France, persuaded the allies to agree to a unified command, and pushed vigorously until the final victory. Leading the French delegation at the Paris Peace Conference, the Tiger insisted on Germany's disarmament and was never satisfied with the Versailles Treaty. He was the main antagonist of Woodrow Wilson, whose ideas he viewed as too idealistic.

Clement XII (1652-1740: Pope 1730-40): During his youth, Lorenzo Corsini bought a prelate's rank from Innocent XI, and eventually held all of the Church's important offices. When he took the papal seat, finances were poor, there was a large deficit, and the subjects were exasperated. As Pope, he encouraged the arts and manufacturing, and modernized commerce laws. He also renewed the public lottery, which brought in a large amount of money. During his second year as Pope, he lost his sight.

Cocteau, Jean (1889-1963): A French writer, visual artist, and filmmaker, Cocteau experimented in most artistic media and was a leader of the French avant-garde in the 1920s. Surrealistic fantasy suffuses many of his films, novels, and plays. His best dramatic works include *Orphée* (1926) and *La Machine Infernale* (1934). His films include *Blood of a Poet* (1933).

Danube: A river that runs through central and southeastern Europe.

Daudet, Alphonse (1840-97): A French writer, Daudet's gentle, naturalistic stories and novels portrayed life in the provinces and Paris. His most famous work, *Letters from My Mill*, was published in 1869.

David (1010-970 BC): The king of ancient Israel who fought off Goliath and was divinely elected to replace Saul. He is mentioned in both the New Testament and the Koran and is believed to be a descendant of Jesus. His reign declined when he committed adultery with Bathsheba and helped murder her husband. Nevertheless, David remained the model for subsequent monarchs of Israel.

de Gaulle, Charles (1890-1970): A French general and statesman, and first president of the Fifth Republic. He served in World War I and was captured in 1916. In *The Army of the Future* (1934), he advocated French investment in mechanized warfare (the same type of machinery that Germany would use to conquer France in 1940). He opposed the Franco-German armistice and fled to London in 1940 to organize the Free French Forces. He later returned to France and assumed a role in political life.

Diocese: The territorial district under the jurisdiction of a bishop.

Dostoyevsky, Feodor Mikhailovich (1821-81): A Russian writer known for combining mysticism with psychological insight in his works. His four great novels were *Crime and Punishment* (1866), *The Idiot* (1869), *The Possessed* (1871) and *The Brothers Karamazov* (1880).

Eastern Fathers versus Western Fathers: In 1054, the schism between the Church of Constantinople (east) and the Church of Rome (west) became final. The separation was characterized by six centuries of disagreements over issues including the Nicene Creed. Introduced by Rome, it stated that the Holy Spirit proceeds not from the Father alone, but from the Father and the Son. Other disputes included disagreements over married clergy, (allowed in the Orthodox faith of the east but not by Roman Catholics), and the rules of fasting. In 1204, the Roman Catholic Church reenforced the division by sanctioning a crusade to capture Constantinople. Thousands of Orthodox Christians died, and later attempts to mend the breach failed.

Ecumenism: A movement promoting worldwide Christian unity through greater cooperation and understanding.

Episcopate: The position, term, or office of a bishop. It also refers to a bishop's area of jurisdiction. As a group, bishops may be called an episcopacy.

Eugene III (Pope 1145-53): An Italian of noble birth, born Bernard of Pisa. He was a friend of Saint Bernard and became a prominent Pope among the Cistercians. He was driven from Rome in 1146 and, while in exile (1146-52), reformed the clerical discipline of western Europe. He led the second crusade and was beatified in 1872.

Faenza: A city in the northern part of central Italy on the Lamone River known for its richly colored ceramics. Called *faience* or *majolica*, the ceramics have been manufactured there since the twelfth century.

Fagiolo, Vincenzo (1918–): Born in Segni, Italy, Fagiolo was ordained in 1943 and made the Cardinal Deacon of San Teodoro in 1994. He has held the position of President of the Disciplinary Commission of the Roman Curia (1990-98), and is President Emeritus of the Pontifical Council for the Interpretation of Legislative Texts.

Florence: Known as Firenze to the Italians, Florence is the capital of Tuscany and is located on the Arno River in central Italy. The city prospered during the Renaissance and was home to Dante, Michelangelo, Machiavelli, and the Medici family, among others.

Franciscan: A member of a religious order founded by Saint Francis of Assisi in 1209.

Franciscans have had a major place in preaching among Catholics and are responsible for developing the Stations of the Cross. Because of their garments, the Franciscans were called Gray Friars, but their vestments are now typically brown.

Frederick the Great (1712-86, king 1740-86): King of Prussia and an enlightened despot who made legal reforms, facilitated trade, and improved education.

Furno, Carlo (1921–): Born in Bairo Canavese, Italy, Furno was ordained in 1944 and made the Cardinal Deacon of San Cuoredi Cristo Re in 1994. He is an alumnus of the Vatican diplomatic academy and has devoted his ecclesiastical career to the diplomatic service. He was the Archpriest of the Patriarchal Liberian Basilica of Santa Maria Maggiore Rome in 1997, and has held the position of Grand Master of the Knights of the Holy Sepulcher of Jerusalem since 1995.

Gagnon, Edoard (1918–): Gagnon was born in Port-Daniel, Canada. He was educated in Montreal and joined the priesthood in 1940. He became the bishop of St. Paul, Alberta, and held various positions in Rome. He was made a Cardinal Deacon in 1985 and later became President of the Pontifical Committee for International Eucharistic Congresses.

Galileo (1564-1643): An Italian astronomer, mathematician, and physicist who laid the foundations for modern experimental science. He accepted the Copernican theory of the solar system that purported that the earth revolved around the sun, and he supported it in his *Dialogue on the Two Chief Systems of the World.* He was tried by the Inquisition and exiled for his beliefs.

Gallicanism: In French Roman Catholicism, Gallicanism is the tradition of resistance to papal authority. It opposes the view that the Pope has complete authority over the universal Church. The two aspects of Gallicanism are royal Gallicanism, which defended the special rights of the French monarch in the French

Church, and ecclesiastical Gallicanism, which attempted to preserve administrative independence for the French Roman clergy. The movement ended in 1870 when the First Vatican Council established the supreme authority of the Pope as dogma.

Gelli, Licio: Called "the Puppet Master," Gelli was the head of the Masonic Propaganda Two (P2) Lodge in the early 1970s and 1980s. The lodge included over a thousand leading political, financial, and government figures, with links to Italian intelligence agencies, senior military staff, and media personnel. He was recently arrested for involvement in many sordid events involving the papacy— including an expatriation movement for Nazis and World War II war criminals, and the Ambrosian Bank scandal.

Genoa: Also known as Genova, Genoa is a city in northwest Italy on the Italian Riviera. It is the country's chief seaport and an outlet for the Po Valley. Historically, the crusades brought the city much wealth.

Genuflection: The act of touching the knee to the floor as a sign of respect or worship.

Giobbe, Paolo (1880-1972): Born in Rome, Giobbe was ordained in 1904 and made a cardinal in 1958. He attended Vatican II and participated in the conclave of 1963.

Giordano, Michele (1930–): Born in San Arcangelo, Italy, Giordano was ordained in 1953 and became Cardinal of San Gioacchino ai Prati di Castello in 1988.

Gramsci, Antonio (1891-1937): An Italian political leader and theoretician, Gramsci was originally a member of the Socialist party and a co-founder of the left-wing paper *L'ordine Nuovo*. In 1921, he helped establish the Italian Communist Party, and was imprisoned for 10 years when Mussolini outlawed the party in 1927. His writings included *Lettere del Carcere*. Published posthumously in 1947, it presented his theory that the dominant class controls society. His works emphasized a less

dogmatic form of Communism, one that many intellectuals preferred to the Soviet Union's version.

Heraclitus (535-474 BC): A Greek philosopher of noble birth, Heraclitus theorized that the only permanent reality was that of change. He advocated that our real and perpetual state was one of "becoming."

Holy Land: The biblical region of Palestine, and the land of the Philistines. Historically, it was on the eastern shore of the Mediterranean and, at various times, comprised parts of modern Israel, the West Bank and Gaza, Jordan, and Egypt.

Hugo, Victor (1802-85): A French writer who went into exile after Napoleon III seized power in 1851. He returned to France in 1870. His two most famous works are *The Hunchback of Notre Dame* (1831) and *Les Miserables* (1862). He was a romanticist specializing in poetry, drama, and narratives. He was elected to the national assembly and senate, and is buried in the Pantheon in Paris.

Innocent III (1160-1216, Pope 1198-1216): Born Lotario Segni, Innocent III was trained as a theologian and appointed cardinal in 1190 by his uncle, Celestine III. His ecclesiastical doctrine stated that the spiritual takes precedence over the physical, and that all earthly things are subject to the spiritual authority of the Pope. Innocent set out to realize his ideal of the pope as ruler of the world, and became the virtual overlord of Christian Spain, Scandinavia, Hungary, and the Latin east; only Philip II of France remained independent. His greatest failure was the Fourth Crusade and his triumph was the Fourth Lateran Council.

Inquisition: In the Middle Ages, the Roman Catholic Church established a tribunal to aid bishops in their duty of investigating heresy. Run by the Dominican Friars, the Inquisition was established by Pope Gregory IX in 1233. The Inquisition's tactics became famous, and stories were circulated of secret trials and torture. Most trials ended with a guilty verdict, and the accused was handed over to secular authorities for punishment, including penance, fines, imprisonment, or death. The Church also acquired a percentage of the guilty person's property. Not to be confused with the Spanish Inquisition, which was begun in 1478 by Ferdinand and Isabella and was controlled by the Spanish Kings.

Iron Curtain: The military, political, and ideological barrier established between the Soviet bloc and western Europe after World War II. It prevented the free exchange of information and ideas.

Jesuits: The Society of Jesus—a Roman Catholic order founded in 1534 by Saint Ignatius Loyola. The order has a tradition of learning and science, and it is known for its foreign missionary work. A Jesuit's training can last for more than fifteen years, and may never result in an ecclesiastical office or honor. Jesuits have no distinctive garments, but are highly disciplined, observe poverty and chastity, and are devoted to the Pope. The Jesuits were a major force in the Counter Reformation, and sought to reclaim Protestant Europe for the Church and to raise the spiritual tone of the Catholic countries, enjoying considerable success in Germany, France, Hungary, and Poland. The Jesuits established schools and colleges in most important cities, and for 150 years were leaders in European education.

John Paul I (1912-78, Pope Sept. 3-28, 1978): Born Albino Luciani, John Paul I vowed to put Vatican II's mandates into effect during his pontificate. He opted for a simple papal coronation ceremony, and died unexpectedly one month after becoming pope.

John Paul II (1920–, Pope 1978-present): Born in Wadowice, Poland as Karol Jozef Wojtyla, John Paul II is the first non-Italian pope since the sixteenth century. He has traveled widely, increasing the international character of the papacy. While continuing to implement the decisions of Vatican II, he has sought to improve relations between Catholics and other religions, especially Judaism. He has, however remained staunchly conservative on topics such as birth control and women's roles in the Church.

John VIII (Pope 872-882): The strongest Pope of the ninth century. He strenuously opposed the activities of Saint Ignatius of Constantinople, and temporarily reconciled the differences between east and west from 879-880 by recognizing Photius as patriarch. He crowned Charles II Emperor, and bribed the Saracens to keep them from entering Rome. He was assassinated by his own relatives.

John XXIII (1881-1963, Pope 1958-63): Born Angelo Giuseppe Roncalli, John XXIII served in World War I in the medical corps and later as a chaplain. As Pope, he made many reforms, including stressing the pastoral duties of the pope, the bishops, and all of the clergy. He actively promoted social reforms, advanced cooperation with other religions, and forbade Catholics from voting for Communist parties. He convened the Second Vatican Council in October 1962. One of the best-loved Popes of modern times because of his love for humanity and his fresh approach to ecclesiastic affairs.

John the Baptist (d. 28 AD): A Jewish prophet and forerunner of Jesus, Saint John the Baptist was the son of Zacharias and Elizabeth (who were related to Mary), and his birth was foretold. He received the divine call to preach, baptized Jesus, and was beheaded at the request of Herod's wife.

Judas Iscariot: One of the twelve apostles, Judas Iscariot was the only disciple from Judea and is remembered as the betrayer of Jesus. Judas went to the chief priests and offered to give up Jesus, for which he was paid 30 pieces of silver. After the Last Supper, he led an armed band to Gethsemane and identified Jesus by kissing him on the cheek. Eventually, he repented and took his own life.

Julius II (1443-1513, Pope 1503-13): Born Giuliano della Rovere, Julius II was appointed as cardinal by his uncle, Sixtus IV, who also gave him many other offices. As a cardinal, Rovere completely controlled Pope Innocent VIII and, consequently, the cardinals elected his bitter enemy, Rodrigo Borgia (Alexander VI), in 1492. He withdrew and went into voluntary exile until Alexander's death. Julius was a warrior and wanted to restore the papal states to the Church. He was a patron of the arts: Raphael painted his portrait, he had many dealings with Michelangelo, and he laid the cornerstone of St Peter's. He was the first Pope to suppress nepotism and abate Rome's corruption. He assembled the Fifth Lateran Council and condemned Gallicanism in the French Church. He also abolished the buying and selling of spiritual benefits or offices in the College of Cardinals.

Laghi, Pio (1922–): Born in Castiglione, Italy, Laghi was ordained in 1946 and made Cardinal Deacon of San Maria Ausiliatrice in 1991. He has held the position of Prefect for the Congregation for Catholic Education and resigned his prefecture in 1999.

Lanza, Andrea Cordero: Lanza is a bishop and the papal nuncio in Jerusalem.

Lavoisier, Antoine Laurent (1743-94): A French chemist and physicist known as the founder of modern chemistry. He attended the Academy of Sciences in 1768, and worked to improve economic and social conditions in France.

Leonardi, Giovanni: Known for working with prisoners and the sick, Leonardi was beatified by Pope Pius IX in 1861.

Lions Club: Founded in 1917 by Chicago insurance broker Melvin Jones, the International Association of Lions Clubs is a civilian service club whose goal is to promote good government, good citizenship, and an interest in moral and social welfare.

Lombardy: A region in northern Italy that borders Switzerland. In the fourteenth and fifteenth centuries, it fell under the Visconti family and the Sforza dukes of Milan (the capital city).

Longbards: Also known as the Lombards, the Longbards were an ancient Germanic people who migrated across Europe and invaded northern Italy in AD 568. The apex of the Lombard kingdom was reached in the seventh and eighth centuries. Converted from paganism to Catholicism under Roman influence, the Lombard culture became a combination of Germanic and Roman traditions. They were conquered by Pepin, Charlemagne's successor, and the iron crown of the Lombard kings was used to crown the first Holy Roman Emperor, Otto I. The Lombardy region of Italy preserves their name.

Machiavelli, Niccolo (1469-1527): Famous for *The Prince* (1532), Machiavelli was a Renaissance Italian politician and theorist who believed that true power could only be achieved and maintained by a ruler who was indifferent to moral considerations. While *The Prince* has several interpretations, many have speculated that his ideal "prince" was modeled after Cesare Borgia. The term "Machiavellian" has come to mean powerful and conniving, with little regard for morals.

Magi: The three Wise Men of the east who followed the star of Bethlehem to Jesus' birth site. They had heard of the Messiah's impending arrival and traveled to the stable, bringing gifts of frankincense, gold, and myrrh.

Magyars: The dominant people of Hungary (although also found in other parts of eastern Europe). They first appeared in Europe during the ninth century and were mistakenly thought to have had similar roots to the Huns and other barbaric tribes. Before settling in Hungary, they were a nomadic people and had conquered a substantial portion of eastern Europe.

Manzoni, Alessandro (1785-1873): An Italian novelist, poet, and ardent Catholic, Manzoni's most important work, *The Betrothed* (1827), followed Sir Walter Scott's style. Set in sixteenth-century Milan, it reveals an in-depth understanding of Italian life, and remains one of Italy's most enduring novels. Manzoni heavily influenced the development of a consistent Italian prose style.

Mark: A Christian apostle and the author of the second Gospel of the New Testament. He is associated with Saint Peter, who supposedly furnished Mark with the facts for his writings. He is the patron of Venice and namesake of its famous cathedral.

Masonic: Anything having to do with freemasonry.

Messina: A city in the northeast region of Sicily. Known as a busy seaport and commercial city, Messina allied with Rome after the first Punic Wars. On December 28, 1908, an earthquake destroyed over 90 percent of the city—including historic buildings such as churches and palaces—and caused over 80,000 deaths. The city was rebuilt with earthquake-resistant structures.

Michelangelo (1475-1564): An Italian painter, sculptor, architect, and poet. From 1540 to 1550, he redesigned St. Peter's church in Rome, completing only the dome and four columns before his death.

Mimmi, Marcello (1882-1961): Born in Italy's Poggio di Castel San Pietro, Mimmi was ordained in 1905 and made a cardinal in 1953. He participated in the 1958 conclave.

Monduzzi, Dino (1922–): Born in Brisighella, Italy, Monduzzi was ordained in 1945 and made Cardinal Deacon of San Sabastiano in 1998. He has held the position of Prefect Emeritus of the Papal Household.

Moses: A Hebrew prophet who led the Israelites out of Egyptian slavery and delivered the Ten Commandments, establishing God's covenant with the people of Israel.

Mother Teresa (1910-97): A Roman Catholic missionary and winner of the 1979 Nobel Peace Prize, Mother Teresa was born in Albania. She moved to India at age 17, became a nun, and taught school in Calcutta. In 1948, she left the convent and founded the Missionaries of Charity—an organization that operates schools, hospitals, orphanages, and food centers in more than 90 countries.

Mussolini, Benito (1883-1945): An Italian dictator and leader of the Fascist movement, Mussolini's ambition was to restore the ancient greatness of Italy. He advocated aggressive nationalism in the *Fasci di Combattimento*, practiced terrorism with armed groups, and set out to forcibly restore order amid strikes and social unrest. After his election in 1921, he allied with Hitler and gave aid to Francisco Franco. Following the defeat of the German armed forces in World War II, Mussolini was tried and executed.

Narcissus: In Greek mythology, Narcissus fell in love with his own image—which he saw reflected in a stream—and drowned himself trying to kiss it. Morally, the story teaches the dangers of overly indulgent self-involvement.

Nasalli, Rocca (1903-88): Born in Piacenza, Italy, Mario Rocca di Nasalli Corneliano was ordained in 1927 and made a cardinal in 1969. He participated in the August and October conclaves of 1978.

Nero (37-68 AD): The mentally unstable Roman Emperor who had both his mother, Agrippina the Younger, and his wife, Octavia, murdered. After a fire destroyed half of Rome in AD 64, Nero held the Christians responsible and began to persecute them. He committed suicide after his cruelty triggered widespread revolts.

Newman, John Henry (1801-90): An English churchman who converted from Anglicanism to Catholicism in 1845, Newman eventually became a cardinal. He wrote *Tracts for Time* (1833), a collection of sermons that provided inspiration to the Oxford movement. He believed in education as moral training, not instruction. His greatest work was *Apologia pro vita sua* (1864), sparked by a comment that the Catholic clergy was not interested in truth for truth's sake. A master of English prose, he wrote refutations of his own Anglican writings, and persuaded many Anglicans to enter the Roman Catholic Church.

Novara: A city in Piedmont, northern Italy, that is an agricultural and industrial center.

Oddi, Silvio (1910–): Born in Morfasso, Italy, Oddi was ordained in 1933. He was made Cardinal Priest of San Agata del Goti in 1969 and also serves as Prefect Emeritus of the Congregation of the Clergy. He was papal envoy to the state funeral of Japanese Emperor Hirohito in 1989.

Olmi, Ermanno: An Italian film director and founder of the Ipotesi Cinema Group. In 1961, he directed and wrote the screenplay for *Il Posto*.

Orwell, George (1903-1950): The pseudonym for Eric Arthur Blair, a British novelist and essayist. His works addressed the sociopolitical conditions of his time, especially the issue of human freedom. His two major works were *Animal Farm*, a satire on the failure of communism, and *1984*, a prophetic novel on the dehumanizing effects of a totalitarian world.

Ottaviani, Alfredo (1890-1979): Born in Rome, Ottaviani was ordained in 1890 and made a cardinal in 1953.

Ozanam, Federico (1813-53): A French Roman Catholic scholar, Ozanam helped found the charitable Saint Vincent de Paul Society. He was a scholar of law and literature as well as a leader in Catholic social theory. His works cover a wide range of material including history and medieval literature.

Padre Pio of Pietrelcina (1887-1968): Descended from a southern Italian farm family, Padre Pio was the first priest to receive the stigmata. Soldiers returning from World War II spread word of his miracles and he became a point of pilgrimage. He heard confessions, healed by touch, and founded hospitals and prayer groups. Pope John Paul II beatified him in 1999 and his canonization is pending.

Pascal, Blaise (1623-62): A French scientist and religious philosopher who founded the modern theory of probability. He was influenced by the theory that emphasizes predestination, denies free will, and maintains that human nature is incapable of good. He believed that mystic faith was necessary to counter reason's inability to act as an adequate tool for solving problems or satisfying dreams. His *Thoughts: An Apology for Christianity* was published posthumously in 1670.

Paul III (1468-1549, Pope 1534-49): An astute church diplomat, Alessandro Farnese chose the name Paul III when he became Pope. He began a new era that included papal involvement in the Counter Reformation, and started a council to reconcile the Protestants and reform the Church—which resulted in the Council of Trent. He was a patron of the newly founded Jesuits, founded the Farnese Palace, continued Michelangelo's decoration of the Sistine Chapel, and rebuilt and repaved many streets in Rome.

Paul V (1552-1621, Pope 1605-21): Born Camillo Borghese to a noble family in Siena, Paul V distanced himself from church factions and immersed himself in the study of law. A stern and uncompromising man, he ruled the church using authoritarian decrees rather than diplomacy. During his papacy, he created controversy by aiming to restore many papal privileges. His accomplishments include overseeing the final touches on St. Peter's, improving the Vatican Library, and creating new institutions for education and charity.

Paul VI (1897-1978, Pope 1963-78): Born Giovanni Battista Montini, Pope Paul VI was the Italian successor of John XXIII. He continued his predecessor's vernacularization of the liturgy and also attempted to reassert papal primacy, despite growing dissent from within the Roman Catholic Church.

Pétain, Henri Philippe (1856-1951): The marshal of France and head of the Vichy government from 1940 to 1944. During World War I, he was the French Commander in Chief, and he became premier during World War II, arranging an armistice with the Germans as France was about to collapse. His government became unpopular due to its collaboration with Nazi Germany, and after the allied victory, Pétain was convicted of treason. His death sentence was commuted to life in prison by Charles de Gaulle.

Pharisees: One of two great Jewish religious and political parties of the second commonwealth, the Pharisees were labeled "separatists" or "deviants." They upheld an interpretation of Judaism that was in opposition to the temple cult. Stressing faith in one God and divine revelation of the law handed down both orally and in writing, they believed eternal life would come to those who upheld the law. They were dominant until AD 135 and influenced modern Judaism and Christianity, despite being labeled as hypocrites in the New Testament.

Piacenza: Located in the northern part of central Italy on the Po River, Piacenza is a city in the Emilia Romagna region. It was a Roman stronghold and part of the Lombard league in the twelfth century.

Pius X (1835-1914, Pope 1903-14): After his succession to the papacy, Giuseppe Sarto found himself in conflict with the French government over its regulation of church affairs. The government declared the separation of church and state and sequestered church property, while Pius X relaxed strictures on Roman Catholic participation in politics. He condemned religious modernism in *Lamentabili* (1907) and *Pascendi* (1907). He took disciplinary measures to eradicate heresy, sought to help the poor, and was widely venerated. He was canonized in 1954 by Pius XII.

Pius XI (1857-1939, Pope 1922-39): Born Achille Ratti, Pius XI's pontificate was marked by great diplomatic activity. He dealt with Mussolini and concluded it was impossible to be both a Fascist and a Catholic. In 1937, he denounced Nazism and spoke out against nationalism, racism, totalitarianism, and their threat to human dignity. His delight in new technology led him to found a Vatican broadcasting station and to improve the Vatican library.

Pius XII (1876-1958, Pope 1939-58): Born Eugenio Pacelli, Pius XII negotiated a concordat with Nazi Germany in 1933. He attacked totalitarianism, and excommunicated Catholics who joined the Communist party. During World War II, he believed that peace could be attained if formal relations were maintained with the combatants. He was criticized for not speaking out against the Nazis.

Pizzardo, Giuseppe (1877-1970): Born in Savona, Italy, Pizzardo was ordained in 1903 and became a cardinal in 1937. He was Secretary of State of the Holy Office from 1951 to 1959, and participated in Vatican II as well as the conclaves of 1939, 1958, and 1963.

Poggi, Luigi (1917–): Born in Piacenza, Italy, Poggi was ordained in 1940 and made Cardinal Deacon of San Maria in Dominica in 1994. He has spent his entire ecclesiastical career in the diplomatic sector and was Archivist and Librarian Emeritus of the Holy Roman Catholic Church until his resignation in 1998.

Poletti, Ugo (1914-97): Born in Omegna, Italy, Poletti was ordained in 1938 and made a cardinal in 1973. He participated in the August and October conclaves of 1978.

Pontius Pilate: The Roman prefect of Judea from AD 26 to 36. He was a ruthless governor and was removed as a result of the Samaritans' complaints. He attempted to evade his responsibility in the trial of Jesus; however, he was the one who ordered Jesus' crucifixion. He committed suicide in Rome.

Potenza: Founded by Romans in the second century BC, Potenza is the capital of the Basilicata and Potenza provinces in southern Italy. Situated in the Apennines, it is an agricultural, commercial, and industrial center.

Prelates: High-ranking clergy, such as bishops or abbots.

Raphael (1483-1520): A major Italian Renaissance painter, Raphael Santi Sanzo's work portrays the balance and harmony of High Renaissance composition. Julius II was his longtime patron, and he was influenced by Michelangelo. In the Vatican, Raphael was responsible for painting the "Stanza della Segnatura." He is also known for the "Temptation of Eve." In 1514, he was named chief architect of the Vatican and designed a number of churches, palaces, and mansions.

Rasputin, Grigori Yefimovich (1872-1916): A Russian peasant who rose to favor by caring for Alexis, the hemophiliac son of Czar Nicholas II. He was a notorious "holy man" whose doctrine of salvation combined religious fervor and sexual indulgence. He was the target of assassins who finally shot him and dumped his body in a canal after failed attempts to poison him.

Ratzinger, Joseph (1927–): Born in Marktl, Germany, Ratzinger was ordained in 1951 and became Cardinal Bishop of the Suburbicarian See of Velletri-Segni in 1977. He has held the position of Prefect of the Congregation for Doctrine of the Faith, and was President of both the Pontifical Biblical Commission and the International Theological Commission. His memoirs, *Milestones: Memoirs 1927-1977*, were published in 1998.

Richard the Lionheart (1157-99): The third son of Henry II of England and Eleanor of Aquitaine, Richard the Lionheart spent most of his life outside England. He is known for his military prowess and chivalrous character, and has become a central figure of romance. In 1190, he participated in the Third Crusade, which produced a treaty allowing Christians to access sites in the Holy Land and Jerusalem. He was captured in 1192 by Leopold V of Austria, was delivered to the Holy Roman Emperor, Henry VI, and was released in 1194 after a large ransom was paid. He surrendered his kingdom, returned to England, and suppressed his brother John's revolt. He was killed in a minor engagement in Europe.

Richelieu, Duc de (1585-1642): Born Armand Jean du Plessis, Richelieu was a French prelate and statesman who served as Louis XIII's chief minister. He gained control of the government and asserted his own domestic policy—which aimed to consolidate and centralize royal authority while disempowering the nobles and Huguenots. Dissatisfaction with his rule became apparant after he increased taxation to support a war. His memoirs, *Testament Politique*, were published posthumously in 1650.

Rosmini, Antonio (1797-1853): An Italian theologian, Antonio Rosmini envisioned a philosophical system based on Roman Catholicism. He foresaw a union between the secular and religious worlds, with the Pope as leader. His writings include *The Origin of Ideas* (1883-1886) and the controversial *Five Wounds of the Holy Church* (1883).

Rossi, Opilio (1910–): Born in New York City, Rossi moved to Italy as a young boy. He was ordained in 1933 and became Cardinal Priest of San Lorenzo in Lucina in 1976. He is Prefect Emeritus of the Commission of Cardinals for the Pontifical Sanctuaries of Pompeii, Loveto, and Bari, and he participated in the August and October conclaves of 1978.

Rotary Club: An organization of businessmen and professionals, founded in 1905 by Chicago lawyer Paul Percy Harris. The club promotes friendly cooperation and high standards of service among business people. It also aids charities and encourages international friendship.

Rubicon: A river in the northern part of central Italy. It is historically known as the river Julius Caesar and his army crossed in 49 BC, starting a civil war against Pompey. "Crossing the Rubicon" has come to mean taking an irrevocable step.

Rumi, Gialal ad-Din (1207-73): A great Islamic Persian sage, poet, and mystic. He studied under the spiritual master of his age, Shams ad-Din Tabrizi. His major work, the *Mathnauvi*, is a six-volume collection on spiritual teaching phrased in the form of stories and lyric poetry. He founded the Mawlawiyya Sufi Order. Known in the west as the whirling dervishes, its members use dance and music as part of their spiritual methodology. His tomb is still a place of pilgrimage.

Sabattini, Aurelio (1921–): Born in Casal Fiumanese, Italy, Sabattini was ordained in 1935 and made Cardinal Priest of San Apollinare alle Terme Neroniane-Alessandrine in 1983. He is Prefect Emeritus of the Supreme Tribunal of the Apostolic Segnatura.

Saint Ambrose (340-97 AD): A writer, composer, and bishop of Milan who imposed orthodoxy on the early Christian Church. He was highly regarded as a governor and only reluctantly accepted his appointment as bishop. He converted Saint Augustine with his eloquent preaching. His famous works were *On the Duties of the Clergy* and *On the Christian Faith*. He became the chief Catholic opponent of Arianism in the west, and persuaded Emperor Gratian to outlaw heresy in the west in 379 AD.

Saint Augustine (354-430 AD): One of the founders of western theology, Saint Augustine heavily influenced Christianity. Born Christian, he lived sinfully in Carthage before returning to his religious roots and becoming a priest. Extreme in his beliefs, Augustine felt that people must ultimately align themselves with God or Satan. His writings have caused great controversy and have influenced many. His major works include his autobiography, *Confessions*, and his dogmatic masterpiece, *On the Trinity*.

Saint Bernard (1090-1153): A French churchman and mystic who was born to a noble family and entered the Cistercian abbey of Citeaux. Devoted to the Cistercians and regarded as their second founder, he established a house at Clairvaux where he remained as abbot for his ecclesiastic career. Renowned for his eloquence, Saint Bernard was a powerful religious influence throughout France and Europe, and often advised popes. He wrote 330 sermons, 500 letters, and 13 treatises. He was canonized in 1170 by Pope Alexander III.

Saint Catherine of Siena (1347-80): An Italian mystic and diplomat, Saint Catherine was a member of the third order of Dominicans. She traveled to Avignon in 1376 and influenced Pope Gregory XI's termination of the "Babylonian Captivity" of the papacy, eventually persuading him to return to Rome. She supported Pope Urban VI during the Great Schism, and advocated a crusade against the Muslims. In 1375, she received the stigmata, which were visible only to her. She never learned to write, but dictated hundreds of letters and a mystic work entitled *The Dialogue of Saint Catherine of Siena*. She was canonized in 1461 by Pope Pius II.

Saint Clement I (pope 88-97 AD): A martyr and one of the Apostolic Fathers, Clement I is the author of the first epistle to the Corinthians. He may have known Peter and Paul, and was highly esteemed in the Church. He assumed authority for the Roman Catholic Church by resolving factionalism in Corinth, and was the first Church writer to use the myth of the phoenix as an allegory of the Resurrection.

Saint Giovanni Leonard (1541-1609): An Italian known for working with prisoners and the sick. He founded the Clerks Regular of the Mother of God, and in 1579, after a disagreement with the clerks, formed the Confraternity of Christian Doctrine. His greatest accomplishment was the publication of a compendium of Christian doctrine that remained in use until the nineteenth century. Pope Pius IX beatified him in 1861.

Saint Gregory the Great (540-604, Pope 590-604): Distinguished for his spiritual and political leadership, Gregory enforced papal supremacy and supported monasticism, celibacy for clerics, and the exemption of the clergy from civil trial. He emphasized the division of Church and state, viewing the Pope as God's chosen spiritual leader and the Emperor as God's chosen secular ruler.

Saint Joan of Arc (1412-31): A French heroine who heard the voices of saints urging her to aid the *dauphin*, who would later become King Charles VII. In May 1429, she raised the Siege of Orleans and persuaded the *dauphin* to be crowned. She was captured by Burgundians and sold to the English, who tried her for heresy and witchcraft and sentenced her to burn at the stake for her crimes. She was canonized by Benedict XV.

Saint John: Believed to be the author of the fourth Gospel, three letters in the New Testament, and the book of Revelation. He was among those closest to Jesus and is thought to have been the disciple "whom Jesus loved." While dying, Jesus committed Mary to his care. He is variously called John the Evangelist, John the Divine, and the Beloved Disciple. His symbol is an eagle.

Saint John of the Cross (1542-91): Born Juan de Yepes, Saint John of the Cross was a Spanish mystic and poet who founded the Discalced (barefoot) Carmelites. He was friends with Saint Theresa of Avila who guided him in his spiritual life. While imprisoned in 1577, he wrote the famous *Spiritual Canticle* and began *Songs of the Soul*. He also wrote *Dark Night of the Soul*, a prose treatise on mystical theology. He was canonized in 1726 by Pope Benedict XIII.

Saint Joseph of Cupertino: Joseph of Cupertino became a Franciscan after other orders rejected him due to his poor education. His ecstatic visions, which began at age eight, set him apart from others within the order and the community. He had a profound spiritual knowledge, and was brought before the Inquisition, but released. He was canonized in 1767 by Pope Clement XIII.

Saint Massimiliano Kolbe (1894-1941): A Franciscan was born in Zdunska, Poland and known as "the patron saint of our difficult century." He was imprisoned in Auschwitz for his anti-Nazi publications and, rather than give up hope, ministered to the other prisoners and even conducted mass. He died by lethal injection after trading places with a man who was to be killed in retribution for an escaped prisoner. His body was burned in the prison camp's ovens. He was canonized in 1982 by Pope John Paul.

Saint Paul (d. 64 AD): A fountainhead of Christian doctrine and a dominant figure in the *Acts of the Apostles*, which, along with the Pauline Epistles, document his life. His epistles contain some of the earliest Christian theological writings, and his views of Church doctrine as the mystical body of Christ and of justification by faith alone were imperative to the formation of the Christian faith.

Saint Peter (d. 64 AD): The leader and spokesperson of the twelve apostles, Jesus called Peter "Cephas" or "Simon," meaning rock in Aramaic. Jesus stated: *"Upon this rock I will build my church."* Peter's successors as bishop of Rome became leaders of the church.

Saint Theresa of Avila (1515-82): The daughter of a Spanish noble, Saint Theresa became a Carmelite nun, a well-known mystic, and a leading figure in the Counter Reformation. She is one of Roman Catholicism's principal saints, and she awakened a religious fervor in Spain that extended to Europe after her death. Her writings include *Life* and *Way of Perfection*, her relics are preserved at Alba, and she was canonized in 1622.

Saint Timothy (d. 100 AD): The son of a Greek father and a Jewish mother, Saint Timothy was an early Christian, and a friend and companion to St. Paul. He became first bishop of Ephesus and, according to tradition, was martyred there. He was also the addressee of two books of the New Testament in which Saint Paul names his coworkers as guardians and transmitters of his teachings, discusses qualifications of the clergy, and warns of future sufferings.

Saint Vincent de Paul (1580-1660): A French priest renowned for his charitable work. The events surrounding his capture by pirates, enslavement in Tunis, and subsequent escape are under debate. He was sent to the French court of Henry IV where he was chaplain to the queen. He brought about a revival of French Catholicism through his activism and his holy life. He inspired the court to take an interest in the poor, and organized several charities. In 1625, he founded the Congregation of the Mission where secular priests were sent to work in rural areas. He also founded the Sisters of Charity, an organization whose members work in the city. He was canonized in 1737 by Clement XII.

Samore, Antonio (1905-1983): Born in Bardi, Italy, Samore was ordained in 1928 and made a cardinal in 1967. He was the special papal representative to Argentina and Chile in December 1978 when the two countries were trying to peacefully resolve their border dispute.

San Remo: A city in northwest Italy on the Italian Riviera just east of Monaco.

Savonarola, Girolamo (1452-98): A fifteenth-century Italian religious reformer, Savonarola joined the Dominican order of priests and attacked materialism through his sermons. An uncompromising figure who criticized the papacy, he was excommunicated in 1497. He was eventually hanged for heresy after being tortured and forced to confess to being a false prophet. He is considered a martyr by many.

Schopenhauer, Arthur (1788-1860): A German philosopher who celebrated the philosophy of pessimism, and influenced both Friedrich Nietzsche and Sigmund Freud. Schopenhauer believed the world was full of unsatisfied wants and pains that could only be escaped by renouncing desire. Temporary relief, however, could be found in philosophy and art. His most important work was *The World as Will and Representation*.

Schotte, Jan Pieter (1928–): Born in Beveren-Leie, Belgium, Schotte was educated in Belgium and the United States. He was ordained in 1952 and became the Cardinal Deacon of San Biuliano dei Fiammighi in 1994. He has been Secretary General of the Synod of Bishops since 1985.

Sciascia, Leonardo: A twentieth-century Italian novelist whose works include psychological analysis, social consciousness, and formal and linguistic experimentation.

Scribes: Jewish scholars and teachers of law as based on the Old Testament and accumulated traditions. The work of the scribes laid the basis for the Oral Law, as distinct from the Written Law of the Torah. The period of their activity is in doubt, but they may have been active from the time of Ezra (444 BC) to that of Simeon the Just. In Talmudic literature, the term may be applied to any interpreter of the Law from Moses to the period just before the compilation of the Mishna.

Scylla and Charybdis: In Roman mythology, Ulysses faced the perils of Scylla (a maiden turned into a monster by Circe) and Charybdis (a terrible whirlpool). These two obstacles bounded a narrow channel, and Ulysses had to make the difficult choice of either losing his ship to Charybdis or sacrificing his crew members to Scylla's voracious appetite.

Sepe, Crescenzio: President of the Pilgrims Office for the Year 2000, and Secretary General of the Central Committee for the Great Jubilee of the Year 2000.

Silvestrini, Achille (1923–): Born in Brisighella, Italy, Silvestrini was ordained in 1946 and made a Cardinal Deacon in 1988. He often serves as head of Holy See delegations to United Nations conferences and for drafting international treaties. He was papal representative to the funeral of Jordan's King Hussein in February 1999, and is currently Cardinal Priest of San Benedetto Fuori Porta San Paolo.

Siri, Giuseppe (1906-89): Born in Genoa, Siri was ordained in 1928 and made a cardinal in 1953. He attended Vatican II and was a member of its board of presidents from 1963 to 65. He participated in both the August and October conclaves of 1978, and was almost elected Pope twice.

Sistine Chapel: One of the most prized structures in the Vatican. Serving as the private chapel of the Pope, it was built in 1473 under Pope Sixtus IV. The artwork covers the chapel from floor to ceiling and features famous works by Michelangelo—including the nine episodes from Genesis across the ceiling and "The Last Judgment" on the altar wall.

Sixtus V (1521-90, pope 1585-90): Born Felice Peretti, Sixtus V was a famous Italian preacher who became a Franciscan at a young age. From 1556 to 1560, he was a counselor to the Inquisition in Venice. As Pope, he brought order to the papal states, and constructed and rebuilt many buildings and churches in Rome. He left a large amount of money in the treasury from taxes, selling offices, and making loans. He sanctioned Phillip II of Spain's attempt to restore Catholicism to England, which ended in the defeat of the Spanish Armada.

Slipyj, Giuseppe (1892-1984): Born in Ternopil, Ukraine, Slipyj was ordained in 1917 and became a cardinal in 1965. His biography, *Confessor between East and West*, was written by Jan Jaroslav Pelikan and published in 1990.

Sodano, Angelo (1927–): Born in Isola d'Ast, Italy, Sodano was ordained in 1950 and became Cardinal Bishop of the Suburbicarian of Albano. He was named Secretary of State of the Vatican City State in 1991 and was the papal legate to the 75th anniversary celebration of the apparition of Our Lady at Fatima in Portugal in 1992.

Solomonic response (d. 930 BC, king 970-30 BC): A reference to the proverbial wisdom of Solomon, king of the ancient Hebrews. One of Solomon's displays of wisdom was the proposal to cut a child in half to appease two women fighting over its maternity: "*And the king said, 'Divide the living child in two, and give half to the one, and half to the other'*" (1 Kings 3:25). He awarded the child to the woman who, upon hearing that the child would be killed and divided in two, begged that the child live and be given to the other woman. Solomon devised that this woman was the real mother, "*And all Israel heard of the judgment which the king had rendered; and they stood in awe of the king, because they perceived that the wisdom of God was in him to render justice*" (1 Kings 3:28).

Somalo, Edoardo Martinez (1927–): Born in Italy's Banos de Rio Tobia, Somalo was ordained in 1950 and made Cardinal Priest of San Nomedi Gesu in 1988. He has served as Prefect of the Congregation for the Institutes of Consecrated Life and the Societies of Apostolic Life since 1992.

Sophocles (496-406 BC): One of the great playwrights of ancient Greece, Sophocles was born at Colonus near Athens and was a military leader and a priest. His most famous tragedy is *Oedipus Rex* (429 BC), in which he told the legend of Oedipus the King, who killed his father and married his mother. Other works include *Ajax* and *Antigone*.

Soubiroux, Bernadette (1844-79): A French peasant girl who, in 1858, claimed to see the Virgin Mary in apparitions at a grotto near Lourdes. Skeptical of her visions, the authorities subjected her to severe examinations and abuse. She was eventually allowed to enter the convent of Notre-Dame de Nevers. She was canonized in 1933.

Spoleto: A city in Umbria, central Italy with Roman ruins. Painting flourished there in the fourteenth and fifteenth centuries, and the city still holds the annual Spoleto Festival of the Arts. The city was destroyed by Emperor Frederick I in 1155, but was rebuilt. Its fourth-century basilica of San Salvatore is a remarkable example of early Christian architecture.

Syria: A country in southwest Asia on the eastern Mediterranean coast, whose capital city is Damascus.

Tardini, Domenico (1888-1961): Born in Rome, Tardini was ordained in 1912 and was a faculty member of the Pontifical Roman Seminary from 1912 to 1929. He declined a cardinalate in 1953, but became a cardinal in 1958.

Teixeira, Pedro (d. 1640): A Portuguese explorer. He commanded an expedition up the Amazon River in the autumn of 1637 and was accompanied on the return journey by the Jesuit priest Cristóbal de Acuña, who wrote an account of the voyage.

Thomas: One of the twelve disciples, Thomas refused to believe in the resurrection until he came into physical contact with Jesus' wounds, hence the term "doubting Thomas." He was said to have been a missionary in Parthia or India, and some churches there claim him as their founder.

Tiber: A river originating from the Etruscan Apennines in central Italy. It flows through Rome and is subject to flooding.

Tiflis: The former name of Tblisi, capital of Georgia, located in southwest Asia. Located in a mountain-ringed basin, Tbilisi is the economic, administrative, and cultural heartland of Transcaucasia.

Traglia, Luigi (1895-1977): Born in Albano Laziale, Italy, Traglia was ordained in 1917 and made a cardinal in 1960. He participated in the conclave of 1963.

Unknown Soldier: The Tomb of the Unknowns is a memorial to the American dead of World Wars I and II, the Korean War, and the Vietnam War. It is located in Arlington National Cemetary and contains the remains of an unidentified soldier from each war.

Universal Judgment: Refers to Michelangelo's painting in the Sistine Chapel entitled "The Last Judgment" (1534). Located at the rear of the chapel, it is considered by many to be his masterwork. The painting depicts Christ's damnation of sinners and blessing of the virtuous, along with the resurrection of the dead and the transport of souls to hell.

Valeri, Valerio (1883-1963): Born in Santa Fiora, Italy, Valeri was educated in Rome, ordained in 1907, and made a cardinal in 1953. He participated in the conclaves of 1958 and 1963 and attended the first session of the Vatican II council in 1962.

Vendors of the temple: An allusion to the passage in the Bible where Jesus drives the money-changers out of the temple: "*And Jesus entered the temple of God and drove out all who sold and bought in the temple, and he overturned the tables of the money-changers and the seats of those who sold pigeons*" (Matthew 21:12).

Viareggio: A city in northern Italy. Located on the Tyrrhenian Sea, it is both a fishing center and a popular beach resort.

Vicar: A member of the clergy who exercises a broad pastoral responsibility.

Vicariate: The office, authority, or district under the jurisdiction of a vicar.

Vico, Giambattista (1668-1744): An Italian philosopher and historian, Vico was the first to formulate a systematic method for historical research, providing the foundation for modern research techniques. Vico regarded history as the study of the birth and development of human societies and their institutions. His major theories were presented in *New Science* (1725), and he revised them in 1730 and 1744. He also advocated the study of language, mythology, and tradition.

Villot, Jean (1905-79): Born in Saint-Amant-Tallende, France, Villot was ordained in 1930 and became a cardinal in 1965. He participated in the August and October conclaves of 1978.

Virgil (70-19 BC): A Roman poet, Virgil wrote his greatest work, *The Aeneid*, as a national epic honoring Rome. It tells the story of the wanderings of Aeneas after the defeat of Troy.

Voltaire, François Marie Arout (1694-1778): A French philosopher and literary figure who personified the Enlightenment and sought justice for victims of religious or political persecution. In 1759, he published *Candide*, a masterpiece of philosophical romance. Voltaire practiced a philosophy of common sense that was blended with skepticism and rationalism. Although he was not well regarded by the Church, he signed a partial retraction of his writings to receive a Christian burial.

Wilde, Oscar (1854-1900): An Irish author and playwright known for his witty plays. He was eccentric in his tastes, dress, and manners, and he became the center of a group that glorified beauty for its own sake. His most famous works include *The Picture of Dorian Gray* (1891), *Women of No Importance* (1893), *An Ideal Husband* (1895), and *The Importance of Being Earnest* (1895). He was found guilty of homosexual offenses in 1895 and was jailed for two years. He lived in France until his death, plagued by ill health and bankruptcy.

Index

Index

Index